D0948577

Detroit Monographs in Musicology/Studies in Music, No. 16

Editor
J. Bunker Clark
University of Kansas

The Symphony

Second Edition

Louise Cuyler

Professor Emeritus of Music
University of Michigan

HARMONIE PARK PRESS   MICHIGAN   1995

Copyright © 1973 by Harcourt Brace & Company
Published by arrangement with Harcourt Brace & Company

Printed and bound in the United States of America
Published by
Harmonie Park Press
23630 Pinewood
Warren, Michigan 48091

Library of Congress Cataloging in Publication Data

Cuyler, Louise Elvira, 1908-
    The symphony / Louise Cuyler. -- 2nd ed.
        p. c.m. — (Detroit Monographs in Musicology/Studies in Music
    ; no. 16)
    ISBN 0-89990-072-0
    1. Symphony. I. Title. II. Series.
ML1255.C9 1995
784.2'184--dc20   95-13538

PHOTO CREDITS   Page 5, Eugene Enrico; page 19, Eric Lessing—Magnum Photos; page 38, from Mozart's "Haffner" Symphony, facsimile edition, c1968 by Oxford University Press; pages 49, 133, 192, The Music Division—The New York Public Library for the Performing Arts, Astor, Lenox and Tilden Foundations; page 120, Library of Congress; page 141, reproduced from *An Illustrated History of Music*, by Marc Pincherle, published by Reynal & Co.; page 160, The Bettman Archive; page 175, University of Michigan Music Library; page 193, G.D. Hackett Photography; page 210, AP/Wide World Photos; page 229, Sandor Acs; page 231, c1962 by Moeck Verlag, D-29227 Celle, copyright renewal c1991.

Acknowledgments

G. Schirmer, Inc. and Associated Music Publishers, Inc. for excerpts from Ives, Symphony No. 3. And from Sibelius, Symphony No. 4. Reprinted by permission.

European American Music Distributors Corporation, for excerpts from Hindemith, *Mathis der Maler*. Used by permission of European American Music Distributors Corporation, sole U.S. and Canadian agent for B. Schott's Soehne. And from Stravinsky, *Symphony in Three Movements*. Used by permission of European American Music Distributors Corporation, sole U.S. and Canadian agent for Schott & Co. Ltd., London.

Hal Leonard Corporation, for excerpts from Dmitri Shostakovich, Symphony No. 1. Reprinted by permission.

W.W. Norton & Company, Inc., for excerpts from Debussy, Afternoon of a Faun. Reprinted from Prelude to "The Afternoon of a Faun"/Debussy, edited by William W. Austin. Reprinted by permission.

Stainer & Bell Ltd., for excerpts from Vaughan Williams, London Symphony. Reprinted by permission.

Table of Contents

Preface

Today the United States is the world's most enthusiastic supporter of symphony orchestras. There are five of surpassing quality and a number of other orchestras of only slightly less excellence in this country. Almost every city of even moderate size supports at least a semiprofessional group, and regional orchestras have done much to assure the appreciation of orchestral music by people who lack access to one of the large, "world class" ensembles. An important umbrella organization, based in Washington, D.C., is the American Symphony Orchestra League (ASOL), which gives "artistic, organizational, and financial leadership and services" to all those who direct and support its more than 800 member orchestras. Of these, as of the listing in the winter 1994 issue of ASOL's magazine *Symphony*, eighty-five have annual budgets in excess of a million dollars, and almost twice that number have budgets of about half to three-quarters that size — a convincing testament to the public support given these orchestras.

There was a time when nearly every high school had a student orchestra, many of them of astonishingly high quality. But with the dwindling support for the arts in our public schools, the number of these orchestras is sadly diminished. In part compensation, as the ASOL list affirms, there are almost 150 youth orchestras, permanently established. And many orchestras provide vital programs in the local schools, to partially offset the lost support for the arts. Thus, most Americans in all walks of life have access to orchestral music and are showing their appreciation by their heartening support of this supplement to their quality of life.

This book is addressed to all lovers of orchestral music, but especially to students and those who prize the status of "informed amateur." The repertory from which orchestral programs are drawn is made up in substantial part of symphonies and their near-relatives, symphonic poems. The purpose of the book is to trace the nearly 250-year development of the symphony as a musical form by citing and discussing representative compositions from each period.

The narrative portions of this book are addressed to student and concertgoer alike. All unusual terms are defined, either in context or in the Glossary. The analyses, which are intended especially for the student, are couched in simple, direct terms. They are keyed to the measure (in a few cases, rehearsal) numbers found in standard pocket scores of many of these works. The student is urged to use these scores, when available, to supplement verbal discussions. And because music is an audible art, recordings of the symphonic compositions should be played as often as possible. For those with access to a symphony orchestra, attendance at live concerts can be the final step in bringing the music to life.

In retrospect, I am grateful to my students at the School of Music of the University of Michigan, during more than forty years of teaching there, for helping me crystallize my thoughts concerning this most durable of forms, stimulating me with probing questions. My continuing gratitude goes to the late Dr. Karl Geiringer of the University of California, Santa Barbara, for his help in preparing the original edition of this book, and to J. Bunker Clark of the University of Kansas for editorial assistance in achieving this second edition of *The Symphony*.

Louise Cuyler

Carmel-by-the Sea, California
March 1995

PART ONE

The Mainstream of Symphonic Development: The Symphony in Austria and Germany

1

The Background
and Heritage of
the Classical Symphony

The symphony for orchestra, which achieved maturity just in time to epitomize the glory of the Classical period, constitutes a double landmark in the evolution of Western music. Along with the opera, it signaled the full emergence of music as a public art. And it offered serious composers a large, autonomous instrumental form capable of sustaining substantial ideas without recourse to extramusical associations. In the thousand-year evolution of Western art music, only two other types—the cyclic Mass of the fifteenth and sixteenth centuries and the opera—can rival the symphony in longevity, flexibility, and catalytic effect on composers. The symphony, lacking any such established patronage as the Church, had to develop its own audience situation: the concert hall. It also generated a powerful, indigenous medium of performance in the symphony orchestra; and it evolved distinctive schemes for shaping and dispersing musical ideas. There was nothing fortuitous in the simultaneous maturation of the symphony and the sonata form, for the symphony became the most vigorous exponent of that form, veritably the sonata for orchestra.

Trends Leading to Development of the Symphony

The symphony, like every other important musical type, was the culmination of a variety of trends. In retrospect, the symphony might be seen as a magnet that, by the middle of the eighteenth century, was attracting every important development in instrumental music into its field. The symphony eventually achieved maturity through the confluence of a number of diverse currents from the past.

3

The Expanding Cult of Instrumental Music

The instrumental performer's transition from disparaged *jongleur* or *ménestrel* of the Middle Ages to respected professional performer in the Classical orchestra was a difficult one, and it encompassed changes in social as well as musical attitudes. Before the fourteenth century, virtually all serious music was planned for vocal performance, largely because the Church, principal patron and employer of musicians, had developed a liturgy that idealized this. Diverse instruments such as trumpets, bells, cymbals, and ancestors of the viol and violin were sometimes used to supplement the voices in church services, as is attested in the written accounts of especially festive celebrations and in such pictorial representations as frescoes and choir-stall carvings. But this occasional use of instruments was extrinsic, not really part of the essential fabric of the music.

The mood of renewal that characterized the sixteenth-century Renaissance was refreshingly secular. Since medieval churchmen had scorned instrumental music, it became an especially attractive medium to Renaissance men of progressive outlook. Virtual extinction of the snobbishness that had denigrated instrumental performance was one of the sixteenth century's vital accomplishments. The fresh attitude encouraged rapid improvement of instruments and development of formalized playing techniques for them. During the sixteenth and early seventeenth centuries, instruments of various sizes and ranges tended to be cultivated in homogeneous families or consorts. Within these groups the prototypes of most instruments that were to comprise the Classical symphony orchestra achieved early prominence. The strings were the first group to acquire sophisticated, practical guise. During the latter half· of the sixteenth century, outstanding specimens of the violin family (violas of various sizes, the violoncello, and the string bass, in addition to the violin itself) were coming from the shops of gifted craftsmen, especially those who worked in Brescia and Cremona in Italy.[1]

To employ the fine new instruments, permanent string ensembles were set up. One of the earliest of these was the famous *24 Violons du Roy* (The King's 24 Violins), established by King Louis XIII of France in 1626.[2] This string band was a five-part ensemble that probably allotted six players to the highest part (violins), four to each of the three middle parts (violas), and six to the lowest part (cellos).[3] This famous orchestra continued in service throughout the reign of Louis XIV (1643–1715), but in time it was surpassed in excellence by an elite smaller group, *Les Petits Violons* (The Small Ensemble of Violins), founded and trained by J. B. Lully, King Louis' famous composer and impresario. The reputation of these highly disciplined ensembles became widespread as travelers spoke their praises; their influence reached Germany and the Low Countries through

---

[1] See David D. Boyden, *The History of Violin Playing from Its Origins to 1761*, 2nd ed. (Oxford: Clarendon Press, 1990), for an exhaustive account of the evolution of instruments of the violin family.

[2] It must not be assumed, however, that King Louis' orchestra necessarily used Italian violins. The preference for those instruments was not firmly established in France until some years later, when Viotti visited Paris.

[3] For a description of this famous group, see Marin Mersenne, *Harmonie universelle* (Paris, 1636), "The Book on Instruments," transl. Roger E. Chapman (The Hague: M. Nijoff, 1957).

San Petronio in 1722. The dispersement of the musicians is as follows: in the center, above altar, 16 or 17 violins in two ranks; to their left and right, tenor viola or cello and theorbo (large lute); in remainder of side balconies, singers. Organ pipes are above to the left and right.

the composer Georg Muffat, who had observed Lully's style when a student in Paris (1663–69) and wrote about it long afterward in his *Florilegium Secundum* (1698). Even England had its 24 Violins of the King, established by King Charles II after he returned in 1660 from his exile in France. Later in England a small band known as the Private Musick was modeled on Lully's smaller, elite group.[4]

In Italy, as might be expected, the tradition of orchestral music initially grew in conjunction with the opera and its religious counterpart, the oratorio. Italy had no single organization to match the great string bands at the French court, partly because Italy still was constituted of a number of cities and city-states that were bitter rivals in everything, including music. In the long view, this Italian multiplicity and rivalry probably constituted a healthier condition for musical development than did the uniformity and royal hegemony that shaped music in France.

But two Italian cities contributed especially to the early development of instrumental music: Bologna and Venice. Bologna, seat of a distinguished medieval university and proud custodian of a long musical tradition, could claim one of the most brilliant permanent ensembles in all of Europe. The great basilica of San Petronio was the home of this group, which was established by Maurizio Cazatti, maestro di capella at San Petronio from 1657 until 1671. San Petronio's music was further nurtured by Cazatti's successor, Giovanni P. Colonna, who died in 1695. The San Petronio orchestra was disbanded for a few years at the close of the seventeenth century, but it became even more brilliant after its reorganization in 1701. A watercolor preserved in the archives of San Petronio (see illustration) permits us to see how the instrumentalists were deployed for

---

[4] We may read about these English ensembles in occasional entries in the memoirs of the famous trio of Restoration diarists: Pepys, North, and Evelyn.

the celebration of the great patronal feast of San Petronio in 1722. According to the church records, 141 musicians were paid for this performance, although the artist, for obvious practical reasons, has shown a more modest number. In general, during the first eight years of the eighteenth century, the number of violins hired for the feast of San Petronio varied from eleven to nineteen. From eight to fourteen violas and five or six cellos were used. Generally there were as many as five violoni (string basses), and the importance of the lowest part (*basso continuo*) is further attested by the constant presence in the orchestral lists of a formidable battery of chordal instruments for "realizing" the harmony suggested by the linear part. These usually included one or two theorboes (large lutes) and four, or even five, organs. The dominance of these chordal instruments assured a certain degree of cohesiveness, but the individual instruments were not encouraged to develop the sturdy independence and disciplined techniques that would be required before instrumental music could truly come of age. Brass and wind instruments were always represented in the lists for the great feasts at San Petronio—generally a pair of trumpets, six trombones, three or four cornetti (wind instruments that often served in lieu of horns as the treble of the brass choir), and at least one oboe.[5]

The real importance of the musical establishment at Bologna lay in its influence as a place for training instrumental performers and composers, for the roster of its distinguished members is a long one and includes the great violinist Corelli. Many of the Bolognese artists eventually moved to other cities in Italy and to foreign courts. Especially significant was the temporary emigration to Germany of two celebrated virtuoso-composers: Giuseppe Torelli and Francesco Pistocchi. During most of the suspension of the San Petronio orchestra (1695–1701), these two Bolognese musicians served at the court of Ansbach, where the music-loving pair, Friedrich III, Margrave of Brandenburg, and his wife, the Electress Sophie Charlotte, presided. Later Torelli took his prowess as a violinist and his early versions of the orchestral concerto and symphony to the court of Leopold I at Vienna.[6] It was through just such cross-fertilization as that accomplished by the talented Bolognese musicians that the taste for instrumental music and the expertise in its production were spread from Italy to the courts of northern Europe. Brilliant native German composers in the generation of J. S. Bach, Telemann, and Handel were direct heirs of this tradition.

Venice, by the early eighteenth century, had lost much of the political acumen and zeal for commerce that had brought such prosperity in earlier years. Fortunately, the city's devotion to music was more enduring. Music at the great basilica of St. Mark was still distinctive, but the most vigorous activity centered around a number of foundling asylums, each with its own superbly trained ensemble of orphan girls. Two composers who were vital to the future of instrumental

[5] See Karl Geiringer, *Instruments in the History of Western Music*, 3rd ed. (New York: Oxford University Press), for a full description of the evolution and capabilities of all instruments in this book.

[6] For a full account of music at San Petronio, see Eugene Enrico, "Giuseppe Torelli's Music for Instrumental Ensemble with Trumpet" (Ph.D. diss., University of Michigan, 1970), or his *The Orchestra at San Petronio in the Baroque Era* (Washington: Smithsonian Institution, 1975).

music concentrated their careers at Venice: Giovanni Legrenzi (1626–1690) and Antonio Vivaldi (1678–1741). Both men composed instrumental pieces that helped to shape many aspects of the early symphony. Vivaldi was especially influential in devising characteristic figurations and passage-work for strings, which persisted in instrumental music for at least half a century after his death. Perhaps Vivaldi's most important accomplishment, however, was his demonstration that instrumental music can sound truly exciting—as dramatic in its own fashion as the opera.

Very soon, other cities and most courts were supporting established instrumental groups. As the eighteenth century neared its midpoint, musical taste was veering more and more in the direction of purely instrumental works. Germany and Austria, where instrumental music was to achieve its splendid maturity, had been heavily infiltrated by musicians from the south, as we have observed. The early works from those countries naturally revealed their Italianate lineage.

The Public Concert

More than any other type of instrumental music, the symphony is a public art. Since it has appeal for many kinds of people, it is best enjoyed in a place that is spacious and easily accessible. Toward the end of the seventeenth century, England moved to establish a stable tradition of concerts available to people of diverse stations and tastes. This democratization of music, in which England continued to be a leader throughout the eighteenth century, was a great boon for instrumental music of every kind.

In France, public concerts were established in 1725, when Philidor founded the series *Le Concert Spirituel* at the Tuileries in Paris. This great concert foundation continued to flourish until the French Revolution and provided an audience for many of the eighteenth century's greatest performing artists and composers. In Germany, Frankfurt-am-Main and Hamburg led in the effort to make music widely enjoyed. By the 1760s, however, Vienna was already assuming the pre-eminent role it was destined to occupy all during the Classical period. America was not far behind Europe, since concerts on a more modest scale were organized before the middle of the eighteenth century in centers like Boston, Philadelphia, and Charleston.

Clearly the day of public music had arrived. The symphony as it evolved after 1750 was a vigorous and glorious response to the new, more democratic musical taste.

The Symphony's Debt to Earlier Forms

Few of the greatest composers were required to be pioneers, since they tended to emerge at fortunate points in musical history, at periods when stimulating new ideas had already been shaped for maximum usefulness by skilled composers who were not themselves able to produce masterworks. Both Haydn and Mozart evolved their great Classical symphonies by drawing on a variety of musical types used and shaped by their predecessors. The fundamental problem for composers of instrumental music, once it had become more than just an alternative medium of performance for vocal pieces, was to generate nonverbal, purely musical organizing factors to stand in lieu of a text, for the text had been the skeleton of Western musical structure from earliest times. Yet the very fact that composers needed to devise musical means for cohesiveness, vivid delineation, and expansion of ideas forced them to be inventive. Even the fledgling sonatas and other instrumental pieces from the earliest years of the eighteenth century show a certain musical integrity that few vocal works can match. At this point, it is well to recall some of the forms used for that early instrumental music, since each made its special contribution to the vigor of the Classical symphony.

The Suite

The idea of a multimovement composition originated in the cyclic Mass which, as early as the fourteenth century, had joined five texts from the Ordinary of the Mass (Kyrie, Gloria, Credo, Sanctus, Agnus Dei) into a composite piece. As instrumental compositions gained in popularity, composers began to combine contrasting dance movements to form similarly composite pieces. In the sixteenth century, dance movement pairs such as the *pavane-gaillarde* were common. Eventually, composers joined several dances of various kinds and often prefaced or interspersed them with short pieces of nondance types. During the seventeenth century, such dance suites were written for lute, various keyboard instruments, and instrumental ensembles; the music was much of a kind, with little distinction accorded by the performing medium. Dance suites were especially popular in Germany where, in 1617, J. H. Schein's *Banchetto musicale* appeared, offering twenty such suites for viols or substitute instruments. Each suite had a *padovana*, *gagliarda*, *corrente*, and *allemande*. The *allemande* generally concluded with a variation (*tripla*) through which the idea of development was injected into instrumental forms. Johann Froberger, who composed fine dance suites for keyboard instruments, was broadly influential since he visited France, England, and Italy. He is generally credited with establishing the fixed order of dances in the suite: *allemande, courante (corrente), sarabande, gigue*. Froberger's effect may be observed in the numerous dance suites for various performance mediums written by J. S. Bach, Handel, and their contemporaries.

The Classical symphony, as is readily apparent, is indebted to the dance suite for an early model of a multimovement, composite instrumental piece. In addition, most symphonies included a movement of dance type—the *menuet* (or *menuetto*)—which, while not a regular movement in the earlier suites, was closely related to the *courante* (or *corrente*)[7] and was very popular at the French court.

[7] Both the *courante* and the *menuet* tend to fuse duple and triple meters, so that a measure needs often to bear some such dual indication as $\frac{3}{4} \frac{6}{8}$. See the discussion of the Menuetto of Mozart's G minor Symphony, K. 550, for an instance of this metric complexity.

Early Sonata Movements

Most of the early sonatas written for one or two melodic instruments (violin, flute, or oboe) and basso continuo (played by a cello, string bass, or bassoon, with a keyboard instrument to "realize" the implied harmony) were multimovement works. Corelli, Vivaldi, Telemann, J. S. Bach, and Handel, along with their lesser contemporaries, all wrote many such pieces. Sometimes a sonata was made up of several dance movements prefaced by an Adagio or Preludio, thus showing a close affinity for the suite, as described above. This type was called *sonata da camera* (chamber sonata), or *partita*. A second type, the *sonata da chiesa* (church sonata), used several movements of nondance type and was considered a more "serious" kind of composition. Several aspects of the sonata da chiesa are reflected in the symphony as it ultimately developed, especially the basic form of many of the movements. Regardless of its type, a movement of one of these early sonatas was likely to show a binary (two-part) form, the implication of two-part division resting largely in a definite change of key. The plan of such a movement, in its simplest guise, was as follows:

PART I				PART II			
Key of X	modulation	cadence in Key of Y	:‖	Key of Y	modulation	cadence in Key of X	‖

This form worked best when Part I commenced with a distinctive, easily recognizable motive and the composer recalled that motive transposed at the start of Part II. This simple binary form carried the seed of the sonata-allegro form, which was the most important and sophisticated design developed for movements in the symphony.

The Concerto

Compositions written in the concerted[8] manner are the most vigorous exponents of the favored sound in Baroque music. The principle of contrast is basic to all pieces called *concerto*, especially contrasting instrumental timbres or opposed dynamics. In the *concerto grosso*, the most popular type, this principle of contrast is the basic instigation of the music: the performing force is divided into a larger body of strings, the *concerto grosso* or *ripieno*, and a smaller body of solo instruments, the *concertino*, made up of from one to as many as four or five different instruments. As the music posits these two groups in rather close and constant alternation, automatic changes from loud (*forte*) to soft (*piano*) are produced. Often, if the *concertino* group includes wind as well as string instruments, a difference of timbre adds another dimension to the contrast.

The concerto grosso was the principal model for distribution of instruments of the orchestra throughout the eighteenth century; the string choir continued to be the foundation of the orchestral sonority, with winds and brass added occasionally for color, emphasis, or simply to increase the volume of sound.

[8] All words with the root "concert" derive from the Latin *concertatio* ("contest"). In musical contexts, the additional Italian implication of *concertare* ("to adjust" or "to adapt") is generally present.

The Italian Overture

The opera, which originated just at the start of the seventeenth century, was the most exciting and successful new type to appear in European music. Early composers developed the orchestra mostly as an adjunct of the opera. Before long, operatic composers felt the need to devise a purely instrumental piece as a curtain-raiser, which they titled *ouverture* or, in certain cases, *sinfonia*. At first these prefatory pieces were brief and unsubstantial. Eventually, however, they gained in interest and importance, and many music historians point to the opera overture, especially as it was cultivated by Neapolitan composers early in the eighteenth century, as the true model for the symphony. Alessandro Scarlatti (1659–1725) was the most skillful and prolific of these Neapolitan composers. His opera overture (or *sinfonia*) is likely to pose three sections in a tempo scheme of fast-slow-fast. This alternation of tempo does, indeed, foreshadow the eventual order of three of the movements of the Classical symphony. Only the dance movement (menuetto) is lacking.

Perhaps this quite obvious affinity has been overemphasized, however, for the Classical symphony, as has been stated already, pays deference to many different forms from the Baroque period. The opera overture might even be viewed as an impediment to the maturation of the symphony, for two reasons. First, the overture had, as its basic function, to attract immediate attention and to pique interest for the pièce de résistance to come: the opera itself. The ceremonial, occasional quality of the opera overture clung to the symphony for many years, tending to inhibit its emergence as an innovative, autonomous form. Second, "learned" development, a hallmark of the mature symphony, was alien to the opera, which was, in the eighteenth century at least, written to divert. The kind of sophisticated musical amplification found in the best symphonies of Haydn and Mozart could develop only after the symphony had lost the aspects of an auxiliary composition.

Some Pre-Classical Symphonists

We cannot be sure on just what models Haydn structured his earliest symphonies. We can, however, cite a number of skilled composers who were active during Haydn's youth and whose embryo symphonies may well have been known to him. As we become increasingly aware of the profusion of works bearing some such title as Symphony or *Sinfonia* and written during the three decades following 1735, we are less and less willing to point to any particular composer or group as Haydn's progenitors. It may be remarked with conviction only that the seeds of the symphony were in the wind and that they found wonderfully fertile soil in Joseph Haydn's talent.

The pioneers of the symphony worked in diverse situations, but it is significant that their places of origin or activity were all within easy traveling distance from Vienna. Consideration of several representative members of this transitional generation of symphonists may well commence with Giovanni Battista Sammartini (1701–1775), who was based at Milan. This ancient Sforza stronghold was under Habsburg rule during most of Sammartini's lifetime and thus had close connections with Austria. His popularity was apparently wide since manuscripts and early editions of his music have been found in such dispersed locations as Paris, Amsterdam, Basel, and London.[9]

Sammartini's symphonies are primarily for strings. Horn parts are included in some early sources, but these appear to be optional, perhaps added later. A specific part for the viola is often lacking, and the lowest part is shared by cellos, string basses, and an implied keyboard instrument.

A Symphony in G of Sammartini, which Churgin[10] places among works written between 1735 and 1740, is sprightly and manifests several forward-looking traits. For one, it has four movements, in contrast to the more usual three of the pre-Classical symphony; but the fourth is a Menuetto, which may have been added at a later time, since it appears also in other contexts.

The opening *Allegro ma non troppo* resembles the design (incipient sonata-allegro) used for many first movements of Haydn's earlier symphonies. A double bar with repeat marks at measure 17 suggests the type of binary sonata movement described above. The opening measures have grouped, incisive chords in violins underlaid with scales, the kind of ceremonial opening found in so many pieces derived from overtures. Ahead of the double bar, a modulation to the dominant key, D major, takes place and is confirmed by a strong cadence. Immediately after this cadence, starting the second part of the design, the opening flourish is recalled, but at the level of D major. This movement exceeds many of the earlier models in that, after measure 33, the first section in G major is recalled, virtually intact. Few of the earlier sonata movements achieved so rounded a form through recapitulation of the entire opening portion.

The second movement, Grave, is not an autonomous piece, but a link between the opening movement and the *Allegro assai* that follows. The Grave has only 6 measures, but its texture contrasts strongly with the surrounding movements: it is based throughout on the trochaic (♩♪) rhythm of the French overture, and the key is somewhat unstable because of the changing inflection of various pitches (C♯-C♮ and B♭-B♮ especially).

The *Allegro assai* resembles the first movement in form but is even closer to Haydn's early sonata design, since the opening material returns at the dominant level within the first section, ahead of the double bar.

The final movement, Menuetto, uses the early two-part design, in which the initial key returns for the close but without reference to opening material.

Another important member of the pre-Classical group of symphonists is Georg

[9] That reliable editions of Sammartini's symphonies are now available is due largely to the work of Bathia Churgin and Newell Jenkins. Various articles and publications of these two scholars furnish a wealth of information about Sammartini. Eighteen symphonies adjudged early (before about 1740) are included in Churgin, ed., *The Symphonies of G. B. Sammartini*, vol. 1, "The Early Symphonies" (Cambridge: Harvard University Press, 1968) — hereafter abbreviated Churgin SSI.

[10] Churgin SSI, pp. 46 and 151-60. This symphony is available also in miniature score, ed. Newell Jenkins: *Sinfonia in G Major for String Orchestra* (Edition Eulenberg).

Mathias Monn (1717–1750). Monn belongs to the Viennese school, since he was probably born at Klosterneuburg, near the Austrian capital, and certainly began his musical studies in the choir of the famous monastery there. His brief career centered at Vienna, where the last decade of his life coincided with Haydn's residence there as a choirboy at St. Stephen's Cathedral. The young Haydn was most likely familiar with some of Monn's *divertimenti*, symphonies, and other instrumental pieces.[11]

Monn's Symphony in D major,[12] composed in 1740, is a remarkably substantial composition. First, it has four movements arranged in the order that was to become typical in the Classical symphony: Allegro, Aria, Menuetto, Allegro, all of them in the key of D major. The use of instruments (transverse flute, bassoon, horns, violins, and basso continuo) is individual. During the opening portion of the first movement, each wind instrument doubles one of the string parts to achieve an integrated *tutti*, in contrast to a deployment that separates and contrasts the two choirs. A second section (meas. 10–16) poses a contrasting texture when the flute is accompanied by violins. This portion commences with a passage unstable as to key, built up of sequential figures hinting at E minor, D minor, C major, and A minor, before the expected dominant key of A major is established firmly during the 4 measures preceding the customary double bar (Ex. 1-1).

EXAMPLE 1-1   Monn, Symphony in D/I;[13] meas. 10–19,
                               second thematic group

---

[11] See *Denkmäler der Tonkunst in Österreich* (DTÖ), vol. 31: *Wiener Instrumentalmusik vor und um 1750*, ed. Karl Horwitz and Karl Riedel (Leipzig, 1908; reprint, Graz, 1959), for a representative group of works by Monn and other early symphonists.

[12] Ibid., pp. 37-50.

[13] Specific movements will be designated hereafter in this fashion: No. 47/I = first movement of No. 47.

This Allegro has no palpable reprise of opening material, although the initial key of D major is re-established before the close of the movement. The final Allegro is similar in design, but it does include an unmistakable recall of the opening section, a forward-looking gesture.

Of all the composers active around Vienna near the middle of the eighteenth century, none looms larger in retrospect than Georg Christoph Wagenseil (1715–1777). His Symphony in D major,[14] written in 1746, is as mature and full-fledged a symphony as any to be discovered before Haydn's early maturity, although it has but three movements—Allegro, Andante (Aria), Tempo di Menuetto. The opening Allegro, which is 72 measures, comes close to a fully rounded sonata-allegro design. The first portion (up to the :‖) has a strong, assertive second key (A major), which contrasts with the multitonal implications of the parallel portion of the Monn symphony cited above. Furthermore, this A major section has a distinctive, cohesive second theme rather than a motivic group, as in the Monn. Wagenseil displays considerable ingenuity in developing and extending materials. A turn toward A minor, such as was found also in the Monn symphony, is present in this first movement of Wagenseil. In both cases, it is introduced so as to contrast the minor with the parallel major mode, and not as part of a system of mixed mode, such as was to be developed by later composers.

[14] Ibid., pp. 16ff.

Of all the pre-Classical composers, none has achieved the widespread recognition accorded the musicians who served at the court of Mannheim in the Rhineland district of Germany. The principal reason for their current reputation lies in the enthusiasm and articulateness of their "discoverer" and advocate, Hugo Riemann.

Early in the twentieth century, when serious investigation of eighteenth-century music had barely commenced, Riemann, in his persuasive essay "*Die Mannheimer Schule*" ("The Mannheim School"),[15] brought these composers and their music to public attention, citing them as principal models for Haydn and his contemporaries. While we should not now belittle the importance of Riemann's pronouncements, we may need to temper them. Musicians would probably have seized less avidly on these men of Mannheim had more music of contemporary symphonists been known and available. At the present time, we regard these Mannheim composers—Johann Stamitz (1717–1757) and F. X. Richter (1709–1789) in particular—as important members of an extensive group that paved the way for Haydn and Mozart. The atmosphere at the Mannheim court was quite cosmopolitan, for Stamitz was a Bohemian and Richter a Moravian. Others of their colleagues were Austrians, and all of them had close ties to both Italy and Paris.

A candid assessment of the repertory of Mannheim symphonists, made now with fuller knowledge of compositions of such men as Sammartini and Wagenseil, suggests that their flair for the orchestra set them apart. Of all the Mannheim orchestral effects, none has received as much attention as the famous crescendo, which seems to have electrified listeners, especially those who came from afar. Mannheim composers frequently interpolated crescendo portions into their symphonies, the length of the passage varying from a single measure with a compressed, electric effect of crescendo-decrescendo ($\prec\!\!\!\prec\ \succ\!\!\!\succ$) to prolonged crescendo passages of 10 to 12 measures. During the longer passages, certain conditions are likely to be present. (1) The harmony is static or moves in a circle to return where it started, thus slowing down the essential "harmonic rhythm." (2) The passage is propelled by a certain figure maintained in repetition or sequence, so that "musical events" are held to a minimum and listeners may concentrate on the dynamic quality. (3) Longer passages of crescendo tend to occur at unessential points in the design, such as transitions, extensions, or just portions of temporizing. In Ex. 1-2, which shows a typical passage, a full cadence in D major is taken (meas. 13) and is extended during the 4-measure crescendo passage while the low strings maintain the tonic note D.

Stamitz's symphonies generally have four movements, with the Menuetto most often third. Richter favors the three-movement design, often with a Menuetto as finale. Both composers are likely to place the second (slow) movement in some such deviant key as the relative, dominant, or subdominant, although there are

---

[15] See Hugo Riemann's preface to the volumes devoted to these composers in *Denkmäler deutscher Tonkunst in Bayern*, series 2, vol. 3, parts 1-2 (1906-07).

EXAMPLE 1-2   Stamitz, Sinfonia ("La Melodia Germanica")
                                           No. 1/I, meas. 12–16[16]

plenty of instances of a single key maintained for all movements of a given work.

The overall designs used for single movements resemble those described earlier for Sammartini, Monn, and Wagenseil. The Mannheimers did, however, devise certain distinctive gestures, which were imitated by later composers.

1. A head-motive or brilliant opening flourish, probably copied from the famous *premier coup d'archet* of the Paris orchestra, is likely to occur in detached form at the beginning of the first movement. This distinctive material is not, in most instances, subject to frequent manipulation and recall, as are other materials. Rather, it is reserved for specific and important spots in the design, such as conclusive cadences or principal points of recapitulation.

2. Principal elements (themes) are generally built up from brief, associated figures or motives whose identifying character is likely to be rhythmic rather than melodic.

3. If material from the opening section is recalled toward the close of the movement, it is likely to be with some such mutation as a transposed sequence of its elements—although the original (tonic) key is always restored for closing sections.

4. Movements that make frequent use of crescendo passages are likely to be longer than usual, since the crescendo passage is generally in excess of the basic material. Such movements were models for later composers who often extended a movement with passages designed merely to exploit the sound of the orchestra.

Having briefly surveyed certain aspects of selected symphonies from the middle years of the eighteenth century, we may now turn to the works of Haydn and Mozart with some awareness of the rich heritage from which their symphonies emerged.

---

[16] See *Mannheim Symphonies*, ed. Riemann, 2 vols. (New York: Broude Bros., n.d.), vol. 1.

2

The Earlier Viennese Period:
Haydn and Mozart

Gifted composers have often appeared in pairs, even in clusters, as witness the talented coterie of men who were contemporaries of Josquin des Prez, or the parallel careers of J. S. Bach and Handel. The obvious inference is that talent fosters talent, and the marvels of the years between 1732 and 1797 surely support such a view. During this period, there were born, within five hundred miles of one another, four composers whose long shadows extend even to our own day. As a group, they marked out the course of Western music for at least a century. Two of them—Franz Joseph Haydn (1732–1809) and Ludwig van Beethoven (1770–1827)—were recognized and widely influential within their own life spans. The other two—Wolfgang Amadeus Mozart (1756–1791) and Franz Peter Schubert (1797–1828)—had far less immediate influence, perhaps because their music was so intensely personal, and because they lacked certain qualities of opportunism and practicality.

Haydn and Mozart enjoyed a lovely, generous friendship that made their compositions of the 1780s splendid examples of reciprocal stimulation. Beethoven labored alone, as befitted a Titan; essentially, he moved others but remained aloof from his contemporaries. Schubert's career forms a brief, lyrical coda to the era we like to call the Viennese period, for all these composers spent major portions of their lives in the Austrian capital.

In the symphony, each of the four discovered an amenable, expressive, useful form. Haydn and Beethoven chose the symphony to carry much of their noblest music; together, they brought this orchestral form to its zenith. Mozart's symphonies, on the other hand, must yield first place to his piano concertos and his operas. Perhaps 5 of Mozart's surviving 41 symphonies are of supreme quality. Schubert found the orchestra inflexible and troublesome until the very end of his life. Only his B minor ("Unfinished") and his C major ("Great") symphonies are masterworks in the grand tradition of his Viennese predecessors.

Numerous historians have cited the debt owed to Joseph Haydn by composers who came after him; this is obvious and indisputable. Few, however, have remarked that those preceding Haydn also have an obligation to him. For who would show interest today in the genial but merely diverting music of Sammartini, the Mannheimers, and other pre-Classicists, except that their embryo symphonies appear to foreshadow certain traits of such masterpieces as Haydn's Paris and London symphonies? This is true regardless of whether Haydn was consciously influenced by these men as models. Haydn was not only the most durable and influential composer of his own generation; by his ultimate achievement, he increased the stature of dozens of lesser musicians who had gone before him or were his contemporaries.

Fortunately Haydn preferred the symphony (along with the string quartet) over all other instrumental forms. The earlier serenades, cassations, and divertimenti that had so delighted contemporary audiences, the orchestral concertos of Vivaldi and his successors, the learned fugues of Fux and Bach—all these were absorbed into Haydn's mature quartets and symphonies. Those who doubt man's essential perseverance and capacity for growth could well spend time contemplating the more than one hundred symphonies of Haydn's legacy. The progress from his earliest sturdy, attractive, but genre works to his confident, sophisticated, individual London symphonies is a record to cheer the most skeptical.

The Symphonies of Haydn

Seldom has a composer matched Haydn in his tenacious consistency, his conservative hoarding of skills, once he had mastered them. Although his early symphonies only slightly indicate the glories to come, it is possible to observe, in an overview of the total corpus of the symphonies, many traits that persisted throughout the years, others that developed plausibly and logically from one period to another. Hence we shall begin with a synoptic view of all Haydn's symphonies.

Chronology of the Symphonies

A number of devoted, long-time Haydn scholars (Geiringer, Robbins Landon, Larsen particularly) have probed the matter of chronology over the course of almost half a century, but several problems concerning dating still remain. This uncertainty relates mostly to works written before Haydn was well known, and such details are of concern primarily to Haydn specialists. The numbering of the symphonies as established by Mandyczewski in 1907, in the first volume of Breitkopf and Härtel's uncompleted *Gesamtausgabe* (Collected Edition), is still essentially valid and in use today. It will serve in the present discussion. The careful student will be wise, however, to examine the detailed information concerning any particular Haydn symphony as it is included in Appendix I of H. C. Robbins Landon's *The Symphonies of Joseph Haydn*. And everyone should maintain an attitude of healthy skepticism about dates, especially for works completed before 1766. The effort to fully reconstruct Haydn's earlier years and to recover authentic scores and parts is constantly being pursued. Every now and then an obscure monastery or library yields a hidden treasure that forces revision even of data that had seemed secure.

Several plans for grouping Haydn's symphonies have been proposed,[1] and each has its special rationale. For our discussion, Haydn's successive patrons or sponsors provide the basis for an informal grouping. Haydn wrote to please his employers, and, until the late 1770s, he composed for immediate performance. Only during his last fifteen or so years did the matter of sale to a publisher raise the question of a work's broad appeal. By that time, Haydn was independent from his patrons and reasonably secure from the blandishments of entrepreneurs. Still, Haydn was a captive of his environment during the greater part of his creative life, although his music attests that this situation was not without its advantages.

Haydn had written a great deal of music—Masses, sonatas, trios, divertimenti, and so on—before he undertook to compose his first symphony. The reason seems not to be that he held this form in special awe, since the qualities of the symphony of the 1750s were shared by most other kinds of instrumental music. Rather, it was that the musical resources for performing a symphony were available only in particular circumstances, such as the musical organization attached to a princely household. Haydn seems to have written symphonies as soon as he had access to such resources. In 1758, he joined the establishment of the Bohemian Count Ferdinand Maximilian von Morzin, who maintained a winter palace at Vienna and a summer residence at Lukaveç. The first five symphonies (as numbered by Mandyczewski) were almost certainly written while Haydn was serving the Count Morzin. To these may probably be added about a dozen other works bearing numbers prior to 36.[2] These early symphonies are sprightly, skillfully constructed, but not significantly superior to similar pieces written by the pre-Classical symphonists cited in Chapter 1.

Haydn was engaged in May, 1761, to become Vice-Kapellmeister at the court of Prince Paul Anton Esterházy, a Hungarian nobleman of enormous wealth, prestige, and fine musical taste. In 1762, Prince Anton died and was succeeded by his brother, Prince Nicolaus, who was Haydn's employer and patron for 28 years, until the Prince's death in 1790. His devotion to music and his discerning taste were responsible for the maintenance of a musical household that was a principal factor in Haydn's extraordinary development. Haydn was promoted to the post of Kapellmeister in 1766, the same year that saw the opening of

---

[1] See Karl Geiringer, *Haydn: A Creative Life in Music*, 3rd ed. (Berkeley: University of California Press, 1982)—hereafter, "Geiringer H." See also H. C. Robbins Landon, *Haydn Symphonies* (London: BBC, 1966), a useful synopsis of information contained in his major study *The Symphonies of Joseph Haydn* (London: Universal Edition, 1955). The larger Landon study is abbreviated hereafter "Landon SJH," the synopsis "Landon HBBC."

[2] See Landon HBBC, p. 12 and Landon SJH, pp. 776-77.

Concert hall at Esterháza, the palace of the Esterházy princes, where Haydn performed most of his works.

Esterháza, the Prince's new palace, which was equipped, eventually, with a theater, several smaller audience halls, and living quarters for the musicians. Until late in Haydn's life, Esterháza provided a place for the performance of the majority of his works.

The improved performance situation and Haydn's promotion to the more prestigious post were very stimulating for the young composer, but they tended to turn his attention, from time to time, away from the symphony, toward opera. Those digressions were not without their fruits, however, for Haydn's symphonies written after such deviations showed fresh vitality from the kind of tension, drama, and sharp contrast that are native to the opera. About 1780, Haydn's public life began. Although he did not travel much until 1791, after the death of his Prince, he did, during the ten years before that time, write important symphonies for other situations than Esterháza and for other patrons.

The first three of the Esterházy symphonies, Nos. 6, 7, and 8, bear the programmatic titles "Le Matin" ("Morning"), "Le Midi" ("Noon"), and "Le Soir" ("Evening") and may have been suggested to Haydn by some such earlier work as Vivaldi's set of four concertos known as "The Seasons." The derivative flavor is supported by many traits of the three symphonies, which use, in several of their movements, a *violino concertante* (solo violin) and, likewise, a *violoncello concertante*, after the fashion of the concerto grosso. Many affective chromatic passages recall similar figures in works of J. S. Bach, Vivaldi, and certain Italian operatic composers. The opening of the second movement of "Le Matin," with its slow-moving, chromatic bass line, and the poignant line assigned to the *Violino I principale* (solo) in the Recitativo movement of "Le Midi" are typical examples. The opening Adagio of "Le Midi" with its permeating trochaic rhythms (♩♪♩♪♩) recalls the French overture of Lully's day. And the shared cadenza of "Le Midi" again points to the earlier concerto form.

Haydn's preoccupation with the Baroque idiom was short-lived, however, for the C major Symphony No. 9 reverts to the prevalent Austrian style, and some seventeen other symphonies of similar flavor were written before Haydn's promotion to the post of Kapellmeister.

During the next ten years Haydn wrote at least two dozen symphonies, most of them bearing numbers in the 30s, 40s, and 50s.[3] His encounter with the *Sturm und Drang* ("storm and stress") movement occurred during the middle years of this period, as many writers have pointed out. Haydn's interest in the movement is reflected in several subjective traits of his symphonies at that time: more expressive subjects, a certain impetuousness, especially in final movements, and a propensity for the affective qualities imparted by chromatic inflections, vacillating keys, and abrupt changes in texture or dynamics. Many of these symphonies have titles—"Lamentation," "Farewell," "Mourning," and so on. Most of the titles are found in early copies and reflect the renewed interest in "the word," which was an aspect of eighteenth-century rationalism.

Two circumstances of the years surrounding 1780 exerted fortunate influences on the quality of Haydn's symphonies. The first was the composer's renewed interest in chamber music, especially the string quartet, which brought flexibility and grace to all his writing. The second was Haydn's friendship with Mozart and the stimulating influence the two men exerted on each other, which quickened after the younger musician became a permanent resident of Vienna in 1781. The affinity with Mozart is strong in several of the symphonies bearing numbers in the 70s, conspicuously in No. 78 in C minor, written in 1782. The opening movement, Vivace, has a first subject that Mozart himself might have written, since he was to use so many like it; for example, the opening of his Piano Concerto in C minor, K. 491. The wide-spaced angular lines in measures 2 through 4, and the sharp contrast in the insinuating chromaticism of the next 4-measure phrase both were hallmarks of Mozart's manner with the minor mode (Ex. 2-1a). The sprightly second subject, in E-flat major (Ex. 2-1b), also has a Mozartian flavor.

---

[3] Landon HBBC, pp. 21-25; Geiringer H, pp. 236-39, 259ff.

And the skillful intertwining of both these subjects in an imitative portion inserted into the Recapitulation section (meas. 142–156) suggests similar passages in the string quartets of both men.

EXAMPLE 2-1a   Haydn, Symphony No. 78/I, meas. 1–8

EXAMPLE 2-1b   Haydn, Symphony No. 78/I, meas. 55–59, second subject

Haydn's first major contact with foreign patrons inspired the symphonies written between 1785 and 1789. This period saw the composition of the symphonies numbered 82 through 92. Nos. 82 through 87 comprised a set of six written for the Concerts de la Loge Olympique at Paris. Nos. 88 and 89 were a pair that reached the Paris publisher Sieber through the violinist Tost, to whom Haydn may have passed them. The set numbered 90 through 92 was perhaps commissioned by the French Comte d'Ogny. Some confusion exists, however, since in 1787 Haydn offered them also to the Prince Oettingen-Wallerstein. And No. 92 is now known as the "Oxford," a designation acquired several years after its composition in 1788, because Haydn himself conducted it at Oxford in July 1791, when he received his honorary Doctor of Music degree there.

To these Paris symphonies should probably be added another large orchestral work, commissioned in 1785 for the Lenten observances at the Cathedral of Cádiz: *The Seven Last Words of Our Savior on the Cross*. Although the total structure of this splendid piece (Introduction, seven "sonatas," and a finale, "The Earthquake") is closer to that of an instrumental cantata, it matches in quality and scope the other more literally symphonic works of this period.

Haydn crowned his instrumental writing with the twelve magnificent symphonies, Nos. 93–104, written between 1791 and 1795 for his two English visits. These were composed at the behest of J. P. Salomon, a London impresario, and the group divides naturally into two series, with Nos. 99–104 composed for Haydn's second visit.[4]

Haydn wrote no symphonies after his return to Austria from England; but his two great oratorios, *The Creation* and *The Seasons*, bear somewhat the same relationship to his purely orchestral symphonies that we recognize more readily between Beethoven's Ninth ("Choral") Symphony and his preceding eight.

An overview of this incredible list of symphonies, the most ample legacy in this form from any composer, must produce first of all a sense of awe and respect. Beyond this, it emphasizes what a man of intelligence, musicality, and consistent ambition can achieve if he is always responsive to circumstances and opportunities. Haydn's symphonies are essentially musical dialogues with his hearers. He adapted his language to their capacities and was shrewd enough never to expand his vocabulary beyond the ability of his audience to understand. No composer has been more articulate or more widely revered by his contemporaries.

Haydn's Orchestra

The string choir was the cornerstone of the orchestra when Haydn began composing symphonies—as it had been for almost a century before him and as it remained far into the nineteenth century. Haydn was himself a skilled violinist and often participated in the performances at Esterháza. Consequently, his string parts have a confident, practical quality, which he developed first in the string quartets. The viola, generally given the least distinctive role, often reinforced the *bassi* (cellos and string basses) in a higher octave. In the early symphonies, the string bass was the foundation of the basso continuo part and thus of the orchestra; but in actual performance, a bassoon or cello reinforced the bass line, even if it was not specified, and the harpsichord "realized" the harmonies inferred from the notes of the linear bass part. In the early 1770s the specific instrumentation of Haydn's bass parts began to be written out fully in his scores. And from this time, the harpsichord was less and less essential. Many of Haydn's symphonies require the use of a double bass with a low compass of Great C (as opposed to Contra E, the lowest note on the ordinary string bass today).

During Haydn's lifetime string instruments underwent several structural alterations, and the Tourte bow with a slightly concave stick, in place of the older arced one, emerged. These changes had little influence, however, on the character of his string writing. Even so, Haydn's parts for the violin in particular are advanced and innovative, utilizing the full compass of the third octave and such special effects as *pizzicato, ponticello, con sordino*, even *col legno*. Some of the earlier symphonies include parts for a solo violin or violoncello, in the style of the older concerto grosso, as we have noted.

Much of the vitality of sound in Haydn's ¸_chestral works emanates from the horns. Not only did he lavish great care in devising suitable parts within the

[4] See Geiringer H, pp. 326ff., and Landon, HBBC, pp. 49ff., for specific comments on each of the London symphonies. All available details concerning each symphony are found in Landon SJH, pp. 435-593.

restricted capacities of the natural horn, but he circumscribed essential harmonic movement in the symphonic plans to conform to the horn's limitations. Although Haydn used only two horns in most of his symphonies, he did specify four in No. 13, written in 1763. More often, the brass choir was augmented by a pair of natural trumpets, sometimes called *clarini*. Since the limitations of eighteenth-century horns and trumpets were similar, this collaboration was reasonably successful.

Two oboes were the foundation of the woodwind sound and were required from the earliest symphonies. Sometimes, as in No. 22, a pair of English horns was used in place of oboes; and occasionally flutes were specified as a possible alternative. One flute (in addition to oboes) was required for the second and third movements of No. 24, and for No. 31. But the flute did not appear in authentic scores with any consistency until considerably later. Two clarinets were specified in some of the London symphonies (Nos. 99, 100, 101, 103, and 104), although they were available in the Esterházy orchestra much earlier. The bassoon acquired a particular part (as opposed to its mere reinforcement of the bass), early in the 1770s, and gained greater importance as additional high woodwinds—flutes and clarinets—became fixtures in the ensemble.

Kettledrums, of a smaller size than today and requiring hand adjustment for a change of tuning, were part of the orchestra for all Haydn's symphonies. These were tuned to the tonic and dominant of any particular movement and were generally written as they sounded (rather than transposed, with C and G uniformly symbolizing the appropriate tonic and dominant pitches, as was so often the case).

The size of the string section available to Haydn in various situations has considerable importance in adjusting present-day orchestras for effective performance of Haydn's music. There is no information about the size of Count Morzin's group, but orchestras in similar circumstances had, at most, six violins, one viola, and one string bass.[5] Esterháza, in 1761–75, regularly employed five violins or violas, one cello, and one string bass.[6] Clearly these were supplemented by players from other musical groups employed at Eisenstadt, if one is to judge from the *concertante* (solo) string parts in such works as the symphonies "Le Matin," "Le Midi," and "Le Soir." In later years, the Esterháza lists show as many as thirteen violins and violas, and at least two each of cellos and string basses.

Paris, the musical hub of Europe in the days just before the Revolution, had a much more pretentious orchestra. The one for which Haydn wrote his so-called Paris symphonies probably employed as many as forty violins and ten string basses. Haydn did not, however, hear the performances at the Concerts de la Loge Olympique, and his parts for strings seem not to have changed in character because of the increased resources.

At London, Salomon's orchestra, which was the performance medium for most

[5] Landon SJH, p. 110.
[6] C. F. Pohl, *Joseph Haydn* (Berlin, 1875), vol. 1, p. 261.

of Haydn's London symphonies, employed as many as sixteen violins, four violas, three cellos, and four string basses.

Haydn's Key Schemes

The group of keys from which Haydn selected the initial tonal levels for his symphonies was conservative indeed, especially in comparison with the plans for his string quartets and keyboard sonatas. As has already been suggested, the presence of natural brass instruments in the orchestra was seriously inhibiting, and Haydn's choice of key must have been influenced greatly by consideration for the horns and trumpets.

More than a third of all the symphonies are in the keys of C or D major, and it is no coincidence that natural horns and trumpets are at their very best when crooked at these levels. Most of Torelli's trumpet concertos, for example, are in D major. The C (alto) horn, which sounded as written, provided the highest pitches available on an eighteenth-century brass instrument and was extremely brilliant. Haydn demonstrated his partiality for this intense horn sound by writing twenty C major symphonies.

The keys of G, E-flat, B-flat, and A account for another third of all the works. Only infrequently did Haydn use the minor mode for an initial key; he apparently preferred to reserve it for contrast within the body of a movement. The few symphonies that do center in a minor key are likely to have affective, even lugubrious titles, such as No. 26, in D minor, *Lamentatione;* No. 44, in E minor, *Trauersymphonie* ("Mourning Symphony"); No. 45, in F-sharp minor, *Abschieds-symphonie* ("Farewell Symphony"). Haydn seldom availed himself of the melodic flexibility found in the optional inflections of the sixth and seventh scale degrees of minor mode (in C minor, for example, A♭ or A♮, and B♭ or B♮, with the choice suggested by the direction of linear motion). Rather he posed the minor mode to contrast with the major in color and often emphasized this. Their differing attitudes toward the minor mode reveal an essential contrast between Haydn and Mozart: Mozart found wonderful motility and compliance in the variable forms of the minor, as we shall see in his G minor Symphony.

Most of Haydn's symphonies written after 1766 have four movements. A slower movement (Andante, or Adagio, or Allegretto, often with some such expressive addition as "cantabile" or "piu tosto andante") is most often placed second, and a Menuetto with Trio third. In a number of cases, the order of these middle movements is reversed. The Finale is uniformly a fast movement, frequently cast in some kind of duple time (2/4, 6/8, 4/4, for example). The key relationship among the four movements is conservative indeed, even as late as the London symphonies. Most often, the slower movement is placed in a closely related key, such as the dominant or subdominant, or the relative minor or major.[7]

Only about a half-dozen of Haydn's symphonies digress even slightly from the conservative plan just described. No. 60 (1774–75), which has six movements,

---

[7] The string quartets of Opus 76, which display such daring key digressions, were written after Haydn returned from England and after his London symphonies.

is not really a symphony, but a kind of suite based on the incidental music to a play, *Il Distratto*. An opening Adagio-Allegro di molto is in C major and the subsequent Andante in G. A Menuetto and Trio use C major again, but a short Presto employs C minor. An Adagio in F and a Prestissimo in C major round off the work.

No. 80 (1783–84) uses the key scheme D minor/B-flat major/D major/D major for its four movements. This represents the first genuine departure from Haydn's closely circumscribed plan, since B-flat major is the submediant key to D minor. But probably the most colorful juncture comes when the second movement cadences strongly in B-flat, then proceeds to D major for the start of the Menuetto. No. 83 shows a parallel scheme, with its four movements in G minor/E-flat major/G major/G major, respectively. Symphony No. 99, one of the London symphonies, uses E-flat major for the first and fourth movements, but G major (which we may term the "mediant-made-major") for the Adagio. After this, the Menuetto is in E-flat, but its Trio is in C major. The last symphony, No. 104, has an opening Adagio-Allegro in D minor/D major, and a return to D major for the final Spiritoso. Between these two movements are an Adagio in G major and a Menuetto/Trio in D major/B-flat major.

Haydn's Choice of Forms

The element of music commonly termed "form" governs the dispersion and organization of musical materials within the time span required for the entire composition. Organized form provides a sense of unity and cooperation among the disparate elements of a movement and is especially important in longer movements. Form has been of primary concern during periods when composers took a rational approach to writing music. Of all periods, the second half of the eighteenth century has put the highest value on the reasonable.

From very early centuries, the prime organizing force in Western music has been repetition, along with its more sophisticated counterpart, recall after intervention of contrasting material. All plans of formal organization used by Haydn and his contemporaries derive from these fundamentals.

Haydn relied, from time to time, on formal plans that had already served composers well for at least two centuries. One was the variation form in which a theme is first stated simply, then restated a number of times, always with embellishment, amplification, or transformation. The variation form is most likely to occur in slow movements. A second archaic type for him was the fugal movement, in which a number of instrumental parts treat the same material, but enter with it successively, in a series of reasonably spaced imitative entries. Fugal movements were considered old-fashioned in Haydn's day, but he appears to have found such orderly techniques as imitation especially useful when his music most tended to be emotional or subjective, notably in the 1770s. Later, Haydn learned to infuse imitation in smaller doses into the whole texture of his symphonies, with the result that parts were interdependent and subtly unified.

The majority of Haydn's symphonic movements employ one of two design types that were perfected during the eighteenth century. The less sophisticated was the partite form (sometimes called "rondo"), which is successor to the ancient *rondeau* forms of troubadours and trouvères and developed more immediately from the *da capo* aria. In its simplest guises, this kind of structure is *binary* (two-part) or, more frequently, *ternary* (three-part). The binary form is often symbolized AB, each letter representing a musical portion typically 16 to 24 measures in length. It is evident that the binary design is "open-ended" and is used most effectively when more music is to follow. The ternary form, generally symbolized ABA, is immediately seen to be a "closed" or autonomous form. Each letter of a ternary design may symbolize a section of considerable length, and many of Haydn's slow movements are cast as large ternary designs.

Sometimes the partite design was expanded by Haydn and others to encompass more than three parts. Always, however, the design depended for unity on recall of material. The more common large partite, or rondo designs, are these: ABACA, or ABACABA. When such forms are organized with a rational scheme of key relationships, they are satisfying indeed. They often served Haydn well for the slow movement, the dance movement (Menuetto), and the finale.

That form which more than any other is the product of eighteenth-century rationalism is the sonata or, more properly, the *sonata-allegro design*.[8] Haydn almost invariably employed this form for the first movements of his symphonies, and he brought it to a high degree of flexibility and sophistication.

Haydn's sonata-allegro design is always a ternary structure with the three main divisions cast as follows:

FIRST SECTION: *Exposition*

This opening portion reveals the essential ideas from which the remainder of the movement derives. It always has two contrasting key areas. Area I generally opens with some distinctive and easily identifiable material. This material may be expanded to the requisite length by a process of motivic growth; or by frequent infusion of fresh germinating material; or, in Haydn's mature works especially, by fusion of materials into a *theme* that shows a palpable small structure of organized phrases. Area II is always marked by its contrasting key level. It may or may not be marked by introduction of fresh material. The Exposition invariably closes with a strong cadence at the second key level and is further identified by a double bar with repeat marks (:‖).

SECOND SECTION: *Midsection, often called Development*

This second division of the movement may open with any one of a number of gestures. If its allusion to the earlier Baroque sonata form is strong, it is likely to begin with a recall of the opening material of the movement, posed at a stimulating new key level. At other times, a colorful chordal progression or an abrupt dynamic change sets the section into motion. The indispensable quality at the start of the Midsection is energy to stimulate activity in the portions to

---

[8] See William S. Newman, *The Sonata in the Baroque Era*, 4th ed., and *The Sonata in the Classic Era*, 3rd ed. (both New York: Norton, 1983).

follow. The Midsection offers opportunity for sophisticated composers to demonstrate virtuosity in transformation and development of ideas. In a very few instances, Haydn introduced a new theme or idea in the midst of this portion, at just about the midpoint of the entire movement. Eventually, the Midsection must evolve into a texture that prepares for the natural, easy return of the opening material of the movement. This section of active Retransition is likely to be the most ingenious and intense part of the movement.

THIRD SECTION: *Recapitulation*

This portion recalls most or all of the chief musical events of the Exposition, but centers vital materials in the original key. Any key digressions that occur during Recapitulation are brief and likely to use relaxed levels, such as the subdominant or submediant keys. If the movement is a long one, a closing section emphasizing the principal key is generally appended to bring the music to a convincing close.

During his forty-year preoccupation with the sonata-allegro form, Haydn took the design on some surprising excursions, delighting in rejection of the obvious. Certain features of the basic design remained malleable and unpredictable to the very end of his days, and much of the fresh vitality of Haydn's music stems from his scorn for the stereotype. Here are a few characteristic facets of Haydn's sonata design:

1. *Choice of thematic types.* Haydn's thematic material for sonata-allegro movements is likely to be cast in one of two fundamental molds. Routinely in earlier symphonies, but intermittently throughout his life, he used the *thematic group*, developed from one or more motives that are capable of germinating surprisingly long portions. Symphony No. 47/I offers a splendid illustration. Strings and horns present the essential idea in an opening dialogue (Ex. 2-2):

EXAMPLE 2-2   Haydn, Symphony No. 47/I, meas. 1–5

This is extended immediately into a passage of 13 measures. Starting at measure 25, Area II develops from the nucleus of the opening motive: the rhythm ♩. ♪. This is the beginning of an interlocked part in the key of D major, which is closely related to Area I (Ex. 2-3).

The second fundamental type of material used by Haydn merits the designation *theme* (as opposed to thematic group). To achieve a theme, several palpable

EXAMPLE 2-3   Haydn, Symphony No. 47/I, meas. 25–30

phrases are organized into a larger unit (often called a *period*), with a series of clear punctuating cadences. Haydn used this type of essential material throughout his life, but it became increasingly prevalent as Classical taste suggested more carefully balanced structures. The Presto portion of No. 101/I offers a clear example of a three-phrase period, which serves as the principal theme of Area I (Ex. 2-4).

EXAMPLE 2-4   Haydn, Symphony No. 101/I, meas. 24–39

Constant variety in the type of thematic unit chosen, even within a single movement, became a source of liveliness and stimulation in most of Haydn's symphonies.

2. *Application of the so-called monothematic principle.* As many commentators
have pointed out, Haydn liked to recall an initial idea as the germ for a subsequent theme or other structural factor. This practice was a valuable source of
unity. Most commonly, the opening motive of Area II was patterned on that
of Area I but always, of course, with appropriate change of key. Symphony
No. 44/I is typical of many similar movements. The *Allegro con brio* opens with
a forceful theme in E minor (Ex. 2–5):

EXAMPLE 2-5   Haydn, Symphony No. 44/I, meas. 1–4

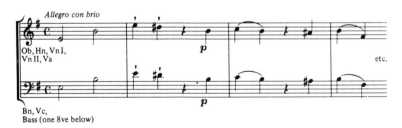

Later, Area II begins with a recall of the same theme, but in G, the relative
major (Ex. 2-6).

EXAMPLE 2-6   Haydn, Symphony No. 44/I, meas. 42–45

Once Area II has been set in motion with a recall of the Area I subject, any of a variety of musical events may ensue, and Haydn is especially adroit in concocting such sections. If only the head-motive of the material is recalled, Area II may progress quickly into a portion that exploits various kinds of orchestral play, such as rapid scales, passages of tremolo, dialogue between choirs, or any of the other orchestral effects with which Haydn became so adept. Not infrequently, however, a new thematic idea follows the recalled material, so that Area II acquires its own distinctive theme to balance Area I.

As a variant of this kind of thematic recall, the second principal portion of the sonata design, the Midsection, may commence with reference to the opening subject, as has been described earlier. But this variant was genuinely Baroque and anachronistic in Haydn's day. If recall of the same material begins both Area II of the Exposition and the Midsection, as sometimes happens, the common material takes on the quality of a cyclic theme, which was to be developed by nineteenth-century composers.

3. Use of a slow introduction before a sonata-type movement. The slow introduction as preface and backdrop for a sonata-allegro–type first movement was favored by Haydn, especially in his later years. All the London symphonies except No. 95 have such preambles. Often the prelude highlights certain qualities of the sonata movement by stressing their opposites in a system of dichotomies, such as slow/fast, minor/major, triple/duple meter, chromatic/diatonic. Only occasionally is material from the introduction recalled during the sonata portion of the movement.

Symphony No. 99

Haydn's Symphony No. 99, one of the most distinctive of the London symphonies, illustrates vividly many of the traits that have been discussed. An analysis of this work follows.

FIRST MOVEMENT: *Sonata-allegro with Introduction, in E-flat major*

Introduction (*Adagio*)

This prelude is divided almost equally into two portions that are connected at measures 10–11 with a vivid enharmonic change: the first cadential pause is taken on the note C♮ in octave unison, with an implication of the submediant of E-flat minor; at the next measure, the C♭ is realized enharmonically as B♮, used eventually as root of a dominant-seventh chord to effect a quick modulation to E minor and, in sequence, another to C minor. At measure 13, the C minor triad is followed by a German augmented-sixth chord, A♭-C-E♭-F♯, which progresses as usual to a G triad (V) in the next measure. From this point (meas. 14), G is maintained as a bass note with the implied V of C minor reinforced by the superimposed harmonies. A pause on G as dominant of C minor at measure 17 is negated abruptly by interjection of the full dominant-seventh harmony of the key of E-flat, for the beginning of the *Vivace assai*. The dual key implications of E-flat and C minor are responsible for the tension and motility of this prefatory section.

The sonata-allegro design (*Vivace assai*)

Exposition
  Meas. 19–47 Area I
    19–26 Theme 1
    27–34 Theme 1 repeated
    34–47 Extension and modulation to B-flat
  Theme 1 (Ex. 2-7) is interesting because it is structured from four 2-measure units (2 + 2 + 2 + 2) of which the first three are interrelated by rhythmic sequence. Because the fourth unit is new, it gains impetus for the cadence and connection to the repetition of the entire Theme 1 at full orchestra.

EXAMPLE 2-7   Haydn, Symphony No. 99/I, meas. 19–26, Theme 1

  A vigorous new motive based on the rhythmic pattern | ♩ ♩ ♬♬ | begins as the cadence of measure 34 falls, and becomes the impetus for the extension and modulation to B-flat major.
  Meas. 48–89 Area II
    48–64 Theme 2a
    64–70 Bridge
    71–81 Theme 2b
    81–89 Codetta
  All of Area II demonstrates Haydn's extraordinary skill in reusing material. Theme 2a commences with a recall of Theme 1, but at the dominant level. After 4 measures, this dissolves in a passage of brilliant orchestral play. Just before the cadence (meas. 64) the mode turns toward B-flat minor, and the bridge that

follows uses the same rhythmic motive (♩ ♩ ♫♫) as the extension to Area I. Eventually (meas. 67), another rhythmic motive (♫♫ ♪ ♫♫ ♪) is borrowed from Theme 1. Theme 2b (Ex. 2-8) progresses without break into a brief closing section (Codetta).

EXAMPLE 2-8   Haydn, Symphony No. 99/I, meas. 71–75, Theme 2b

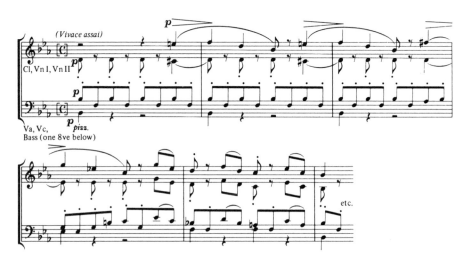

Midsection

The Midsection is set into motion with a recall of Theme 1, posed over G major harmony as V of C minor; and the next 2 measures paraphrase the same material, confirming C minor with the same German augmented-sixth chord heard at measure 13 in the Adagio. Measure 91 (Ex. 2-9) shows one of Haydn's favorite devices: F♮ in the first violin figure and F♯ in the viola conflict in a pungent, pointed cross-relation that serves to activate the new section.

EXAMPLE 2-9   Haydn, Symphony No. 99/I, meas. 90–93,
                              beginning of Midsection

Once this arresting motto has prepared the key of C minor, the Midsection proceeds, in the usual fashion, to carry easily identifiable materials from the Exposition through a variety of keys and some striking mutations. Preparation for the Recapitulation (Retransition) is accomplished mostly through use of a motive from Theme 2b, projected eventually (meas. 134–137) over B-flat as a dominant pedal point in cellos and basses.

Recapitulation

Theme 1 occurs as an 8-measure unit, not repeated but stated with full orchestra. The extension (meas. 145–56) parallels that used in the Exposition, except that no modulation takes place. Theme 2a (the recall) is omitted, and Area II commences at measure 157 with Theme 2b, used in the key of E-flat. The closing portion is closely patterned on the parallel section in the Exposition.

SECOND MOVEMENT: Quasi–Sonata-allegro

Exposition

Meas. 1–34, Area I

  1–16   Theme 1; a lyric subject made especially motile by the varying lengths of its component phrase units (4 + 2 + 6 + 4).

  16–26 Theme 2a, with extension; starts in a recall of Theme 1 but develops along its own lines.

  27–34 Theme 2b; commences with a distinctive head-motive, which is recalled in subsequent sections of the movement (Ex. 2–10).

EXAMPLE 2-10   Haydn, Symphony No. 99/II, meas. 27–28

Vn I, Ob

Midsection

The Midsection starts in D minor with innocuous, slow-moving harmony, but soon arrives (meas. 43) at a recall of Theme 2b in C major. The remainder of this short (19-measure) Midsection is less a "development" than a section of shifting harmonies, activated by the sextuplet figure that begins at measure 47. Its close and connection with the Recapitulation is dramatic, however: the cadence pause at measure 53 is on a B major chord, which implies the dominant of E minor; the Recapitulation with its reference to Theme 1 in G major follows without connective, leaving the preceding dominant chord open and unfulfilled. Haydn used this device again and again to refresh the stereotyped sound of the progression V–I, a cliché of eighteenth-century music.

Recapitulation

Theme 1 recurs in a slightly altered guise. It is followed by Theme 2b in G major. This material is greatly extended and returns full orchestra at measure 89 to close this sonata-style movement.

THIRD MOVEMENT: Menuetto/Trio

The Menuetto, in E-flat, is a ternary form (ABA) with the reprise at measure 45. The vigor comes mainly from the key of the Trio, in C major. The Trio is cast in an open-ended binary design, with preparation for return to the Menuetto (*da capo*).

FOURTH MOVEMENT: *Free Rondo-Sonata*[9]

This movement is typical of many closing movements in Haydn's instrumental compositions, which are hybrids showing characteristics of both rondo and sonata designs. The rondo-like elements of this movement include (1) cheerful themes cast generally in symmetrical phrases, (2) emphasis on one piece of material—here the opening theme, (3) lack of the double bar with repeat, which generally marked the sonata design. The principal sonata-like trait is the exploitation of thematic development throughout the movement. The entire movement emanates from several ideas—melodic or rhythmic—implicit in the opening measures. The fact that it is a somewhat longer movement than the first (272 as contrasted with 202 measures) stresses the growing importance Haydn attached to the Finale.

In examining this movement, citation of a number of highlights will be most useful. Each reader may then draw his own conclusions about the total design.

Theme 1, meas. 1–24, is extended immediately by imitative entries (cello-bass, viola, then violins) and, eventually, by routine orchestral play.

Theme 2a, meas. 51–67, begins with recall of Theme 1 in the cello-bass part. Theme 2b emphasizes dactylic rhythms (♩♫).

Recapitulation occurs at measure 113, with return of Theme 1, and the remainder is a brilliant play on many of the ideas proposed in the opening section.

Perhaps the most forward-looking trait of this Finale is the integration of the development process into all portions of the movement, in contrast to reservation of such processes for the Midsection, as in the typical sonata-allegro design. We shall see how nineteenth-century composers came to enlarge upon Haydn's model.

The Symphonies of Mozart

Mozart's brief life transpired like a play-within-a-play in the midst of Haydn's long, productive career. Mozart's influence on the older artist was exceptionally strong, and we may view Mozart as an uncommonly lovely gift to Haydn, who was not fortunate in his personal relationships. Mozart in turn revered his older peer and held for him a singularly uncomplicated affection, such as he could never summon for his own father. Haydn had a healthful stabilizing effect on the *Wunderkind* who had survived the blandishments of London and Paris, but not without a residue of uncertainty and disillusionment.

Neither the symphony nor the string quartet occupied a central role in Mozart's total oeuvre. As his personal style crystallized, his dependence on a dichotomy or dualism of elements became increasingly apparent. While a dichotomy can be set up artificially within any of the components of music, it is implicit in certain performance mediums, notably the solo concerto with orchestra and works for voices and orchestra. Consequently, most of Mozart's masterpieces are

---

[9]Occasionally "sonata" is employed as an abbreviated form of "sonata-allegro," especially when the word is used in combination, as here.

found among the 23 concertos for piano and orchestra, and the operas. Probably many church compositions (Masses, vespers, motets, and the like) should be grouped with the operas in the second category, for many a treasure lies buried among these sacred works, which are heard so infrequently in the United States.

In recognizing these circumstances, we neither disparage nor discount Mozart's symphonies. We simply indicate at the start that there is plausible reason for the modest number of Mozart's major symphonies. And we may anticipate that his best symphonies will manifest certain traits native to the concerto or the opera.

Of the 50-odd symphonies written by Mozart, a few have been lost, but 41 survive in the collected edition.[10] No more than ten of these are truly significant works, and perhaps only five are supreme Mozart.

The first symphony, K. 16 in E-flat, was written when the neophyte composer was only nine and engaged in a concert tour designed to conquer England. Johann Christian Bach, youngest son of the old cantor, was enjoying enormous success in England at the time, and he served as Mozart's mentor during his visit. Not surprisingly, Mozart's earliest symphonies were written in the shadow of the older man's compositions, which, in turn, were of Italianate flavor since Bach had lived in Italy before moving to England. The influence of Italy in Mozart's music intensified during the next few years, after Mozart himself visited that eighteenth-century musical center. When Mozart moved permanently to Vienna in 1781, he had written the large majority of his symphonies—about 35 according to the Köchel list (excluding dubious or incomplete works). But his major symphonies—the "Linz," the "Prague," and the three masterworks of 1788—were products of his Vienna years.

The succession of Mozart's symphonies written before 1773 shows no logical pattern of growth and progressive mastery, such as one observes in Haydn's first sixty or so works. The reason is that the young Mozart, like his models in Italy, viewed the symphony lightly: it was a delectable hors d'oeuvre, useful mostly to whet the appetite for more serious fare to come. Although Mozart was a "serious" composer from at least the age of fourteen, his major symphonic compositions had to await his change from Italian to Austro-German in his view of large instrumental works. Haydn was the principal force in effecting this conversion, but there are indications in some of the symphonies of the early 1770s that Mozart was ripe for that change.

During the autumn of 1773 and early winter of 1774, Mozart composed three symphonies that foreshadow the quality of the final three he would write in 1788. These are K. 183 in G minor, K. 200 in C major and K. 201 in A major. Each shows traits that were to become Mozart hallmarks within ten years. The "Small" G minor, K. 183 (as opposed to the "Great," K. 550), for example, was Mozart's first symphony in a minor key; Mozart was to find particular magic in the minor

---

[10] "K." or "K.V." followed by a number in designating a Mozart work indicates *Köchel Verzeichnis:* L. von Köchel was the first (1862) to establish a chronological index (*Verzeichnis*) of Mozart's compositions. Köchel's numberings are still followed, although Alfred Einstein has made some changes and emendations.

mode, as we perceive in the magnificent G minor String Quintet, parts of the *Requiem,* and the "Great" G minor Symphony itself. Here are some of the individual traits and devices that emerge in the first movement of this little symphony, K. 183.

1. Use of the agogic motive or theme (one using conspicuously longer values than surrounding material), especially when posed as an epigram or motto. This is typified by the opening subject, projected in whole notes in the oboes (Ex. 2-11).

EXAMPLE 2-11   Mozart, Symphony No. 25 (K. 183)/I, opening motive

In future works, such as the "Kyrie" portion of the *Requiem,* or the fugal play on the opening theme in the Finale of the "Jupiter" Symphony, short motives like this one become subjects of interesting imitative sections.

2. Free recall of material, generally through its rhythmic quality. In this movement, motives comprised of four whole notes occur with some frequency and always suggest the opening motto, even though the melodic shape is quite new.
3. Use of the unresolved dominant chord in a dramatic "open cadence." Here, the second key level of the Exposition—B-flat, the relative major—is assumed without preparation after a pause on V of G minor (meas. 28–29).
4. Establishment of the second principal key level of the Exposition far ahead of the statement of Theme 2. Here, measures 29–58 are devoted to asserting the key of B-flat; Theme 2 enters at measure 59. In this case, and others like it, Area II is binary, with the first portion devoted to key establishment and the second reserved for presentation of a new Area II theme.
5. Bridging the double bar at the close of the Exposition. In this movement, the material appearing just before the double bar (meas. 82) is continued during 4 measures after it, thus obscuring the traditional cadence. This is a very forward-looking device.
6. Use of linear modulation. Measures 80–87 effect a linear (that is, with harmony only implied) modulation from B-flat major to C minor.

The other three movements of K. 183 are attractive, but they are genre pieces.

The second of the symphonies of the 1773–74 group, K. 200 in C major, has the kind of ceremonial opening found in many symphonies and overtures written in the Mannheim-Paris tradition: full unison statement of a short subject followed by scalar passages set in imitation. This first movement reserves Theme 1 until measure 13; then it turns out to be based on the "sarabande" rhythm (♩♩ ♩. ♪) with weight in the middle of the triple measure, which Haydn, too, had favored. The most notable feature of this opening movement is the recall of Area I material just before the close of the Exposition. This gesture gives the Exposition section a certain affinity to ternary design and became almost routine in Mozart's mature works.

The first movement of the third of the symphonies of 1773–74, K. 201 in A major, has an opening portion that leads into a prolonged pedal point on A at measure 13. A quick turn to E major at measures 22–23 creates imbalance in length between Area I and Area II, for this latter portion is 54 measures to the double bar. Such imbalance is a source of litheness and vitality in many Mozart works—although it is most likely to be applied in a smaller context, to successive phrases. As was the case in K. 183, the double bar is bridged by using the same material before and after it. And like K. 200, this sonata-allegro design recalls Area I material during a concluding portion, in a small Coda that brings the entire movement to a close.

Mozart's choice of instruments for the wind choir of his orchestra was less consistent than Haydn's, perhaps because he rarely composed for a particular situation, as did Haydn at Esterháza. But during the summer of 1778, Mozart received a commission to write a symphony for the Corpus Christi program at Le Concert Spirituel, that venerable Parisian institution, which was still flourishing. This opportunity to write not only for a specific orchestra but for the most prestigious one on the Continent inspired Mozart to turn out his first symphony in the grand manner, one that called for an instrumentation worthy of the formidable band available at Le Concert Spirituel. The symphony Mozart wrote for this occasion was K. 297 in D major, and the orchestral group was as large and inclusive as any used during the eighteenth century: pairs of flutes, oboes, clarinets, and bassoons; horns and trumpets; timpani; and the usual string component.

The key of D major, which was so felicitous for the winds, served Mozart more often than any other key, even C, for his symphonies. Following this "Paris" Symphony, both the "Haffner" and the "Prague" used it. Mozart was less daring than Haydn in his choice of keys, perhaps because Mozart's melodic and harmonic texture is more liberally infused with chromatic tones than Haydn's; and "neutral" keys (D, C, E-flat for Mozart) are more effective foils for these decorative tones than are more complicated tonalities such as B major or E major.

That both Mozarts, father and son, took the Paris commission very seriously is attested by a passage in a letter of February 11–12, 1778, from Leopold Mozart to Wolfgang, who was pausing at Mannheim en route to Paris:[11]

> From Paris the name and fame of a man of great talent resounds throughout the whole world. There the nobility treat men of genius with the greatest deference, esteem and courtesy; there you will see a refined manner of life, which forms an astonishing contrast to the coarseness of our German courtiers and their ladies; and there you may become proficient in the French tongue.

As it turned out, the composition that Mozart produced for Le Concert Spirituel is grandiose but not musically significant. It may, however, have con-

[11] All excerpts from Mozart's letters are taken from *Letters of Mozart and His Family*, transl. and ed. Emily Anderson (London, 1938; 3rd ed., London: Macmillan, 1985).

A manuscript page from Mozart's "Haffner" Symphony

vinced Mozart that the symphony was a viable form, one on which he could well lavish more of his talents, for he wrote no more genre symphonies.

In 1782, Mozart, who was then firmly settled at Vienna, composed the so-called "Haffner" Symphony (K. 385). Although full of sprightly charm, it is in the spirit of a serenade, like another of Mozart's quasi-symphonies, *Eine kleine Nachtmusik* (K. 525) of 1787.

In 1783, Mozart composed, apparently in great haste, the first of his "serious" symphonies, which is designated the "Linz" (K. 425). On October 31, Mozart wrote to his father from Linz, while he was en route from Salzburg back to Vienna:

> On Tuesday, 4 November, I am giving a concert in the theater here and, as I have not a single symphony with me, I am writing a new one at breakneck speed, which must be finished by that time . . . .

This C major symphony is the first of Mozart's with a slow introduction, although some of the "ceremonial" openings of earlier works approximated such a preface. We recall, also, that the so-called "Dissonance" Quartet (K. 465), a work from the same period and also in C major, begins with a dramatically contrasting Adagio to usher in a somewhat routine Allegro. This was the period when Mozart became intimately acquainted with the works of J. S. Bach and his sons, and when his admiration for Haydn crystallized. The influence of all these men may be seen in the "Linz" Symphony. While he was no eclectic, even Mozart needed a year or two to refine various influences and make them part of his own unique manner.

Three more years passed before Mozart made use of his new-found adeptness in the symphonic form. His "Prague" Symphony (K. 504), in D major, received its first performance on January 19, 1787, in Prague. This is a symphony of three movements (the Menuetto is omitted); as in the "Linz," an impressive Adagio introduces the Allegro. This opening is especially Mozartian in melodic and harmonic language, for Mozart found a freedom to digress in such a preliminary portion that was not available within the more prescribed confines of a sonata-allegro movement. The Adagio opens with the keynote D stressed in a figure that imitates the so-called drag rhythm of the side-drums:

etc.

We shall encounter a like figure in the "Jupiter" Symphony. At measures 4–6, three quick key changes are suggested: B minor, G major, and E minor. After this, a lyric theme with many flexible and fleeting chromatic inflections ensues. At measure 16, the mode turns to D minor, which is colored strongly with its submediant, B-flat major, in measures 18–19. A modulatory passage at measures 20 to 27 converges on A, the dominant of D, stressed as a pedal point in the low strings, timpani, and horns (meas. 28–33). The last two bars before the onset of the Allegro are activated by long-short (trochaic) rhythms.

The Allegro begins with a syncopated figure in the first violins, recalling the start of the G minor Symphony, K. 183. Beneath this, the other strings enunciate the first phrase of Theme 1; the second phrase is brilliantly juxtaposed in winds, constituting the kind of orchestral dualism that Mozart preferred. The contours of Theme 2 (meas. 97ff.) seem to be derived from the first melodic material of the Adagio, which may be a conscious seeking for unity on Mozart's part. In the Midsection in particular, Mozart's new expertise with counterpoint comes into full play. And all through this Allegro, his mastery of orchestration is seen in the frequent use of "louvered texture," in which instruments enter and exit frequently, thus lightening the opaque orchestral sound.

In the light of Mozart's meager rate of production for the six years after 1782 (only three symphonies, even counting the "Haffner"), his incredible accomplishment during the summer of 1788 is especially surprising. Within scarcely two months, Mozart wrote three symphonies that transcend all his former symphonic works and at the same time apotheosize the whole genre of Classical instrumental music. No one has discovered why the symphonies were written, nor is it known if they were performed during Mozart's lifetime. Perhaps their extraordinary quality rests in the very fact that these are in no sense occasional pieces but highly personal documents, which Mozart must have written for the music's sake and not for some sponsor or commission.

The first of the trio, K. 543 in E-flat major, bears the completion date of June 26, 1788; the G minor, K. 550, and the C major ("Jupiter"), K. 551, followed within six weeks. Three works could scarcely differ from one another more strikingly, although all bear the indelible mark of Mozart's genius. The orchestral complement is different in each, which serves to emphasize that instrumentation, even at that comparatively late date, was not fully standardized. The G minor symphony, a chamber work in many respects, especially in the linear textures that predominate and in the independence of single parts, has neither trumpets nor timpani. Mozart no doubt deliberately omitted these incisive "vertical" timbres to emphasize the intimate quality of this loveliest of all Classical symphonies. But the G minor's woodwind choir is the fullest used in any of the three symphonies: one flute, oboes, clarinets (added later by the composer), bassoons, and two horns, which complement the woodwinds. The E-flat and C major symphonies both use one flute, bassoons, horns, trumpets, and timpani, but the former adds to these two clarinets, the latter two oboes. A five-part string choir is, of course, the foundation in all three works.

Symphony in E-Flat Major (K. 543)

In his E-flat symphony, Mozart draws on his mature symphonic style as it emerged in the "Prague" Symphony; at the same time he makes use of several Haydn mannerisms. The preliminary Adagio, plotted in two contrasting sections, prefigures Haydn's prefatory Adagio for his Symphony No. 99 (see p. 30), which also shows a binary scheme. Mozart's musical language and means of implying the partition are quite his own. The first portion, measures 1 to 14, is ordered by its lowest part, cellos and basses: essentially, this bass line moves upward from E♭ to B♭ (the dominant note) and then maintains B♭ through six bars. The distance from E♭ to B♭ is traversed diatonically (E♭–F–G–A♭) until the immediate approach to B♭, when a single chromatic note (A♮) intensifies the final juncture. During the second portion (meas. 14–25), activity increases through a combination of the trochaic rhythm (♩♪♩) and scale figures. The most intense point is reached with a diminished-seventh chord, A–C–E♭–G♭, at measure 21. Out of this volatile and active harmony emerges a linear figure (flutes, bassoons, Violin I) that emphasizes the pungent, active, nondiatonic intervals of the diminished seventh, augmented fourth, and chromatic semitone. The outcome, though, is the cliché progression of I_4^6–V, for the approach to the key of E-flat and the Allegro portion of the movement.

The Allegro is a straightforward sonata design with clear, attractive themes, a few contrapuntal touches that remain unobtrusive and not conspicuously "learned," and full play of effective orchestral devices. The Midsection is brief and the Recapitulation uncomplicated.

The Andante is mostly a lyric episode with a theme that depends on recurrent trochaic rhythms grouped in pairs (♩♪♪♩) for its impetus. A vivid enharmonic modulation around the midpoint of the movement is a true Haydnesque touch that refreshes the prevalent key of A-flat major: at measure 91, the mode changes to A-flat minor, and in the next measure a linear modulation to B major takes place. The key of B major is really the enharmonic equivalent of C-flat, which is the mediant of A-flat minor. But this "reasonable" explanation does not dispel the fresh, pungent effect of the shift from flats to sharps and the 7-measure episode in B major-minor that follows.

The Menuetto is without artifice or tension, since even the Trio remains in the initial key of E-flat major. The Finale (Allegro) recalls Haydn once more, its gypsy flavor bringing to mind the *all'ungarese* movements in the older master's chamber music. Affinity for the Andante movement develops when enharmonic modulations from flat to sharp keys emerge between measures 50 and 64 and measures 200 and 212. These modulations are more than "eye music," for they involve, in each case, keys a third apart and related through a change of mode.

Symphony in G Minor (K. 550)

Mozart's G minor Symphony occupies a totally unique position in the whole oeuvre of Classical instrumental works. For many people, it stands as the consummate art work of the late eighteenth century; few would deny it a place among the supremely great compositions of all time. Assessing the source of its quality is difficult and probably not even desirable; but perfect balance among all its elements, the result of a great artist's intuitive knowledge of "when" and "how much," is one of this symphony's great treasures. Instruments are used with special magic, such as the initial entry of the wind choir, which stresses the first open cadence (first movement, meas. 14–20); or the lovely bassoon transition, commencing as this cadence concludes (meas. 20–22). All through the symphony, the horn parts are bewitching, especially if we consider that the natural horn had, at best, only eight or nine different notes.

Mozart's knack for the dichotomy—for using musical elements in dualistic schemes—is more evident in the G minor Symphony than in any other of his works. It is conspicuous in his distribution of the orchestra; each choir is conceived of as an entity (occasionally several entities), and only rarely does the type of sound we call a "mixture" develop. Even a casual glance at a few passages for full orchestra in the first movement illustrates this vividly; for example, measures 14 to 20, 34 to 42, 114 to 125. The strength of the dichotomy emerges also in Mozart's contrast of the diatonic passage with the chromatic. The two principal themes of the first movement illustrate this. Theme 1 (Ex. 2-12a) is structured from the diatonic members of the key of G minor. Theme 2 (Ex. 2-12b), on the other hand, is made lithe and insinuating by frequent infusion of chromatic tones, although it is strongly centered in B-flat, the relative major key.

EXAMPLE 2-12a   Mozart, Symphony No. 40 (K. 550)/I, Theme 1, meas. 1–9

EXAMPLE 2-12b   Mozart, Symphony No. 40 (K. 550)/I, Theme 2,
                       meas. 44–51

An especially wonderful passage, contrasting the diatonic with the chromatic simultaneously, occurs in the final segment of the Retransition leading to the Recapitulation in the sonata design of the first movement (meas. 160–65). Here the bassoons sustain the dominant note D, while the clarinets and the flute interlock in a chain of imitative segments cast, in the clarinets, in descending chromatic thirds. Another infusion of the chromatic occurs at measures 281 to 285, just in time to start the final cadence group in G minor.

Three other features distinguish the first movement of the G minor Symphony. First, there is the permeating quality of the two-note appoggiatura figure at the start of Theme I (Ex. 2-12a). A suggestion of this pointed, propulsive figure is rarely absent from the texture, the principal exception being the few measures devoted to stating Theme 2 (meas. 44–57). The absence of the figure there helps to set Theme 2 apart from surrounding texture. Often this figure (termed X hereafter in this discussion) is subject to various sophisticated mutations. For example, as Theme 2 is extended (meas. 58–61), the figures in the woodwinds and first violins are derived from X. Later (meas. 72–84), X is subject to the contrapuntal device of augmentation. In every case, even a touch of X is sufficient to evoke the opening theme.

Another feature of the first movement is the frequent use of the general pause, a dramatic touch that reminds us of Mozart's preoccupation with the opera during his last years. Finally, Mozart makes conspicuous use of recall of initial material to round off principal sections of the sonata design. The section just cited (meas. 71–85), which uses X at the Area II key level, B-flat major, gives a pseudo-ternary shape to the Exposition. Measures 268 to 273 constitute a parallel section in the Recapitulation. And measures 287 and 288 provide a last recall before the final cadence group.

The Andante of K. 550 is no passive lyric episode, but a real tour de force of contrapuntal and chromatic writing that matches the first movement in artifice. This Andante is cast in a modified sonata-allegro design, with a unique developmental episode inserted into Area II of the Exposition. This movement is briefly discussed below, beginning with the Exposition.

Area I, meas. 1–19: Theme 1, in E-flat major, is stated, then restated (meas. 9–19) with contrapuntal mutation (inversion of parts, augmentation) and extension.

Area II, meas. 20–52: The new key, B-flat major, is assumed without preparation, but this part moves almost immediately into a developmental episode that recalls material from Area I as it moves through a remarkable succession of implied keys (C minor, G-flat, and D-flat major). At measures 34 to 36, the second principal key level, B-flat major, is reestablished in cliché fashion through the German augmented-sixth chord, Gb-Bb-Db-E♮. This prepares for presentation of the second principal theme, from measure 37 onward. This ingenuous idea is stated sparsely, mostly in strings (meas. 37–43), but it is suddenly refreshed by one of Mozart's chromatic episodes (meas. 44–47). The effect of such chromatic infusion, so invigorating in Mozart's late music, is not unlike that of the famous loud chord in the Andante of Haydn's "Surprise" Symphony. The early part of the Midsection of this Andante of the G minor Symphony recalls the developmental episode in its Exposition. Retransition is accomplished with still another chromatic passage (meas. 65–73), based on a cycle of major-minor seventh chords. The Recapitulation is somewhat abbreviated, appropriately so after the somewhat devious portions that preceded it.

The Menuetto of the G minor Symphony is one of Mozart's finest. It stresses the implicit 2-measure syncopation that is a feature of the true minuet:

The Trio, in G major, belongs to the horns and is shaped to their capacities.

The final *Allegro assai* uses a sonata-allegro design with rondo-like themes. A certain affinity with the X-motive of the first movement may be seen in the opening phrase of Theme 1 (Ex. 2-13).

EXAMPLE 2-13   Mozart, Symphony No. 40 (K. 550)/IV, Theme 1

Symphony in C Major ("Jupiter," K. 551)

Many of the qualities of the G minor Symphony are present, too, in the C major "Jupiter." However, the key of C major, which Mozart used so frequently for earlier symphonies, appears to have made him less individual—more skilled but still a ceremonial composer. The opening measures attest to this, and subsequent portions are closer to the "Linz" and "Prague" than to the G minor Symphony. Two notable features of the first movement are the turn to C minor for a sudden change of modal color (meas. 81–82), just after Theme 2 has occurred; and the unexpected presence of a third theme, perhaps to be called "closing theme" (meas. 101–07), just short of the close of the Exposition.

While the *Andante cantabile* is cast in a small sonata-allegro design, its real distinction lies in the exquisite embellishment and mutation of materials. The Midsection (meas. 45–59) is appropriately brief, since the entire movement is, essentially, an elaboration of two or three simple ideas.

In the Menuetto, the chromatic lines of the melodic portions counterbalance the stable, repetitive horn and trumpet parts. In the Trio, the opening phrases are stimulated by metric imbalance between their two segments:

Of the four movements of the "Jupiter," the Finale (*Allegro molto*) has probably been singled out most frequently, although for a surprisingly naïve reason: the first recall of the opening subject (Ex. 2-14a) is in form of a little fugal episode (meas. 36–53) that includes a separate imitative entry for double basses (Ex. 2-14b). This fughetta is an effective texture for early recall of the principal subject; but surely, at this late point in Mozart's career, one need feel no surprise

EXAMPLE 2-14a   Mozart, "Jupiter" Symphony (K. 551)/IV,
                            opening subject

EXAMPLE 2-14b   Mozart, "Jupiter" Symphony (K. 551)/IV, meas. 36–53

at his injection of counterpoint into virtually any portion of a composition. Mozart's own string quartets of the 1780s are permeated with contrapuntal episodes, as are Haydn's. And all the late symphonies show effective contrapuntal portions that, if less obvious than the little fughetta of the "Jupiter," are still characteristic of Mozart's finest textures. Instead of singling out the fughetta passage, we should view the Finale of the "Jupiter" as a brilliant summation of almost all Mozart's most sophisticated techniques evolved to enliven his sonata-allegro designs. Much more significant than the fughetta, for example, is the preparation for the Recapitulation and the key of C, which takes place between measures 216 and 224 (Ex. 2-15). This is a genuinely bitonal passage with dual implication of the keys of E minor and C. Brahms, as we shall see, recalls this very passage, under like circumstances, in the Finale of his First Symphony.

Mozart wrote no more symphonies after the summer of 1788; and while Haydn was beginning his first English visit, Mozart died, to the grief and desolation of his older friend. Mozart's influence is as obvious in Haydn's last symphonies as was Haydn's in most of Mozart's works of the last ten years of his life. Musical reciprocity has produced no other comparably felicitous circumstance.

EXAMPLE 2-15   Mozart, "Jupiter" Symphony (K. 551)/IV, meas. 216–25

3

The Later Viennese Period: Beethoven and Schubert

Historians who advocate a strictly evolutionary view of music are confounded by the emergence of a Titan like Beethoven. He is an anomaly that defies categorizing. His compositions were the catalyst for musical attitudes of the entire nineteenth century, yet the works themselves stand proudly detached—from their successors as from each other.

Beethoven found in music the noblest means of enunciating the sublime, and he freed music for all time from necessary reliance on a text. When, in such late works as the Finale of the Ninth Symphony and the *Missa Solemnis*, he made conspicuous use of voices, Beethoven used the vocal component as a resource for contrasting timbres and increased sonority; the integrity and articulateness of the music did not rely on the presence of words. Beethoven marked himself as essentially an instrumental composer when he chose the string quartet, the most intensely instrumental of all genres, for his final, consummate works.

Beethoven was spared the necessity of serving a single patron, as Haydn had served the Prince Nicolaus, or Mozart the Prince Archbishop Colloredo of Salzburg. For the day of a musician's position of servitude largely vanished with the eighteenth century, rendered archaic by the same upheaval in ideas that precipitated the French and American Revolutions. Such wealthy noblemen as the Princes Lichnowsky and Lobkowitz, the Archduke Rudolf, and the Count Rasumovsky took pride in giving financial aid to Beethoven. Their generosity has proved to be the price of immortality, for their names live through the ages in the dedications of Beethoven's works. In the broadest sense, however, Beethoven addressed his music to all mankind, and his giant accomplishment has dwarfed all subsequent composers.

Ludwig van Beethoven

The Symphonies of Beethoven

Beethoven was born, it would seem, to write symphonies. Although he had composed a considerable body of music—mostly chamber works and sonatas—before he undertook his first symphony, his whole musical style crystallized and became assured with the completion of that first work in 1800. Beethoven's nine symphonies have stood for more than a century and a half as ideals for others to emulate. There is neither an uncertain composition nor a genre work among the nine. Each is a confident, individual statement from an artist for whom music was the supremely expressive language. Beethoven restored music to the proud pinnacle it had occupied in earlier times when, along with arithmetic, geometry, and astronomy, it was included in the quadrivium of liberal arts. He proclaimed himself a *Tondichter* (tone-poet). In so doing, he set himself apart from his craftsmen-forebears of the eighteenth century, and he placed his art on a par with literature, philosophy, and religion, as a means to uplift, instruct, and heal mankind. Beethoven's nine symphonies, along with his sixteen string quartets, are the supreme testament to their composer's fiery confidence in music.

The customary three-period partition of Beethoven's creative life is even less meaningful than usual when it is applied to the symphonies, which follow a somewhat irrational and independent chronology. The writing of the first six symphonies was accomplished within approximately eight years between 1799 and 1807–08. The seventh and eighth were completed about four years later; and the ninth occupied Beethoven intermittently for about seven years after 1817. Even the opus numbers assigned by the publishers and the numbering tend to be misleading, because the periods of composition generally overlapped and first performances were often delayed. The time of the first sketches for the Fifth Symphony, for example, coincided with the time (1804–05) of completion of the Third ("Eroica"), although the Fifth itself was not finished until 1807. Meanwhile, during 1806, the symphony now designated the Fourth was written. The Fifth Symphony did not receive its first performance until the famous concert of December 22, 1808, in Vienna, at which time the Sixth ("Pastoral") Symphony also was performed for the first time. But on that occasion, the designating numbers were reversed, with the present No. 6 shown as No. 5. Clearly, the Third through the Sixth symphonies cannot be viewed as constituting a plausible evolutionary cycle, although some writers have considered them in this fashion. Rather, they demonstrate the multifarious aspects of Beethoven's earlier symphonic style.

During the four-year interval that followed the completion of the Fifth and Sixth symphonies, Beethoven composed major works with symphonic affinities, such as the "Emperor" Concerto and the Fantasy in C for piano, chorus, and orchestra, Op. 80. In 1812, both the Seventh and Eighth symphonies were completed, and two more contrasting works would be difficult to discover. As for the Ninth Symphony, that towering masterpiece, which dwarfed symphonic writing for half a century, in it Beethoven summarized extroverted music; afterward he turned, for the remainder of his life, to the contemplative style of his late string quartets.

Although Beethoven's symphonies fail to show the somewhat toilsome pattern of growth that is often apparent in works of lesser artists, they do reveal a number of consistent traits; and certain of them have striking similarities. Each of the nine is basically a four-movement work. The Sixth ("Pastoral") Symphony, which shows five movements, might seem to belie this; but in this work the third and fourth movements are linked in somewhat the same fashion as a scherzo and its trio, with the conjunction of keys (F major and F minor) confirming the relationship. The Ninth, which is irregular in countless ways, still shows a four-movement plan, even though the Finale is, by itself, a multisectional piece with its own unique plan of organization and is as long as many an entire Classical symphony.

Beethoven never exceeded his Classical forebears either in his choice of principal keys for his symphonies or in intermovemental key relationships. But within the bounds of virtually every individual movement, he explored daringly remote tonal regions and often organized the deviant keys into a rational modulatory scheme. By the time of the Fourth Symphony, his excursions to remote keys were spectacular and had infiltrated principal as well as developmental portions of the designs. Beethoven expanded the modulatory process itself, often using a key change as an opportunity to interject a devious or boldly conceived passage. Elsewhere he replaced the processed modulation with a simple, brusque juxtaposition of keys.

In his uncanny intuition for timing, Beethoven probably found his most individual and useful talent. The pace and dispersion of musical events in a sophisticated composition parallel the unfolding of a fine dramatic work. Significantly, the composition of the third through the sixth symphonies coincided with the composition and primary revisions of Beethoven's only opera, *Leonore* (*Fidelio*); and these earlier orchestral pieces are marked by such drama-inspired effects as the sudden general pause, the deliberate manipulation of temporal organization as in augmentation of the cadence group, and the abrupt interpolation of either a *sforzato* or notes of conspicuously longer value. Certain rhythmic figures appear to have acquired special significance for Beethoven, none more so than the trochaic (long-short) foot, expressed in music in a variety of combinations, of which these are most frequently encountered:

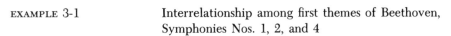

The First, Second, and Fourth symphonies, which have a number of traits in common, all have first themes based on a larger version of the trochaic rhythm: $\frac{4}{4}$ 𝅗𝅥. 𝅗𝅥 . Ex. 3-1 shows how these three themes relate to the basic trochaic foot and to one another.

EXAMPLE 3-1   Interrelationship among first themes of Beethoven, Symphonies Nos. 1, 2, and 4

Beethoven employs a substantial introduction in slower tempo to preface the basic sonata-allegro design for the first movements of the First, Second, Fourth, and Seventh symphonies. The reduction of the preface to two quick tonic triads at the start of the Third ("Eroica") Symphony is an immediate indication of the bold stance characteristic of that entire work. Many writers have suggested that this assured manner heralds the arrival of Beethoven's mature second period; but such a view is not necessarily supported by the retrospective nature of several subsequent works. Interesting variants of the rather discursive introductions cited above are the openings of the finales of the First and Third symphonies. In both these cases, the brief prefatory material derives from an embellished dominant-seventh chord, dispersed cumulatively in passage-work for the strings. In the first instance, the first violins alone structure a linear passage that ascends gradually from g' to g''. In the second instance, the dominant chord, B♭-D-F-A♭, accrues gradually in a brilliant tutti for all the strings: the passage starts indeterminately on the note D, commences to focus with the arrival of A♭ in measure 4, and becomes clear in its dominant intent when the bass strings achieve B♭ between measures 6 and 11. The first movement of the Ninth Symphony has an introduction of sorts, although the tempo of the movement proper (*Allegro ma non troppo*) is assumed at once. Here, the prefatory character of the first 16 measures is suggested by the empty sound of the open fifths posed over A, the dominant note. These are the "ghostly fifths" that so fascinated Wagner. This prefatory portion belongs inherently to the movement proper, since this is the material cited in the reminiscent quotations used during the Finale.

Distinctive traits of individual symphonies are described in the analyses that follow.

Symphony No. 1 in ⌣ Major, Op. 21

Date of composition: probably 1799–1800
Dedicatee: the Baron von Swieten
First performance: April 10, 1800, Vienna, with Beethoven conducting

FIRST MOVEMENT: *Adagio molto/Allegro con brio, in C major*

The prefatory *Adagio molto* opens with a 4-measure passage (Ex. 3-2) as bold and confident as any to be found among Beethoven's earlier works: three chordal pairs suggest, in consecutive resolutions, the keys of F, C, and G major. But the implication of G vanishes immediately when F♮ appears in the violin lines of measure 4, and the remaining 8 measures of the Adagio confirm C major as the principal key of the movement.

EXAMPLE 3-2   Beethoven, Symphony No. 1/I, meas. 1–5

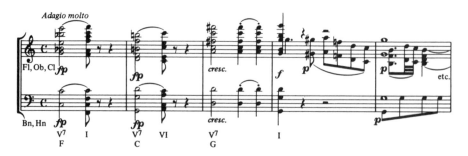

The *Allegro con brio*, which is cast in a conventional sonata-allegro design, displays a number of traits that occur often in Beethoven's later sonata designs. Here is a skeletal analysis of the movement:

Exposition

Meas.	13–52	Area I C major	Theme 1 and its enlargement
	53–109	Area II G major	Theme 2 and its enlargement: meas. 53–87 Theme 1 recalled in G, in position of a closing theme: meas. 88–100 Codetta confirming key of G: meas. 100–09

Midsection

	110–77		Conventional fragmentation and development of materials, culminating in a retransitional passage (meas. 160–72) that predicts A minor; but a quick retransition to C major is effected through a V^7 chord dispersed in longer note values.

Recapitulation

	178–205	Area I C major with transient modulations	Theme 1: meas. 178–88 Added modulatory section based on the figure ♪♪♪♪ | ♩ : meas. 188–205
	206–98	Area II C major	Theme 2 and its enlargement: meas. 206–40 Theme 1 recall, interspersed with closing material, as Coda: Meas. 241–98

Several features of this essentially straightforward design merit comment. The first is the cadence augmentation and embellishment used at the close of each of the first two phrases of Theme 1: successive phrases are fused through a 2-measure link in longer note values in the woodwinds. The tension is increased in each instance when a chromatic tone embellishes the approach to the next level. The first link (meas. 17–18) uses C♯, which effects a quick modulation to D minor for the sequential second phrase; the second link (meas. 23–24) uses A♭, which is borrowed from the parallel minor key. The important purpose of these linking figures is obliteration of the usual cadence relaxation through use of fresh instrumental color and the chromatic tones, and the consequent joining of all three phrases that constitute Theme 1.

A second notable aspect of this movement is the recall of Theme 1 at the second key level (G major) to round out the Exposition portion of the design.

Beethoven may have learned this device from Mozart, who used it frequently. When the Midsection commences abruptly with an A major chord attached to a recall of Theme 1 and immediately following the dominant-seventh chord of C major, it foreshadows many such abrupt chordal juxtapositions that were to be commonplace in Beethoven's later works.

SECOND MOVEMENT: *Andante cantabile con moto, in F major*

This movement is cast in a small sonata-allegro design, in which the principal elements are these:

Exposition

Meas.	1–26	Area I F major	Theme 1 and its enlargement
	27–64	Area II C major	Theme 2 and its enlargement: meas. 27–53 Codetta, based on G pedal in brass and timpani, trochaic rhythms ♫♩♫♩♩ and triplet figures: meas. 53–64

Midsection

	65–100		Characterized by pervasive trochaic rhythm

Recapitulation

	101–26	Area I F major	Theme 1
	127–61	Area II F major	Theme 2
	162–95	Coda	Commences with recall of Theme 1 in first violins, goes on to ruminate on various materials in a portion almost exactly balancing the Midsection in length.

THIRD MOVEMENT: *Menuetto (Allegro molto e vivace), in C major*

After this First Symphony, Beethoven was not again to entitle a third movement "Menuetto" until the Eighth Symphony. In the present instance, the spirit and tempo already suggest the scherzo, which was to supplant the menuetto in the Second Symphony.

The Menuetto portion of this movement is marked by an unusual number of chromatic tones, mostly flats derived from the parallel minor key (B♭, E♭, A♭) or from the key of D-flat, which is maintained with brilliant effect between measures 18 and 33. The key digressions of this Menuetto are as colorful as any found in Beethoven's early works.

The Trio belongs to the wind choir, especially the horns. There is no change of key for this Trio; the extensive tonal digressions of the Menuetto made such constancy desirable. An interesting three-part tonal scheme emerges in this movement, with the principal key, C major, asserted most overtly in the center of the design:

Menuetto	Trio	Da capo
C major, then transiently multitonal levels (C, G, E-flat, C minor, A-flat, D-flat, E-flat minor, C)	C major throughout except for embellished V cadence at meas. 103	Menuetto as before

FOURTH MOVEMENT: *Adagio/Allegro molto e vivace, in C major*

The small sonata-allegro design used for this movement resembles that of the second movement, since a sizable coda again balances the Midsection in length.

Exposition

Meas.	1–6		Prefatory phrase
	7–54(55)	Area I C major	Theme 1 presented as a binary design, with its second part commencing at meas. 30
	56–96	Area II G major	Theme 2 and its enlargement: meas. 56–86. Codetta, recalling opening gesture of Theme 1: meas. 86–96

Midsection

	97–162		Routine developmental section

Recapitulation

	163–90(191)	Area I C major	Theme 1, shortened by omission of former second part
	192–227	Area II C major	Theme 2 and its enlargement
	227–42		Added bridge passage
	243–end		Commences with recall of Theme 1 and continues in brilliant orchestral play based on recalled motives

A distinctive aspect of this movement is the attention centered on the concluding (Recapitulation) section. In the added bridge passage (meas. 227–42), the scale figures of the violins derive from the lead into Theme 1 (meas. 6–7), while the underlying bass line (meas. 227–36) effects a direct chromatic descent from C to F. A pause in the middle of the passage (meas. 236–37) is taken on a full dominant-seventh chord of C major, and the imitative scale figures that follow build up considerable expectancy for the final recall of Theme 1.

Symphony No. 2 in D Major, Op. 36

Date of composition: 1802
Dedicatee: the Prince Lichnowsky
First performance: April 5, 1803, Vienna, with Beethoven conducting

The plausible and obvious evolutionary relationship between the First and Second symphonies is the more notable because it does not happen again: each subsequent symphony is highly individual and, apparently, independently conceived. In the Second Symphony, Beethoven expands several devices that he merely experimented with in the earlier work. He employs much more daring key digressions and expands the scope of the basic sonata-allegro design. The orchestra required for this work is the same as that for the First Symphony: pairs of flutes, oboes, clarinets, bassoons, horns, and trumpets; two timpani; and the usual string choir. But the composer's gift for deploying the instruments with flexibility and imagination is especially marked in this Second Symphony; frequent use of louvered texture and colorful antiphonal dispersion of the choirs signal Beethoven's increasing ease with the large ensemble. In later works, Beethoven depended on instrumental color to provide much of the lively sense of ebb and flow that characterizes his mature music.

FIRST MOVEMENT: *Adagio molto/Allegro con brio, in D major*

The prefatory Adagio is one of the most imposing episodes of this kind Beethoven was to write. But we probably should not attach undue significance to this since he had such complex prior models as the prefatory Adagio to Mozart's "Dissonance" Quartet (K. 465) and the colorful introductions to several of Haydn's London symphonies. Furthermore, the kind of discursiveness of key found here is less significant in free portions like introductions than it is within the regimented confines of a prescribed design such as the sonata-allegro form. Even so, the range of keys is brilliant. An opening pair of phrases (meas. 1–8) is conventional and establishes D major firmly as the key of the movement. After this, a 4-measure passage of unsettled key focus leads to the second portion of the introduction, which starts solidly in B-flat major (meas. 12). Beethoven was to use the specific juxtaposition of D major and B-flat major often in his later works, always with arresting effect. (See especially the Violin Concerto, the first orchestral tutti; and the "Archduke" Trio, Op. 97, the first turn toward the second thematic area.) The rapid scales, the most lively element in this second portion, suggest a series of transient key changes but converge (meas. 23) on a D minor triad dispersed in an orchestral tutti; and the section concludes on a massive tutti on the note A, the dominant of the key of D. From this point (meas. 24) to the end of the Adagio, A is maintained as the bass tone (pedal point), while the overlying parts provide active preparation for the *Allegro con brio* that follows.

The *Allegro con brio*, which, like all Beethoven's opening movements, uses a sonata-allegro design, has some obvious affinities with the first movement of the First Symphony. The resemblance between the first themes of the two works has already been cited (see Ex. 3-1 above). Other relationships are these: (1) the concluding portion of Theme 2 of the Second Symphony (meas. 88ff.) is derived rhythmically ($\quad$) from Theme II of the earlier work; (2) a recall of Theme 1 at the close of the Exposition section rounds out the opening statement in each work; (3) a sizable coda (meas. 302–60 in the Second Symphony) again balances the Midsection in length. A striking dissimilarity lies in the character of Theme 2, which, in the Second Symphony, begins with an incisive military subject in horns and winds (Ex. 3-3).

EXAMPLE 3-3   Beethoven, Symphony No. 2/I, meas. 73–76, Theme 2

Another notable feature in this first movement of the Second Symphony is the interpolation of a digressive quasi-developmental passage (meas. 96–112) into the Exposition section, just ahead of the recall of Theme 1. To introduce the brilliant closing section of the first movement, Beethoven uses a direct chromatic ascent through an octave from D, in cellos and basses (meas. 326–34).

SECOND MOVEMENT: *Larghetto, in A major*

This movement has the skeletal form of a sonata-allegro design, but alludes also to the variation form through the profusion of thematic embellishment and elaboration. Thematic materials are especially lovely; they unfold in the seemingly effortless realization found only in the works of a great master. The principal design elements are these:

Exposition

Meas.	1–47	Area I A major	Theme 1: meas. 1–32 Extension and modulation: meas. 33–47
	48–99	Area II E major	Theme 2a: meas. 48–82 Theme 2b: meas. 82–99

Midsection

	100–57		Commences with Theme 1, in A minor and embellished. The entire section has the flavor of a variation.

Recapitulation

	158–211	Area I A major	Theme 1: meas. 158–89 Extension and digressive modulations for added interest: meas. 190–211
	212–63	Area II A major	Parallels the same section in Exposition except for key change
	264–end	Coda	The head-motive of Theme 1 is recalled here for a ruminative closing segment.

THIRD MOVEMENT: *Scherzo Allegro/Trio, in D major*

This Scherzo, especially the opening statement, offers typical instances of the louvered texture Beethoven came to employ with such skill. The orchestral color shifts with each successive measure, changing as follows during the first strain: measure 1, tutti; measure 2, Violin I; measure 3, tutti; measure 4, Violin I; measure 5, horns; measure 6, Violin I; measure 7, oboes and horns; measures 8 and 9, tutti, etc. Several changes of key or mode enliven subsequent portions: D minor and B-flat major for the second strain (meas. 17ff.); and F major toward the close of the Scherzo (meas. 53ff.). The Trio, which remains basically in D major, is colorful through its stressing of the note F♯, first by reiteration in the strings (meas. 85–89), and then through use of the full F-sharp major triad (meas. 89ff.). An interesting "mirror" relationship of keys is thus suggested in this movement, since B-flat, the principal digression in the Scherzo, and F-sharp, the principal digression in the Trio, are equidistant (a major third) on either side of D, the key note.

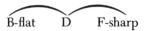

B-flat   D   F-sharp

FOURTH MOVEMENT: *Allegro molto, in D major*

This Finale is cast in the hybrid sonata-rondo design that Beethoven employed often. As usual, the rondo-like elements are the sprightly, unpretentious themes and the predominance of a particular theme through its persistent recall. The constant development of materials and several unexpected tonal digressions suggest the sonata form. Two other aspects of the movement merit attention. The first is the use of a 2-measure head-motive in connection with Theme 1, which gives its phrases a lively imbalance deriving from the 2 + 4-measure phrase units. The second is the effective use of agogic stress through the frequent insertion of longer note values, beginning, in particular, with the Coda. The skeletal outline of this brilliant rondo-sonata design is as follows:

Meas.	1–51	D major	Theme 1, as a bipartite design (Part II starts at meas. 26)
	52–107	A major	Theme 2, extended with key digressions to A minor and C major, and an imposing section of Retransition
	108–84	D major, then transiently multitonal	Theme 1, recalled during two phrases; the section then dissolves without break into development at meas. 119 a..d continues in the fashion of a conventional Midsection until the next recall of the principal theme.
	185–235	D major	Theme 1 restated as a two-part design

236–93	D major	Theme 2 restated at tonic level
294–335	D major	Theme 1, extended with developmental episode and pausing, with fermata ($\frown$), on the V^7 chord (meas. 334–35)
336–end	Brilliant cycle of transient keys before D major is reestablished	(Coda). This vivid conclusion starts with the first of the agogic chords mentioned above: the F-sharp major triad that succeeds immediately the V^7 of the preceding close. The entire coda is colorfully inflected with unexpected key levels and decorative chromatics.

Symphony No. 3 in E-Flat Major (The "Eroica"), Op. 55

Date of composition: 1804

Dedicatee: the Prince Lobkowitz. An earlier dedication to Napoleon, which Beethoven had planned before the French general declared himself Emperor, was abandoned. This is attested by an early copy of the "Eroica"—not an autograph but with notes in Beethoven's own hand—that is preserved in the library of the Gesellschaft der Musikfreunde at Vienna. This copy still reveals an inscription on the title-page: "intitulata Bonaparte," which is partially erased and now barely legible.

First performance: April 7, 1805, Vienna, with Beethoven conducting. (An informal performance had taken place three months earlier.)

Beethoven's "Eroica" Symphony, his first composition in the grand and spacious style we now associate with him, had a mixed reception at its first performance. One critic thought it a "tremendously expanded, daring and wild fantasia"; but Czerny, a major pianist of the day, recalled that at the first performance an auditor from the gallery called, "I'll give another *Kreutzer* [a small German coin] if the thing will stop." Another faction, which included Beethoven's special coterie of friends and many cognoscenti of the day, held that this was "the true style of high-class music"—and their opinion has, of course, turned out to be the prophetic one. The "Eroica" announced, in vehement tones, that the day of music as an exalted art that approached a religion had come. Music has never been the same since then.

Our present-day surfeit with the voluptuous sounds of late Romantic music, not to mention the cerebral inventions of the serialists, makes difficult a candid assessment of such direct, eloquent music as Beethoven's "Eroica." The essential quality of the work derives from nobility of idea and an unfettered plan for dispersal of materials within the confines of a traditional design. That critic who called the symphony a "wild fantasia" sensed this freedom and, although he may not have understood the music, he was basically right about it. The bold, generous quality of the symphony is apparent in its opening statement (Ex. 3-4). Two E-flat major triads in a full orchestral tutti dispense impatiently with the traditional introduction. Then the "Eroica" motto is revealed in simple grandeur, but is truncated summarily with the chromatic note C♯.

EXAMPLE 3-4   Beethoven, Symphony No. 3/I, meas. 1–8, opening motto

After the injection of this audibly "foreign" C♯, 6 measures are occupied with restoring the key of E-flat. Then a sizable portion explores the potential of the "Eroica" motto in the kind of self-germinating section Beethoven had learned to structure so successfully. The heroic scope of the first movement is indicated by its total length: 691 measures, as compared with 327 for the *Allegro con brio* portion of the Second Symphony.

The pathos of the second movement, inscribed *Marcia funebre*, undoubtedly helped endear the entire symphony to the Romantic generations that followed Beethoven. In a sense, this symphony was Beethoven's own encounter with the *Sturm und Drang*, even though it was a quarter of a century delayed. The Scherzo is larger in scope than that of the Second Symphony, principally because the *da capo* recall after the Trio portion is enlarged, varied, and enlivened with the injection of a sudden *alla breve* (duple meter) section at measure 381. The Finale is cast in a variation form, the first such movement to appear in Beethoven's symphonies. An analysis of the four movements of the "Eroica" follows.

FIRST MOVEMENT: *Allegro con brio, in E-flat major*

Sonata-allegro design

Exposition

Meas.	1–45	Area I E-flat major, with modula- tions	Prefatory chords and motto, plus bridge: meas. 1–14 Theme 1, its enlargement, and modula- tion: meas. 15–45
	45[1]–83	Transitional episode	A palpable bridge between the two principal themes, of unusual length and with a characteristic motive to activate it.

[1]Frequently the cadence of a concluding part overlaps the beginning of a new member. In such cases, the same measure number appears for the end of one part and the beginning of the next.

| 83–148 | Area II B-flat major, with much chromatic embellishment | Theme 2: meas. 83–108 In contrast to the seamless sweep of Theme 1, this second theme is fragmentary and tentative in quality. Closing portion: meas. 109–48 |

Midsection

| 148–397 | | This Midsection can be regarded as beginning before the double bar, thus forecasting a time when this visible end to the Exposition section will be abandoned. It is clued by the recall of Theme 1 at the level of B-flat. The heroic length of this portion (250 measures) marks it as Beethoven's first tour de force of virtuosic development. |

Recapitulation

398–448	Area I E-flat major, with modulations to F and D-flat	Theme 1 and its restatement at various key levels
448–86	Transitional episode	As in Exposition, except for key, which prepares the return to E-flat
486–550	Area II E-flat major	Theme 2 restated at tonic level: meas. 486–512 Closing portion: meas. 512–50
551–end	Grand Coda	Initiated by a recall of Theme 1 in E-flat, this massive coda includes daring key deviations: to D-flat and C major within 10 measures of its beginning. Its length (140 measures) counterbalances the extended Midsection.

SECOND MOVEMENT: *Marcia funebre (Adagio assai), in C minor/major*

This *Marcia funebre*, which takes the place of the traditional slow movement, is cast in the type of large ternary design used routinely for a Menuetto or Scherzo: the middle portion (in C major), indicated *Maggiore*, ("Major") is in lieu of the usual Trio. We might recall that a March, even one with lugubrious overtones, may be regarded as a dance form. Hence the choice of design is not unsuitable.

The *Marcia funebre* portion has a five-part design (ABA'B'A") with sections conspicuously unbalanced as to length (16 + 14 + 6 + 14 + 18 measures). The Maggiore is unified by the persistent triplet rhythm $\frac{2}{4}$ ♩ ♫ ♫ ♫ ♫ .

The reprise of the Marcia, after the Maggiore, is greatly enlarged: 142 measures, as opposed to 68 in the primary statement.

THIRD MOVEMENT: *Scherzo (Allegro vivace), in E-flat major*

This Scherzo closely resembles the parallel movement of the Second Symphony, but exceeds it in the extended and varied *da capo* portion, which includes a brief *alla breve* insert (meas. 381–84). The design is a routine Scherzo with Trio, in which the horns are conspicuous, especially in the Trio.

FOURTH MOVEMENT: *Finale (Allegro molto), in E-flat major*

The basic materials for this imposing and daring set of variations are derived from Beethoven's music for *Prometheus*. They must have pleased the composer especially, since he used them in two other contexts: in a *Kontretanz* (country dance) and again in the Piano Variations, Op. 35. The *Prometheus* excerpt (Ex. 3-5) yields two fine linear subjects; the first (to be designated Element 1) is its robust bass part, the second (to be designated Element 2) is the melodic upper part.

EXAMPLE 3-5   Beethoven, Symphony No. 3/IV,
                                     Prometheus themes used for variations

The series of variations is prefaced by the brilliant flourish in the strings described earlier in the chapter. Some of the distinctive aspects of the movement are these: the cumulative variation technique that withholds important material (here Element 2) until later portions of the design; variety in length of the variation segments; and occasional deviance from the central key of E-flat.

The plan of the Finale of the "Eroica" follows:

Meas.		
1–11		Opening flourish in strings, based on dominant-seventh chord B♭-D-F-A♭.
12–43		Statement of Element 1 as the initial subject of the movement. The principal burden of the statement falls to the strings, pizzicato; but the material is kept asymmetric by interjections in winds and brasses at measures 29–31 and 37–39.
44–59 repeated	Variation 1	Element 1 in second violins, marked *dolce,* is embellished with a simple contrapuntal associate, mostly in eighth-notes, that is scored in repartee between cellos and first violins.
60–75 repeated	Variation 2	Element 1 moves to first violins; the new contrapuntal associate, in lower strings, is in triplets.
76–116	Variation 3, plus transition	Element 2 enters for the first time—in oboe, clarinet, bassoon; Element 1 is in horns and cellos-basses pizzicato; remaining strings and flute have support. At measure 84 the instrumentation changes and increases, with Element 1 in two trumpets and Element 2 in first violins and violas. At measure 92, the 8-measure phrase of the two principal Elements is interrupted by a series of 4-measure phrases in decreased instrumentation, the close of each marked by a fermata. The transitional passage of meas. 108–16 serves to prepare for the first key change (C minor) and the first of the fugal episodes.
117–210	Variation 4 Fugal episode	The first section to depart from the initial key of E-flat major, this portion begins in the relative minor key, and it

achieves a colorful intermediate level at measure 175, when the key of B minor is reached. A series of fugal entries, based on Element 1, is regular only through the fourth, in cellos and basses (meas. 137); from this point the texture is free until Element 2 enters, in B minor, with the modulation just cited. A brilliant transitional and modulatory passage leads to Variation 5.

211–65	Variation 5	The key is now G minor and Element 1 in low strings is overlaid and complemented by a new Hungarian-style countersubject in vigorous trochaic rhythm $\frac{2}{4}$ ♩ ♪♪♩ | ♩ ♪♪♩ | ♩. ♪♩ ♪♪♩ |etc. A transitional episode based on Element 2 and in C major closes this section and prepares for the second fugal episode.
266–348	Variation 6 Fugal episode	This variation begins in C minor with a small double fugue in which successive entries combine Element 1 in a wind instrument and Element 2 in a string choir. Subsequent portions exploit other contrapuntal devices, and a massive tutti commencing about measure 334 prepares for the restoration of the key of E-flat major.
349–430	Variation 7 Poco Andante	The woodwinds begin with a more tender version of Element 2, once more in E-flat. This long section explores more and more complicated rhythms and climaxes in the G pedal point of measures 420–30.
431–73	Conclusion Presto	This rousing conclusion proceeds without break from the previous section. Materials from each of the two Elements are used in fragmented form, but brilliant, characteristically orchestral passage-work provides most of the impetus toward the close.

Beethoven's "Eroica" Symphony was an important landmark in the evolution of musical style as well as in the composer's own artistic growth. But Beethoven's later works did not necessarily bear the mark of this masterpiece. Certain of its techniques, notably that of extended development, became Beethoven's for life; but he never recaptured the confident, exalted mood that produced the "Eroica." The next three symphonies must be regarded as a group, for Beethoven apparently turned from one to another in writing them; their numbers represent the probable order of completion. This is borne out especially by a sketch book in the Lansberger collection of autographs, which intermingles sketches for the Second, Fourth, Fifth, Sixth, and, surprisingly, the Ninth symphonies. Of the three that followed the "Eroica," the Fourth is retrospective in many qualities; the Fifth might be viewed as the "logical" successor to the "Eroica"; and the Sixth is unique: in it Beethoven shows a strain of gentleness and tenderness that he rarely disclosed.

Symphony No. 4 in B-Flat Major, Op. 60

Date of composition: 1806
Dedicatee: the Count Oppersdorf
First performance: March, 1807 (probable)

The retrospective quality of this symphony is revealed immediately in the presence of a weighty Adagio as preface to the first movement. This has certain resemblances to the introductory Adagio of the Second Symphony. It does, however, display at least one forward-looking trait: the shape and rhythm of the first principal theme of the *Allegro vivace* are foreshadowed by the persistent eighth-note figures (♪ 𝄾 ♪ 𝄾 ♪ 𝄾 ♪) that start at measure 6 of the Adagio. An abbreviated survey of the four movements of the Fourth Symphony follows.

FIRST MOVEMENT: *Adagio/Allegro vivace, in B-flat major*

The Adagio begins full orchestra on the note B♭, but turns, at the second measure, to the key of B-flat minor, with a profusion of the minor-oriented pitches G♭ and D♭. At about the midpoint of this introduction (meas. 18), a division into two parts is suggested when the note G♭ changes enharmonically to F♯, initiating a series of colorful modulations.

The *Allegro vivace* is cast in the usual sonata-allegro design, a less devious and more conventional one than that found in the first movement of the "Eroica." The similarity of its Theme 1 to those of the First and Second symphonies has been cited (Ex. 3-1 above). Theme 2 (meas. 141), in F, seems slight compared to the lengthy and active transitional section leading to it (meas. 95–140) and the brilliant close (Codetta) that follows it (meas. 161–85). The Midsection is skillfully wrought, deriving interest from vividly juxtaposed harmonies (for example, the C major and A major triads at meas. 202–03), louvered texture, and, finally, a persistent tonic (B♭) pedal point in the kettledrum, beginning at measure 283. This pedal point anticipates the B-flat key level of the Recapitulation by 53 measures and produces stimulating tonal relationships with the music above it during much of this distance. The Recapitulation is an orthodox one.

SECOND MOVEMENT: *Adagio, in E-flat major*

This movement uses another hybrid form—the sonata-variation. The first statement (Exposition) might serve for a conventional sonata-allegro design, since a distinctive Theme 2 in B-flat begins at measure 26. A Midsection is by-passed, however, and a Recapitulation that has the style of a series of variations comes immediately after the terminal cadence of the Exposition (meas. 41). The movement is marked by long, unbroken lyric lines and by the pervasive trochaic rhythms of the accompaniment.

THIRD MOVEMENT: *Allegro vivace, in B-flat major*

This movement is a Scherzo and Trio, distinguished by the invigorating metric displacement found in the opening strain especially. As was the case in the two preceding symphonies, the reprise of the Scherzo (*da capo*) is varied and extended.

FOURTH MOVEMENT: *Allegro ma non troppo, in B-flat major*

Sonata-allegro is probably the proper designation for this movement since two sonata-allegro "signals" are present—the double bar at the end of the Exposition (meas. 100) and a sizable Midsection (meas. 101–88). The conspicuous and protracted recall of Theme 1 after the statement of Theme 2 gives the Exposition a flavor of the rondo, but this recall retains the second key level (F major).

Symphony No. 5 in C Minor, Op. 67

Date of composition: 1805–07
Dedicatees: the Prince Lobkowitz and the Count Rasumovsky
First performance: December 22, 1808, at Vienna

This "Grand Symphony" (as it was called in all the earliest references) has become the single most admired and beloved work in the entire symphonic repertory, but for various reasons. A number of popular legends concerning the "meaning" of the persistent rhythmic motive ♪♪♪ | 𝅗𝅥 have helped endear the work to those of romantic mind. Yet plenty of intrinsic musical qualities have made this middle symphony of Beethoven's nine equally valued by connoisseurs.

At least the sketch of this work was concurrent with the writing of the "Eroica," but a comparison of the first movements of the two symphonies emphasizes how completely Beethoven's music eludes the stereotype. There is the matter of length, for instance: the "Eroica"'s opening movement, with its 691 bars of triple meter, has 2,073 beats—more than twice the total length of the parallel movement of the Fifth with its 502 bars of duple meter. The prime material for the "Eroica" (see Ex. 3-4) is spacious and linear, whereas the nucleus of the Fifth is the permeating motive ♪♪♪ | 𝅗𝅥, whose character is totally rhythmic. The first movement of Beethoven's Fifth Symphony may be his most concise statement of a large-scale design; the only rival is perhaps the opening movement of his F minor String Quartet, Op. 95.

The second movement has a certain resemblance to the *Marcia funebre* of the "Eroica," perhaps through its elegiac mood and the persistence of the trochaic rhythm. The Scherzo, with its fugue-like Trio, is one of Beethoven's finest. And the Finale, in its large-scale sonata-allegro design, is as imposing a piece of musical architecture as many a first movement. More detailed comment on each of the four movements is given below.

FIRST MOVEMENT: *Allegro con brio, in C minor*

The sections, both small and large, of this sonata-allegro design are unusually obvious. Generally they are stressed by a pause or a fermata, or both. The essence of the movement lies in a simple, vivid dualism of metric contrast: "upbeat" motives (usually ♪♪♪ | ♩) belong to initial material—the opening motto and its realization in Theme 1; "on-the-beat" materials belong to Theme 2 or to extraneous portions. Citation of basic materials (Ex. 3-6) and a synopsis of the design follow.

EXAMPLE 3-6   Beethoven, Symphony No. 5/I, basic materials

a) Motto for Theme 1, meas. 1–5

b) Theme 2 with its prefatory motto, meas. 59–66

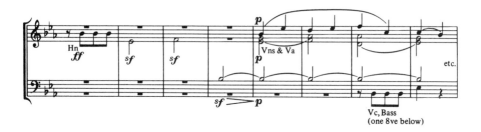

Exposition

Meas.	1–58	Area I C minor	Prefatory statement of the motto-motive: meas. 1–5 Theme 1 develops entirely from the motto used in free imitation, and it produces an illusion of constant eighth-note movement: meas. 6–58

| 59–124 | Area II
E-flat major | A prefatory motto in horns, based on previous motto: meas. 59–62.
Theme 2: meas. 63–110
Close, recall of "upbeat" rhythm: meas. 110–22. |

Midsection

| 125–248 | | This developmental portion uses the two mottos (Ex. 3-6) for basic material. The most vivid section, however, is derived from free temporal manipulation in a section of louvered texture (meas. 196–227). At the start of this passage, a 2-measure segment is the unit of alternation ($\downarrow$ | $\downarrow$). After 14 measures, the alternation doubles speed when a single measure becomes the unit of change. |

Recapitulation

248–302	Area I C minor	Basically a reprise of previous Area I, but prepares key of C for next portion.
303–89	Area II C major	Basically a reprise of previous Area II except for key change. The portion ends abruptly with a colorful modulation to F minor, meas. 380.
390–end	Coda	This close is prepared by a sudden, brilliant diminished-seventh chord, stated full orchestra and attached to the rhythm of the opening motto (meas. 390–95). The next portion (meas. 400–69) is conspicuous because it is constructed entirely of "on-the-beat" rhythms. This proves to be a foil for the concluding portion, which recalls the opening motto with its "upbeat" rhythm.

SECOND MOVEMENT: *Andante con moto, in A-flat major*

This movement uses a variation form in which the unusually lengthy and sophisticated thematic unit imparts a serious character often lacking in such a design. The theme is cast in a hybrid three-part design (ABB′) that is unusual because the reprise of the second material as the third part is transposed to C major, the key of the "mediant-made-major" in relation to the initial key of A-flat. This transposition serves to refresh the key of A-flat when it returns for the start of each successive variation. The three variations begin at measures 50, 98, and 185 respectively.

THIRD MOVEMENT: *Allegro, in C minor*

This is the customary Scherzo with Trio design, although the sections are not so marked. The opening strain of the Scherzo recalls the metric contrast between the two basic ideas of the first movement, since its first phrase begins on an upbeat, but the complementary second phrase begins solidly on the beat (Ex. 3-7). At measure 19, the horns introduce a driving rhythm ♩ ♩ ♩ | ♩. that recalls the motto of the first movement.

EXAMPLE 3-7   Beethoven, Symphony No. 5/III, meas. 1–26, theme of Scherzo

The reprise of the Scherzo is varied even more than usual: the opening subject is carried pizzicato in strings, culminating in a 50-measure passage constructed over a C pedal point in one kettledrum, constantly reiterated in the basic quarter-note rhythm. This ominous, driving passage leads without pause into the brilliant finale.

FOURTH MOVEMENT: *Allegro, in C major*

This imposing but conventional sonata-allegro design has a profusion of attractive, easily identifiable themes, perhaps to compensate for the first movement, which was structured from short motives. Both Area I and Area II are binary designs, and each of the four parts has a strong characteristic thematic component with a triumphant, martial quality, in accord with the prevailing quadruple rhythm (Ex. 3-8).

EXAMPLE 3-8 Beethoven, Symphony No. 5/IV, principal thematic components

Theme 1a, meas. 1–6

Theme 1b, meas. 26–28

Theme 2a, meas. 45–46   Theme 2b, meas. 64–65

The Midsection begins to recall the motto rhythm of the first movement at measure 122; at measure 153, this rhythm takes on the shape it had in the Scherzo, through the change to 3/4 time, and this episode serves as direct retransition to the Recapitulation.

Symphony No. 6 in F Major (The "Pastoral"), Op. 68

Date of composition: 1807–08
Dedicatees: the Prince Lobkowitz and the Count Rasumovsky
First performance: December 22, 1808, at Vienna

Beethoven's Sixth Symphony, which is somewhat of an anomaly among the nine, is the most readily apprehended of all. That it was admired from the first is attested by a notice in the famous German musical journal *Die allgemeine musicalische Zeitung* for January 1810, which begins: "This wonderful, original, lively work, which undoubtedly can take its place beside his [Beethoven's] other masterworks . . . ." Beethoven may have yielded with some reluctance to the temptation to include a section of descriptive music in this symphony, since an early part for Violin I bears the following inscription and partial disclaimer from the composer:

Pastoral Symphony
or
Recollections of country-life
(More expression of feeling than tone-painting)

It is quite true that this symphony may be enjoyed as absolute music without recourse to the "program" suggested by the titles of movements—except in instances of such obvious tone-painting as the bird calls at the end of the second movement. These are shown in a musical example included in the same journal cited above (see Ex. 3-9).

EXAMPLE 3-9   Beethoven, Symphony No. 6/II, bird calls

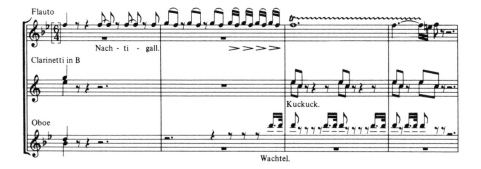

The first movement, *Allegro ma non troppo,* with the subtitle "Cheerful feelings aroused on arrival in the country," is as ingenuous and unpretentious as its inscription suggests. Even the customary tension between the first and second principal themes is wanting, and only the new key, C major, really marks Area II.

The second movement, *Andante molto mosso* in B-flat, is inscribed "Scene at the brook." The pleasant, undulating 12/8 rhythm, and the simple, tuneful subjects evoke the pastoral setting, and climax in the calls of nightingale, cuckoo, and quail (*Wachtel*), as in Ex. 3-9.

The third movement, in F major and subtitled "Joyful gathering of the countryfolk," is really a Scherzo in Beethoven's customary boisterous manner, with a subsection in duple time (2/4) to provide contrast. This movement moves without break into the Allegro—"Thunderstorm"—where the parallel key of F minor provides a plausible link with the Scherzo. The "thunderstorm" is evoked with a profusion of tremolo in the strings and loud blasts from the brasses. The storm recedes finally in an ascending scale passage in flute, which links this movement with the cheerful finale, Allegretto, subtitled "Glad, thankful feelings after the storm."

As for the technical aspects of the various movements, it is easy enough to perceive the customary sonata-allegro and partite designs in this, as in the previous symphonies. However, in the light of Beethoven's obviously relaxed, cheerful temper in writing the piece, perhaps it should be enjoyed in a similarly relaxed mood.

The long interval between 1808, when the Fifth and Sixth symphonies were performed, and 1812, when Beethoven again completed a pair of symphonies, was not one of the richer periods of the composer's creative life. The reason is not readily apparent, but it may well have been simply that Beethoven's muse was weary—understandably so with three great concertos, three master symphonies, the Rasumovsky quartets, and numerous smaller works achieved, all within the brief span of three years. Moreover, political conditions in Austria were extremely unsettled: the final collapse of the long-moribund Holy Roman Empire came in 1806, and extensive occupation of Austria by French troops was a continuing aggravation. Beethoven's wealthy patrons were far less secure during these years and were probably preoccupied with other concerns than music.

The pair of symphonies that Beethoven completed in 1812—his Seventh and Eighth—are contrasting works, the first written in the grand manner, the second recalling the gentler mood of the Sixth, although without its programmatic allusions.

Symphony No. 7 in A Major, Op. 92

Date of composition: 1812
Dedicatee: the Count von Fries
First performance: December 8, 1813, at Vienna

In the first performance of the Seventh Symphony, Beethoven found his most spontaneous and unanimous approval. So great was the success of the work that a second performance, four days later, was arranged immediately; and on both occasions the audience demanded a repetition of the Allegretto movement. The Seventh Symphony is that ideal masterwork that mounts attractive, spontaneous themes in a supporting structure of superb craftsmanship.

FIRST MOVEMENT: *Poco sostenuto/Vivace, in A major*

With the *Poco sostenuto*, Beethoven returned to the imposing introduction he had used for earlier symphonies—but with important differences. The devious key digressions of the prefaces for the Second and Fourth symphonies are replaced here by a cogent "mirror" plan, in which the two principal key digressions (C and F) are a third away on either side of A realized as a minor key; they are, moreover, in a dominant-tonic relationship to each other: F   A   C.

I   V

This scheme gives the *Poco sostenuto* a tight organization often lacking in such prefatory sections. Furthermore, the essential materials are as attractive and individual as those in the subsequent sonata-allegro design (Vivace). There is the opening 2-measure motive in oboe, which is explored successively by horns, flute, and bassoons; next come the active scale passages, which lead urgently to the second melodic idea, again in oboe (meas. 23) but in C major and extended to 6 measures. This idea gains in importance when it is recalled at the second deviant key level—F major—just ahead of the dominant bridge to the Vivace. The structure of this bridge derives from temporal artifice: rhythms are so manipulated as to move smoothly from the 4/4 meter of the introduction to the 6/8 of the Vivace.

The Vivace is cast in the customary sonata-allegro design and the entire movement is unified by two persistent traits: a profusion of pedal points that tend to provide stabilization, and a pervasive active 6/8 rhythmic group ♩.♪♪ . Detailed analysis follows:

Exposition

Meas. 63–110	Area I A major	After four measures of activating rhythm, Theme 1 is stated as a binary design, then is repeated in a full tutti over an A pedal point. The turn away from the key of A comes suddenly, in meas. 109.
111–30	Area II C-sharp minor/ E major	The first phrase in C-sharp minor acts as a bridge to the true Theme 2, at the dominant level, commencing at meas. 119.
130–76	Coda E major/ C major	At meas. 136, this close recalls the key of C major, proposed so effectively in the Introduction.

Midsection

177–277	Although the traditional double bar with repeat (:‖) is still used here, its effect is annulled by a transitional passage starting 6 measures before it and continuing 2 measures after it.
	The Midsection begins in C major, a key that has already assumed great importance in prior parts of the design.

Recapitulation

278–386	This reprise is enlivened by modulations to D and G, commencing with the reprise of Theme 1 at meas. 301.

| | Theme 2 commences in A minor but shifts to the parallel major mode with its second phrase. |
| 389–end | Grand Coda, distinguished by a 22-measure sustained dominant pedal point in horn (meas. 401–22). |

SECOND MOVEMENT: *Allegretto, in A minor/major*

This splendid movement, favorite of audiences for a century and a half, uses a hybrid design—ABA′B′-A″ (the last two parts form a coda)—in which the A element is itself a variation form. The thematic element that is the seed of these attractive variations is a 24-measure segment with an ABB relationship among its three component 8-measure phrases. The first statement of the theme is homorhythmic in three-voiced texture of the lower strings (Viola, Violoncello I and II with Basses). Although none of the three voices emerges as prime in the initial statement, the highest part (Viola) becomes the most important in subsequent variations: it is extracted and placed in the highest part (Violin II) for the first variation. It keeps this highest position during the increased instrumentation in the next variations. The B element, in A major, contrasts the square, duple A section with its pervasive triplet rhythm. At the reprise of the primary thematic element, the original Viola part is again moved—to the lowest position in the harmony—and an active complementary part in Violin I and Viola is added. This variation brightens when the mode turns briefly to major, just ahead of a contrapuntal variation that begins as a small *fughetta* with successive entries of the theme in Violin I, Violin II, Cello and Bass, and Viola. The countersubject of this little fugue becomes the predominant part in the full orchestral statement of the theme that closes this A section. More modest recalls of B and A then close the movement, combining to form a coda.

THIRD MOVEMENT: *Presto/Assai meno presto*, in *F/D major*

This is perhaps the finest scherzo movement of any in Beethoven's symphonies. The Scherzo itself (Presto) is magnificently self-propelling and offers brilliant examples of louvered texture in the instrumentation. As was the case in the Fifth Symphony, a simple contrast of "upbeat" and "on-the-beat" motives provides much of the kinetic energy. The Trio, focused in the vividly contrasting key of D major, offers the most conspicuous examples of "on-the-beat" material. The theme of this Trio is, according to an early authority, based on a Lower-Austrian pilgrimage hymn (*Wallfahrtgesang*), shown in Ex. 3-10.

EXAMPLE 3-10   Beethoven, Symphony No. 7/III (Trio), tune of pilgrimage hymn

This Scherzo assumes a larger form than usual, since the Trio intervenes twice, making a large five-part design: AB (Trio) A'B'A''.

FOURTH MOVEMENT: *Allegro con brio, in A major*

This Finale uses a sonata-allegro design, but is conspicuously partite in its general effect. The liveliness of the movement derives from several unexpected key changes and transposition of material; on the whole, the materials are as intensely duple as those of the first movement's Vivace are triple.

Symphony No. 8 in F Major, Op. 93

Date of Composition: 1812
Dedicatee: the Empress of Russia
First performance: February 27, 1814

This symphony was completed at Linz—"in the month of October 1812," according to the heading on the original manuscript score. It is somewhat. neglected by orchestras today, which is unfortunate because it is one of Beethoven's most attractive large-scale works. The symphony lacks the customary slow movement, having an *Allegretto scherzando* and a *Tempo di Menuetto* for its middle pair of movements.

The *Allegretto scherzando* is notable because it is in duple time (2/4) rather than the triple time found in most Beethoven scherzos, and because it is written in a fugal style not often encountered in such pieces. The movement has come to be associated with the invention of the chronometer (metronome) by Johann Nepomuk Mälzel, a clever German organist-turned-inventor. Schindler, in his book on the early life of Beethoven, was responsible for propagating a story concerning the origin of Beethoven's fugal subject: it was, he contended, based on a canon that was sung spontaneously by a group of musicians (Beethoven, Salieri, and Weigl) who had gathered to see a demonstration of Mälzel's newly perfected metronome. The story may be apocryphal; but it does remind us that Beethoven's own metronomic markings for tempi in various movements of the symphonies did not appear until 1817, when the primitive "time machine" of Mälzel had achieved acceptance. These markings were first set down in an 1817 issue of *Die allgemeine musicalische Zeitung.* An additional anecdote concerning Mälzel is that he succeeded in devising an improved ear-trumpet for his deaf friend, Beethoven.

The first movement of the Eighth Symphony, *Allegro vivace e con brio,* in F major, uses a sonata-allegro design of rather modest length (373 measures). There is no introduction, and Theme 1 begins immediately. It is a genial, uncomplicated tune stated first as a pair of complementary phrases in contrasting instrumentation—tutti, then woodwinds. Ideas implicit in the opening strain are then developed. The most sophisticated portion of the Exposition is a section preparing for Theme 2. This section suggests D minor and C minor before it eventually leads, without break, into C major and Theme 2. An incisive preparatory phrase (meas. 70) implies duple meter: etc., but a legato complementary phrase immediately restores the prevailing triple meter.

The subsequent sections of the movement are written in Beethoven's suavest manner. The most colorful spot is probably the start of the large coda (meas. 302), which uses the minor mode submediant level of D-flat major during its first portion.

The *Allegretto scherzando,* in B-flat major, the facile second movement whose gay character does not belie Schindler's claims about its origin, is actually cast in a simple partite design: ABAB' Coda. But the constant use of imitation obscures the partite structure, and the pervasive effect is that of a recurrent fughetta. This little scherzo might be grouped with the second movement of the first Rasumovsky quartet (Op. 59, No. 1), which is also in B-flat, as an illustration of how sophisticated a composer Beethoven had become, even when he wrote in jocular mood.

The use of a Menuetto as third movement is, of course, an anachronism. This piece is a trifle heavy-handed, leaving us with the impression that Beethoven may have lost his taste for such elegant, stylized dance types. The effective part for horns in the Trio is, however, in Beethoven's best manner.

The final *Allegro vivace,* in F major, continues the scintillant mood but shows some artful, and typically Beethovian, touches. All the elements of Theme 1 are activated by contrast between duple and triple rhythms. This distinction is proposed at the very outset by the rhythm of the opening subject:

Theme 2, on the other hand, is marked by harmonic artifice: it is prefigured by first violin at the unexpected level of A-flat major (meas. 48); but, 12 measures later, the same subject is recalled in flute and oboe, this time at the expected dominant level of C major (meas. 60). The design is a large rondo form, with liberal infusion of development, and is considerably longer than the first movement.

With the writing of his Eighth Symphony, Beethoven had finished his composition of large-scale works for orchestra alone. The Ninth Symphony belongs with the *Missa Solemnis,* as the apotheosis of his grand style. For the most part, Beethoven occupied his last years with writing sonatas—duo sonatas as well as those for piano alone—and string quartets.

Symphony No. 9 in D Minor (The "Choral"), Op. 125

Date of composition: 1817–24, but mostly 1822–24
Dedicatee: the King of Prussia
First performance: May 7, 1824, at Vienna with Schuppanzigh and Umlauf as
    conductors

The power and scope of such an art work as Beethoven's Ninth Symphony daunt our capacity to comprehend it. The initial reaction of anyone who listens for the first time co this titanic masterpiece is a sense of wonder that it could have originated in the mind of a single man. This awe is only slightly diminished by the knowledge that the Ninth Symphony was the culmination of a lifetime of thought. Sketchbooks from Beethoven's very earliest years reveal his lifelong interest in Schiller's "Ode to Joy"; and fragments of various motives of the Ninth Symphony are scattered sporadically among working drafts for compositions covering a quarter of a century. Even so, Beethoven's serious, continuing work on the Ninth did not commence until 1817, and, at first, he may have planned it as one of another pair of symphonies. The use of a choral finale seems not to have been part of the original plan, but an idea that developed when the earlier movements were nearing completion. Even after the first performance, Beethoven considered supplanting it with a purely orchestral finale. The theme used subsequently for the Finale of the String Quartet, Op. 132, was originally planned for the Ninth Symphony.

The four movements of the Ninth Symphony are discussed below. Beethoven wrote them as independent movements, as he had done with his earlier symphonies. Only when the work was nearing completion did he perfect the plan for the choral finale and thus pose for himself the problem of linking this movement plausibly with the other three.

FIRST MOVEMENT: *Allegro ma non troppo, un poco maestoso, in D minor*

During his later years, Beethoven showed an increasing predilection for the sounds and techniques of music of the past. We see this first in his inclusion of fugal episodes in so many of the compositions written after approximately 1814. And, alluding to earlier practice in subtler fashion, he began casting essential materials as brief, embryonic ideas, unachieved in first presentation, so that exploration and fulfillment of them would provide logical, necessary impetus for growth. In 1826, as still another extension of his studied archaism, Beethoven was to revive the essence of the old ecclesiastical modes, in the "Lydian" Adagio of his String Quartet, Op. 132.

This interest in the past is revealed in several facets of the Ninth Symphony. In the first movement, two simple, intrinsic sounds serve to stimulate all of Area I and much of the remainder of the sonata-allegro design. These sounds are the primitive open-fifth intervals of the background, perhaps suggested to Beethoven by medieval organum; and the brief motive with anacrusis (upbeat) ♪ | ♩, which, in one form or another, breeds most of the linear thematic material. Both sounds are proposed during the introductory 16 measures. To these two basic ideas are added the propulsive rhythm already encountered in the Fifth Symphony: ♪♪♪ | ♩; and a second animating rhythmic unit, ♪♩♪, which often occurs in combinative figures, such as the kettledrum part, ♪♩♫ | ♪♪, at the close of the first thematic presentation (meas. 27–30), or the figure extending Theme 2: ♫♩♪♪ (meas. 102–07).

Although a sonata-allegro design provides the skeletal framework for this first movement, so pervasive is the principle of germinating growth that many of the "signals" of the sonata form tend to be obscured. Most of the material is distinctive for its rhythmic, rather than its melodic, character; but two palpable small themes may be identified as basic components of the design. These are shown below in Ex. 3-11a and b.

EXAMPLE 3-11   Beethoven, Symphony No. 9/I, principal themes

a) Theme 1, meas. 17–22

b) Theme 2, meas. 74–80

Of the 158 measures given over to the Exposition section of this sonata-allegro design, only about 20 have material that is thematic in the sense of a "tune." Realization of this gives a clue to the texture of Beethoven's mature music: the larger portion of any design—including this first movement of the Ninth Symphony—is generated by motivic growth, causing such "filler" portions as extensions, episodes, transitions, and the like, to occupy the greater proportion of the space in the plan. A piece so structured generates a strong implicit sense of inner unity, as contrasted with the impression of variegated mosaic design imparted by most music from the Classical era.

The traditional repeat marks at the close of the Exposition section are not used. A double bar is present, but the Midsection actually begins 2 measures ahead of it (meas. 162) with a recall of the open fifths over A, as at the beginning of the movement. This gives a brief illusion of reprise, before the Midsection evolves (meas. 184) into a traditional developmental episode. Thus Beethoven makes a suave, fleeting gesture of compliance with the long-established tradition of restatement of the Exposition section.

SECOND MOVEMENT: *Molto vivace, in D minor*

The principal motive of the Scherzo, based on the rhythm ♩. ♪♩ , was the first idea for the Ninth Symphony to take concrete shape. The Scherzo portion itself shows a large sonata-allegro design occupying 395 measures without its Grand Coda. But the extremely rapid tempo and the permeation of all portions with the active basic rhythm make it seem shorter. Theme 2 of the Scherzo (meas. 93) overlies a C pedal point that uses the basic rhythm ♩. ♪♩ . This simple second theme is inconspicuous in this context, but takes on added importance when, converted to duple meter, it emerges as the principal material of the Trio (meas. 416ff.). The frequent use of imitative episodes and truly virtuosic scoring for the orchestra make this Scherzo the most scintillant portion of the symphony.

THIRD MOVEMENT: *Adagio molto e cantabile, in B-flat major*

The free variation form used for this Adagio has produced one of the loveliest of all Beethoven's slow movements. The composer avoided the ingrained tedium of the ordinary variation sequence by posing not one but two well-contrasted themes on which to base subsequent transformations. These two themes are presented initially in a pair of keys that Beethoven so often favored juxtaposing: B-flat major and D major. Subsequently, other keys (G major and E-flat major) are used, avoiding another disadvantage of the variation chain—monotony of key. In the deceptively simple metamorphoses Beethoven is able to achieve, themes are not so much embellished or varied as induced to assume fresh and improbable contours, which then seem to have been implicit in the materials as originally presented.

FOURTH MOVEMENT: *Presto/Allegro ma non troppo/Allegro assai,*
in D minor/major

This grand finale, in the style of a cantata for instruments and voices with the overlay of a large rondo design, apparently cost its composer more travail than any other of his works. As we have observed, the idea of setting Schiller's "Ode to Joy" had been with Beethoven for many years; but the decision to link it with the Finale of the Ninth Symphony may have come as late as 1823. Even after the "Joy" theme had assumed its now familiar contours, the problem of how to link it—or, indeed, a choral finale at all—with the previous three movements seemed nearly insoluble. Anyone who harbors the illusion that musical composition is easy or spontaneous would do well to familiarize himself with

Beethoven's sketches for this choral movement, for they reveal the slow, painful stages of molding the ideas into their final, flawless guise. (Thayer, in his *Life of Ludwig van Beethoven,* reproduces some of these sketches.)

Beethoven's eventual plan for fusing the Finale to the other movements also provided a unique design for the fourth movement itself. His implement of linkage was recitative, which had served many a generation of operatic composers for a similar purpose: in opera, passages of text declamation to music (recitative) have the dual aim of enunciating the plot and fusing such disparate portions as arias, choruses, even ballets. When we hear how superbly recitative fulfills Beethoven's needs in this Finale, we are likely to forget the long, painful interval of frustration that preceded the composer's inspiration to use it.

The Finale is cast in two large, unbalanced sections: the orchestral "ante-exposition," or prelude, and the movement proper, which is a gigantic rondo shared by orchestra, chorus, and vocal soloists. In the orchestral prelude, the voice of the recitative is a combination of cellos and string basses; in the instrumental-choral portion it is a solo baritone, who declaims, "O friends, not these strains! But let us voice something more agreeable and full of joy!"

The instrumental ante-exposition occupies only 207 measures and alternates the recitative with interjections of recalled motives from the three preceding movements; the climax is the superbly exultant Joy theme (Ex. 3-12). The recitatives in this first, instrumental version are so clearly, though implicitly, "questing" as to make the addition of words in the subsequent section almost superfluous.

EXAMPLE 3-12   Beethoven, Symphony No. 9/IV, meas. 92–115, "Joy" theme

The plan of the orchestral ante-exposition is this:

Meas. 1–7   Introductory phrase in winds and brass, peremptory in quality to dispel the effect of the Adagio movement, but forecasting the contour of the recitative

       8–16   Recitative in cellos and basses

       16–25   Modification of the introductory phrase

25–29	Modified recitative
30–38	Opening of first movement recalled
38–47	Recitative
48–55	Opening of Scherzo recalled
56–62	Recitative
63–65	Opening of Adagio recalled
65–76	Recitative, partially accompanied and with transformation in its opening strain.
77–80	Embryo of the Joy theme, the principal subject of the movement
81–91	Recitative with implied affirmation in orchestral chords
92–207	Joy theme explored in a variation chain reminiscent of that used in the Allegretto of the Seventh Symphony. The 24-measure theme is stated first in cellos and basses, unaccompanied. It then increases gradually in complexity and dynamic power through three variations and a massive coda.

The ante-exposition achieves the link with the three foregoing movements. The second large section, 733 measures in total length, first brings back, as a brief introduction, the recitative with the added words, and the Joy theme. It then realizes the Joy theme in a magnificently exuberant rondo, which explores every compositional technique, of the past as well as of Beethoven's own day. We shall comprehend this enormous rondo-finale quite readily if we realize that its basic design is the same one encountered often in Beethoven's more modest final movements: a five-part rondo (ABA'CA'' Coda), in which each part (as symbolized by a letter) has the length, scope, and complexity of many a single composition. In the lettered design shown above, A always represents a return of the Joy theme, often with transformation and amplification. The synoptic outline of this rondo design, shown below, reveals that the principal keys of the large sections are indeed plausible for a rondo design; their sequence is D major, B-flat major, D major, G major, D major.

THE CHORAL-ORCHESTRAL RONDO (*Meas. 237–940*)

Meas. 237–330—A: the first rondo section, in D major

Measures 237–40 are merely preparatory, and the strophic unit begins at measure 241. The musical context of the Joy theme is a 6-phrase unit in 4 + 2-phrase construction a a' b a' b a' . (Schiller's four-line verse is adapted to this by repetition of lines 3 and 4.) This first A of the rondo design includes three full statements of the Joy theme, the last greatly varied, plus a coda whose effect is agogic through its longer note values and chorale-style setting. The cadence and pause at measures 329 to 330 is electric: A major (dominant of the prevailing key of D) is juxtaposed to F major for the pause. This relationship will be seen to parallel that between D major and B-flat major, which Beethoven had used so frequently.

Meas. 331–542—B: the second rondo section, in B-flat major (*Alla marcia*)

The mood changes abruptly for this second section of the rondo design, and the dynamic level is abruptly *pianissimo*. The thematic elements contrast with the "Joy" portion, mostly through the metric change to a 6/8 measure for a fast-moving march rhythm. The voices are used sparsely, and the major part of this section belongs to the orchestra.

Meas. 543–94—A': the third rondo section, in D major

This section is a recall of both text and basic thematic material from the original A portion. The theme is adapted, however, to the 6/8 measure, which is retained from the preceding B section. The metric adaption of the Joy theme to 6/8 from the original 4/4 measure is this:

This brief section is given over entirely to one statement of the basic strophe by the chorus accompanied by full orchestra.

Meas. 595–654—C: the fourth rondo section, in G major, but modulating eventually to F and G minor (*Andante maestoso/Adagio ma non troppo*)

This section introduces a fresh motivic idea at the start and is written throughout in a broad triple meter. The general impression is that this is the "slow" portion of the Finale.

Meas. 655–762—A'': the fifth rondo section, in D major (*Allegro energico, sempre ben marcato*)

Initial text as well as music are again recalled in this last regular portion of the rondo design. To the Joy theme in the sopranos of the chorus is added a countersubject derived from the previous Andante, in the altos, to provide the nucleus of a great double fugue.

Meas. 763–940—Coda (*Allegro ma non tanto*)

This massive concluding section is in the style of a fantasia. Tempo changes are frequent; and recalled music and text are interspersed with portions that seem new, although they are generally derived from materials of the rondo.

The first stanza of Schiller's "Ode to Joy" is given on the following page—in the original German and then in a free English translation.

A manuscript page from Beethoven's Ninth Symphony showing the double fugue in the *Allegro energico* section.

Freude, schöner Götterfunken, Tochter aus Elysium,
Wir betreten feuertrunken, Himmlische dein Heiligtum!
Deine Zauber binden wieder, was die Mode streng geteilt;
Alle Menschen werden Brüder, wo dein sanfter Flügel weilt.

Joy, thou beautiful God-begotten daughter of Elysium,
Fire-enraptured, we approach thy heavenly shrine.
Thy magic binds together what custom has parted,
All mankind become as brothers where thy gentle wings abide.

Those who wish to read a detailed, if decidedly subjective, analysis of the Ninth Symphony may consult George Grove's *Beethoven and His Nine Symphonies*. Although Grove made his observations in 1896, they are still full of personal insight and, more important, reveal a late Romantic view of Beethoven's music.

The Symphonies of Schubert

The most serious deterrent to understanding Schubert's symphonies and appraising them candidly is easy to identify: Beethoven. Schubert was forced to spend all but the final year of his creative life in the shadow of this musical colossus, and Schubert was only too aware of his handicap. The wonder is that the gifted young man did indeed preserve his musical integrity to emerge, at the close of his short life, the most individual of all the Viennese group of composers—a true harbinger of the Romantic era to come.

Schubert's symphonies, like those of Beethoven, have an erratic chronology. Confusion about their sequence and numbering persists even today. The first six, all composed by the time Schubert was twenty, cause no problems; they were written as follows: No. 1, in D major (1813); No. 2, in B-flat major (1814–15); No. 3, in D major (1815); No. 4, in C minor (the "Tragic," 1816); No. 5, in B-flat major (1816); and No. 6, in C major (1817–18). It is now well established and generally agreed that Schubert wrote four more symphonies; but only two of them survive in performable guise. Number 7, in E minor/major, of which there remain only quite full sketches for four movements, was undertaken in 1821. The so-called "Unfinished" is No. 8, written in 1822. The lost "Gmunden-Gastein" Symphony, of which there is unimpeachable record, was written in 1825 and is No. 9; so that the "Great" C major is properly No. 10. The confusion surrounding the last four arose because none was performed or published during Schubert's lifetime.

The mix-up was compounded by the Collected Edition of Schubert's works that was prepared late in the nineteenth century. This edition designated the "Unfinished" as No. 8, but obviously did this more through good fortune than perspicacity. For the same Collected Edition named the "Great" C major as No. 7, even though it was known to have followed the "Unfinished" by six years. Present-day publishers are maintaining the uncertainty, and we may buy one score that designates the "Great" C major as No. 7 (after the model of the Collected Edition), but another that shows the same work as No. 9. This latter number at least represents a proper sequence; but it ignores the undoubted composition, in 1825, of the so-called "Gmunden-Gastein" Symphony. If this lost work were ever to turn up, the situation of numbering would indeed be chaotic.[2]

Schubert's six youthful symphonies are all derivative works, influenced quite obviously by Haydn and Mozart and somewhat less by Beethoven, whose model Schubert may have tried to avoid. The six have many traits in common. All, for example, are four-movement works, and all except No. 6 use a Menuetto as a third movement. Only No. 5 lacks a weighty Adagio or Largo to preface the principal portion of the first movement. There are no surprises at all in the intermovemental key relationships, and Schubert chooses the subdominant key for the slow movements of all except for No. 4, in C minor, which uses A-flat major.

Despite their obvious heritage and their general predictableness, these early symphonies do have some traits that should be cited, for they give occasional glimpses of Schubert as he was to emerge later in his great instrumental works. The Symphony No. 2, in B-flat, is a case in point. The first movement is extraordinarily long—624 measures—with only ten of those devoted to the introductory Largo. The Exposition section alone of this sonata-allegro design is 257 measures to the double bar, and it has an uncommonly colorful key plan. After a Theme

[2] To further complicate the question of sequence and numbering of Schubert symphonies after No. 6 was a lecture presented to the 1978 International Schubert Congress in Detroit. Dr. Otto Biba, a chief archivist at the Gesellschaft der Musikfreunde, containing much of Vienna's musical treasure, asserted that the Great C Major Symphony was composed in 1825, and a year later the score was presented to the Gesellschaft—confirmed by newly discovered orchestral parts bearing the date 1827.

1 in B-flat that Haydn might well have written, the section modulates to C minor (meas. 49) and A-flat major (meas. 70), before Theme 2 in E-flat major is introduced (meas. 80). After this subdominant key level has been firmly established in some 58 measures of orchestral play, a return to A-flat (meas. 138) initiates another modulatory cycle that passes through the keys of B-flat minor, F minor, and D-flat major, before the key of F major, the dominant and traditional key for a second subject, is resolutely prepared (meas. 184). The "new" material at this point is a recall of Theme 1, stated at the dominant level; and the orchestral play of the remaining 84 bars of the Exposition is firmly anchored in F major. The key plan of this peripatetic and trisectional Exposition is shown below.

Theme 1	Theme 2	Theme 1 (recalled)
B-flat major, C minor, A-flat major	E-flat major, A-flat major, B-flat minor, F minor, D-flat major	F major ——————— :‖

The first movement of Symphony No. 3, in D major, is notable because the most prominent element of its prefatory *Adagio maestoso*—the ascending scale figures in sixty-fourth notes—is incorporated into the movement proper: similar scale passages serve as a bridge in the Recapitulation section (meas. 159–74) and appear again just before the close of the movement.

A number of writers have pointed out the similarities between the principal subject of the first movement of Schubert's C minor ("Tragic") Symphony and the parallel subject of Beethoven's String Quartet, Op. 18, No. 4, which is also in C minor. Actually, the rhythmic shape of both these subjects— ¢ ♩♫ | ♫ ♩ ♫ | ♩ ♩ ⁊ etc., for Schubert—is derived from Haydn, who produced a number of themes cast in this very pattern. In the Schubert movement, Area II uses the key of A-flat major, the submediant to C minor and a favorite deviant level for Schubert, as it was also for Beethoven. In this C minor symphony, the anacrusis figure ♫♫ | ♩ (in the second movement ♫♫ | ♩) might be viewed as a rudimentary cyclic motive, since it is to be found in all four movements.

The Fifth Symphony, in B-flat major, a somewhat fragile work, has one of Schubert's exquisite slow movements—this one an *Andante con moto* in E-flat major. This piece might well have served as the musical component for one of his incomparable *Lieder* (art songs), which he was writing in profusion at the same time.

The Sixth Symphony, in C major, gives no foreshadowing of the massive work in the same key Schubert was to produce just ten years later. It does, however, make extensive and colorful use of the woodwinds. Schubert's special way with the woodwinds is a hallmark of the orchestration in his finest instrumental works.

After his Sixth Symphony, a three-year hiatus occurred before Schubert again turned to the symphonic form—in this case to sketch the E minor/major Symphony and then to complete two movements of the "Unfinished" Symphony, in B minor, which has come to be shrouded, perhaps inevitably, in a web of romantic legend. The truth of why Schubert left the work unfinished seems to be simply that his muse ran out; after writing two superb movements, he was apparently unable to devise a worthy scherzo and finale to "complete" the work, which he then put aside. The tentative sketches for a scherzo, which are generally published at the end of the scores of this Eighth Symphony, bear out such a conclusion: the material is commonplace, angular, and certainly not of a caliber to enhance the two completed movements.

The manuscript of the B minor Symphony was discovered, some 37 years after Schubert's death, among the discarded papers of Anselm Hüttenbrenner, an eccentric older brother of Schubert's close friend Josef Hüttenbrenner. By then (1865), the world was more aware of the quality of this composer, all but ignored by his own generation; and Schubert's "Unfinished" Symphony quickly became one of the most beloved of all symphonic works.

The belated admiration is entirely deserved, for in his B minor Symphony Schubert succeeded for the first time in bringing the individuality and charm of his *Lieder* within the more regimented bounds of a large instrumental work. Not only themes but background material and accompanimental figures are distinctive and memorable. Ex. 3-13 shows essential materials of the first movement; the accompanimental line in sixteenth notes beginning at measure 9, well ahead of Theme I, which it supports, is quite as individual as the opening motto, or Theme 1 itself. Likewise, as seen in Ex. 3-13b, the syncopated accompanimental figure for Theme 2, although simple, is vital enough to be recalled by itself, without Theme 2, during portions of the Midsection.

EXAMPLE 3-13   Schubert, "Unfinished" Symphony/I, principal materials

a) Meas. 1–20, motto and Theme 1

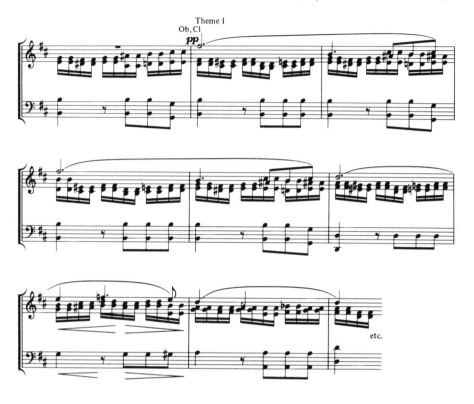

b) Meas. 42–47, Theme 2

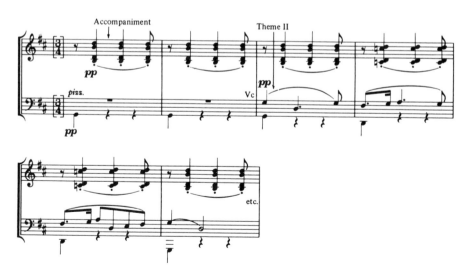

Effortless modulation is often cited as an important trait in Schubert's music. Frequently, the semblance of ease comes from careful plotting of essential materials—the opening motto (Ex. 3-13a, meas. 1-8) gives an excellent illustration. This motto implies multitonality: B minor, the principal key of the movement, is confirmed by the first and last pitches, which are, respectively, its tonic and dominant notes; measure 5 leans toward D, which key is confirmed in the first cadence of Theme 1 (Ex. 3-13a, meas. 19–20); and measure 4 is suggestive of G, which is the key of Theme 2 (Ex. 3-13b). Thus all the vital key changes of the Exposition section are prepared in this masterly motto.

Beethoven's shadow emerges in this first movement mostly in the sudden interpolation of chords marked *Fz* or simply *ff*, often attached to colorful harmony. Such a passage occurs as soon as Theme 2 has been stated but broken off inconclusively with an unresolved dominant chord (meas. 61). The mode is suddenly G minor, and the harmonic succession IV–I$_4^6$–VI is taken, each chord attacked with a violent tremolo in strings.

The other movement of the "Unfinished," *Andante con moto*, is deceptively simple—a charmer with so many traits typical of Schubert that it is almost a distillation of his style. First of all, the key of this binary movement is E major, a happy aural surprise. The themes seem artless and effortless, but are actually formed with great skill. Theme 1 will serve to illustrate this: a 2-measure motive taken pizzicato in double basses overlaps the principal melodic idea in upper strings, which, in turn, overlaps the recurrence of the pizzicato. The result is a 7-measure phrase in 2 + 5-measure construction, but with no cadential punctuation because of the constant elision. To highlight this unbalanced structure, Schubert shifts among parts of the orchestral medium constantly, even detaching the double basses to provide three contrasts of instrumental timbre: string basses pizzicato, tutti strings, and winds.

Although several years intervened between Schubert's "Unfinished" Symphony and his "Great" C major, there is a striking parallel between the two: the use of an opening motto with more than one key implied. The motto for the "Great" C major symphony is seen in Ex. 3-14. It is apparent here that the keys of C major and A minor are proposed.

EXAMPLE 3-14   Schubert, "Great" C Major Symphony/I, opening motto

The result of this opening bitonality is an interesting key scheme for the Exposition section of the ensuing *Allegro non troppo*, which may be illustrated as follows:

Theme 1	Theme 2
C major (meas. 78)	E minor (meas. 134)
	then G major (meas. 174)

Theme 2 is presented successively in the dominant keys of A minor and C major.

The lengthy Andante introduction (77 measures), of which the motto is the opening material, forecasts also the essential components of the Allegro (sonata-allegro) portion: the trochaic and triplet rhythms. Theme 1 develops by alternating these two figures, the trochaic rhythm falling most often to the strings, the triplets to woodwinds.

Theme 2, which belongs uniquely to the woodwinds, also includes triplet figures within the first phrase (see Ex. 3-15 for both principal themes). The lengthy Exposition section, which uses only these simple materials in addition to routine orchestral "filler" passages, is made colorful in its later portion through a bold succession of deviant key levels that are startlingly candid in their effect. Area I (meas. 78–133) is starkly in C major until the very moment of the turn toward Theme 2 and its first key level, E minor. Area II, using Theme 2 as essential material, passes through a surprising succession of deviant keys before G major, the dominant key, is reconfirmed in a strong cadence progression just ahead of the double bar. The principal deviant keys are these:

E minor	G major	E-flat major	A-flat minor	E minor
meas. 134	meas. 174	meas. 190	meas. 200	meas. 216

There is then a long drive to measure 228, the level of G major, which persists as the key to the end of the Exposition.

EXAMPLE 3-15   Schubert, "Great" C Major Symphony/I, principal themes

a) Theme 1, meas. 78–85

b) Theme 2, meas. 134–40

The comparatively brief Midsection stresses the key of A-flat and combines the principal rhythmic ideas of the two themes, fusing them and making them incisive with fine parts for horns and timpani.

In the Recapitulation, Theme 1 gains interest by a series of key digressions that converge, at measure 436, on a G pedal point to approach Theme 2. This is stated at three successive levels—C minor (meas. 440), A minor (meas. 460), C major (meas. 492)—to fulfill again the bitonal prediction of the opening motto. A coda, *Piu moto* (meas. 570), uses material from Theme 1 until it climaxes (meas. 662) in a massive recall of the opening motto, now harmonized and underlaid with the essential trochaic and triplet rhythms.

The second movement, *Andante con moto*, is in a lengthy five-part design that many people have found somewhat tedious and repetitious. This is unfortunate, because the two themes are enchanting. The segments of the design, with designation of materials and keys, follow:

A	*B*	*A'*
Theme 1	Theme 2	Theme 1
A minor	F major	A minor
meas. 1–92	meas. 93–159	meas. 160–266

B'	*A''*
Theme 2	Theme 1
A major	A minor
meas. 267–329	meas. 330–80

The C major Scherzo is vigorous and boisterous. Surprisingly, it has a small sonata-allegro design, with Theme 2 in G (meas. 31ff.) kept colorful by its stressing of the dominant harmony, D-F♯-A. The Midsection begins abruptly in A-flat and explores both principal themes, carrying them through a series of deviant keys until G is reached for retransition at measure 137. The Recapitulation is brief, closing in a strong authentic cadence in C major that highlights the key of A major of the Trio, which follows immediately. If the repeats that are indicated are taken in performance, the Trio is longer than the Scherzo; tedium is to be avoided only by observing meticulously the *Allegro vivace* tempo indication and by stressing such enlivening factors as contrasting dynamics, louvered texture in the instrumentation, and vividly juxtaposed keys. Such movements as this Scherzo are rigorous tests for the conductor.

The Finale, *Allegro vivace*, shows another sonata-allegro design, but this one is extraordinarily long: 1,155 measures. Theme 1, announced at the very beginning, associates trochaic and triplet rhythms as did the first movement, and Theme 2 is related to it (Ex. 3-16).

Like the preceding two movements, this brilliant and attractive piece suffers from want of conciseness. In the composer's defense, we must observe that Schubert, in the last year of his life, was just mastering musical architecture in the grand manner, as evidenced by this symphony and the great piano sonatas in A and B-flat major. Had he been allotted only a few more years, restraint and cogency would undoubtedly have come to his style. We must recall, too, that

EXAMPLE 3-16   Schubert, "Great" C Major Symphony/IV, principal themes

a) Theme 1, meas. 1–14

b) Theme 2, meas. 170–78

had Beethoven died at the same age as Schubert we should have only his first symphony; if Haydn had died equally early, there would be only his tentative earliest symphonies. Even Mozart at 31 had still to write his three great symphonies of 1788, on which his reputation as a symphonist rests. With Schubert's tragic early death, one of music's richest talents was extinguished just at the brink of maturity; and the first flourishing of the Viennese symphony was over. The center of musical activity shifted, for a time, to Germany and to such exotic regions as Russia and Hungary. France, too, had a major role in shaping the symphony of the nineteenth century, as will be described presently.

4

A Time of Temporizing:
Mendelssohn and Schumann

The half-century after Beethoven's death was a somewhat bleak period for the Austro-German symphony. This type of music had reached its apogee under Haydn and Beethoven, and their immediate successors found it difficult to conceive of the symphony as other than a somewhat learned orchestral sonata of four movements. But even as Mendelssohn and Schumann labored mightily to carry on, exciting new concepts of the symphony were being proposed—outside the Austro-German orbit. An interval of contemplation was needed before German composers could assimilate these radical ideas into their own music.

Composers of the next few decades after Beethoven's death were in something of a quandry, especially those in Germany and Austria. On the one hand, there was the magnificence of their heritage, in symphonic music in particular; for a German composer to depart drastically from the directions pointed by Haydn and Beethoven required not only musical gifts, but adventurousness. On the other hand, there was the lure of new ideas, emanating from France in particular. Berlioz's music had the fresh spirit of its times, as we shall see presently; yet embracing such bold concepts as his without self-consciousness was virtually impossible for a German composer of the 1830s and 1840s. To complicate matters still further, those same decades saw the first stirrings of interest in music of a more remote past than that represented by Haydn and Mozart. Two musical events of the years immediately following Beethoven's death set the tone for the decades to follow and serve to epitomize the dilemma of the Romantic composer. In 1829, Mendelssohn conducted the first public performance of J. S. Bach's *Passion According to St. Matthew;* within the same year, Hector Berlioz undertook to turn music away from its Classical models as he wrote his precedent-shattering *Symphonie fantastique.* Thus two main currents in nineteenth-century music were brought into early confrontation, with only the distance between Berlin and Paris to separate them. A composer of extraordinary conviction and talent might have found a middle road, but Beethoven's immediate successors were men of more modest endowment.

For a time, it seemed that the day of the large-scale orchestral work was over. The most popular types of music in the middle years of the nineteenth century were opera and compositions for piano solo. The heyday of the virtuoso had arrived, and spectacular performers (Paganini, Spohr, Liszt, Chopin, among others) titillated the public with musical acrobatics that deflected attention from more intrinsic values. The orchestra, which is inherently the very antithesis of the virtuoso, lost in favor and was often regarded as merely a necessary accouterment for the opera and the solo concerto.

Felix Mendelssohn-Bartholdy (1809–1847) and Robert Schumann (1810–1856) lived their entire creative lives in those uncertain, transitional years. Their symphonies are the only German ones of note during this period; but a just evaluation of them has been complicated by the extreme fluctuations in taste that have, from time to time, tended to disparage both men or, when the pendulum swung in the opposite direction, to inflate their significance.

The Symphonies of Mendelssohn

Mendelssohn, like Schubert, spent his youth in Beethoven's shadow; but he found it less oppressive because his situation (Berlin and Leipzig) was fairly remote from Vienna, and because the fortunate circumstances of his family life provided a certain insulation. Mendelssohn would probably have written the same kind of agreeable, unpretentious music even if Beethoven had never lived.

The symphony was not Mendelssohn's métier, although he had already written twelve little symphonies for strings before he was fourteen. Even the more successful of his later symphonies have the flavor of homage to a past that Mendelssohn always revered. The Symphony in C minor, Op. 11, generally called No. 1, is interesting chiefly because Mendelssohn was only fifteen when he wrote it in 1824. The next one in sequence is the D major "Reformation" Symphony, written in 1830 for the three-hundredth anniversary of the Augsburg Confession (Mendelssohn was a Lutheran by conversion). It was published only posthumously, as Op. 105, and then designated, confusingly, No. 5. This is a somewhat pompous work, self-conscious in its use of material borrowed from traditional Lutheran sources. The Dresden Amen appears twice in the first movement, in both cases as a bridge to Theme 1; and "Ein feste Burg" has a conspicuous role in the introduction to the Finale. Mendelssohn is at his best when he is unpretentious, and the middle movements—a genial Scherzo and an ingenuous Andante—are the most successful parts of the "Reformation" Symphony.

A performance of this work was planned—for Paris of all places. Mendelssohn had ventured to the French capital for a second time in December of 1831, for he had enjoyed some pleasant successes there. But Habeneck's famous orchestra, during rehearsals, took a violent dislike to the "Reformation" Symphony, and the projected performance was called off. The 22-year-old composer was deeply wounded by this rejection, which probably inhibited his future writing of similar pieces.

By far the best of Mendelssohn's symphonies are the two known as the "Scottish" and the "Italian." Today they are designated, respectively, No. 3 and No. 4, with slight regard for any circumstances of performance or publication. Mendelssohn was apparently planning both these works while the "Reformation" Symphony was having its unfortunate trial run, and the delay in bringing them to completion may well be attributed to the fiasco at Paris.

Both the "Italian" and "Scottish" symphonies were inspired by the composer's travels, but they are free from any literal quotations of native materials. That particular aspect of nationalism—borrowing folk materials—had not captured the interest of composers in the 1830s as it was to do a few decades later; at any rate, Mendelssohn was disillusioned about quoted materials after the rejection of his "Reformation" Symphony. Like Beethoven's "Pastoral," Mendelssohn's "Italian" and "Scottish" symphonies are "more expression of feeling than tone-painting."

The Symphony No. 4 in A major (the "Italian") is one of Mendelssohn's finest orchestral pieces. As already noted, Mendelssohn's successful music is always without guile; "unpremeditated" quite justifiably describes the effect of the "Italian" Symphony and a few other works like it—the "Midsummer Night's Dream" music and the Finale of the Violin Concerto, for example. We should simply miss the charm were we to look for devious tonal plans or grandiose musical architecture.

The first movement, *Allegro vivace*, does conform to the sonata-allegro formula, but this design is of minimal importance because the general effect is one of perpetual motion in a nonpartite structure. The cantering 6/8 meter is constant throughout, and notes longer than a dotted-quarter are quite scarce in the melodic parts. Close scrutiny of the Exposition reveals that the timpani, tuned throughout to A and E, are the equipoise for the movement. They are not used at all until the principal theme is restated at full orchestra (meas. 51), so that they acquire prominence by suppression. During the remainder of Area I, which is in the key of A, the two timpani are maintained in the descending fifth (V–I) relationship of E to A. During Area II, in the key of E, the timpani reverse and emphasize the rising fifth, A to E, a potential plagal (IV–I) relationship. But when the A drum begins its long pedal point (meas. 132), the superimposed harmony is the full dominant-seventh chord, B-D♯-F♯-A. The apparent conflict between A in the kettledrum, which resolves to E (meas. 140), and A in the surrounding harmony, which moves simultaneously to G♯, is the source of considerable piquancy. It also permits maximum use of the timpani, which were still hand-tuned in Mendelssohn's day and so fixed in their initial tuning.

The second movement, *Andante con moto*, is Mendelssohn at his best. There is the plaintive feeling of a cortège, mostly through the constant staccato eighth notes in cellos and string basses; and the superimposed first theme in D minor could probably have been written by no one else (Ex. 4-1). This whimsical, wistful little march sounds faintly archaic because it uses the natural form of the minor mode, with the unraised seventh scale degree (C♮).

EXAMPLE 4-1   Mendelssohn, "Italian" Symphony/II, Theme 1

The third movement is a Menuetto with Trio, although it is not so designated. The Trio, in E major after an A major Menuetto, is scored with skill and imagination; and the written-out reprise of the Menuetto is both expanded and varied. The symphony closes with a dashing A minor Saltarello—an Italian jumping dance.

The Symphonies of Schumann

Robert Schumann was far more affected by the conflicting currents of his day than was Mendelssohn; and he was the first German composer of importance to make manifest the Romantic era's fascination with "the word." As a consequence, his essays and critical articles are almost equal in importance to his music. Schumann was extraordinarily generous, passionate, and unrestrained. Had he lived and worked outside Germany, where the shadow of a glorious musical past was overpowering, Schumann might have been as uninhibited a radical as Berlioz. As it was, his effort to reconcile the conflicts of his age may have contributed to his ruin, for he finished his days in an insane asylum.

Schumann's symphonies, written during his later middle years, were spared much of the effusiveness of his youth and the insecurity of his late maturity. The fresh originality of his rhythmic ideas is a vital force in all his music. Unfortunately, in his orchestral works, clarity of rhythm is often obscured by nonidiomatic or downright clumsy scoring.

In its mood, Schumann's Symphony No. 1 in B-flat major, completed in 1841, is a successor to Beethoven's "Pastoral" Symphony. Very likely it was inspired by a poem about the spring of Böttger, and Schumann once considered giving each of the movements a title alluding to some aspect of the springtime. Before the work was finished, however, he changed his mind, and the only vestige of the Böttger poem lies in the affinity between the rhythm of the opening motive in the brasses and the meter of the poem's refrain:

Im   Tha - le blüht   der   Früh - ling   auf
(In the valley spring is bursting forth)

After a somewhat heavy prefatory *Andante un poco maestoso,* this same rhythm in halved values becomes the nucleus of Theme 1 in the *Allegro molto vivace,* which is the sonata-allegro portion of the first movement. The remainder of the symphony continues in genial but unremarkable fashion until the dashing Finale, its most characteristic and successful movement.

Schumann's next symphony in sequence is his D minor, which is designated No. 4 today. It was completed in original form soon after the Symphony No. 1, and was performed under the title *Symphonische Phantasie* ("Symphonic Fantasy") on December 6, 1841, at Leipzig. Feeling less than satisfied with this initial performance, Schumann put the work aside; he reorchestrated it twelve years later, at which time it was designated No. 4. Since this may be Schumann's finest large orchestral work, it has been chosen here for detailed comment.

This is the first German symphony with extensive, successful mutation of the sonata-allegro and partite designs as they had been handed down by composers of the Classical and post-Classical eras. It is also one of the earliest German works to seek unity among its movements by studied means. (Non-German composers, discussed later in this book, definitely led the way in both these areas of experimentation.)

Schumann seeks cohesion among the four movements of his D minor symphony through at least four perceptible devices:

1. He provides a basic motive (which we may call X) at the start of the work. This X-motive is recalled in every movement, although its derivation in the Scherzo is indirect and tenuous.

2. He truncates or otherwise alters the design of each movement so that it is less than autonomous and must attain fulfillment as part of the entire symphony.

3. He casts the Finale as a kind of grand fantasy, overlaid, it is true, with a free sonata-allegro design. During this closing section, not only the X-motive but a number of other materials from the various movements are recalled and given new contexts.

4. He uses the key of D as a focal point for each of the four movements. The first one is quite candidly in D minor, but there are striking tonal digressions, and the closing portion turns to the major side of the mode. The Romanza hovers between D and A minor and even closes without determining which is to prevail (the A major triad at the close might be considered V or I). The Scherzo is in D minor, but its Trio, in B-flat major, gives needed variety. The Finale is in D minor/major.

A discussion of each of the movements follows.

FIRST MOVEMENT: *Ziemlich langsam/Lebhaft*[1] (*Quite slow/Lively*)

The X-motive appears in both the introduction (*Ziemlich langsam*) and the sonata-allegro (*Lebhaft*) portions. This motive comprises the five contiguous pitches F–E–D–C♯–D and serves to circumscribe the key of D minor. In the Introduction, it appears immediately after the pitch A has been taken in a full

[1] Schumann was one of the first composers to use German (rather than Italian) tempo indications.

The concert hall in Leipzig

orchestral tutti; it is sounded by first bassoon and second violins, which are reinforced a sixth below by second bassoon and violas (Ex. 4-2).

EXAMPLE 4-2   Schumann, Symphony No. 4/I, X-motive

During subsequent portions of the Introduction, the X-motive is heard frequently, sometimes at the original pitch level and sometimes in transposition; in each case, its distinctive linear shape is unmistakable. Toward the end of the Introduction, the movement quickens from eighth to sixteenth notes in a bridge to the movement proper (*Lebhaft*).

Up to the conventional double bar, the *Lebhaft* prepares a classic sonata-allegro design. Theme 1 (Ex. 4-3a) uses figures derived from the X-motive, and Theme 2 (Ex. 4-3b) resembles Theme 1, but it is in F major. Such relationship gives the movement Haydnesque overtones.

EXAMPLE 4-3   Schumann, Symphony No. 4/I, Theme 1 and Theme 2

a) Theme 1, meas. 29–32

b) Theme 2, meas. 59–63

Area I (meas. 29–58) is almost equally divided between a first portion in D minor that states and expands Theme 1, and a second portion that modulates, somewhat clumsily, to F major. Area II complements the sixteenth-note figures of Theme 2 (Ex. 4-3b) with fresh rhythmic counterpoint— ♪♪♪ | ♪.♪♪ ♪.♪♪ etc.; a strong F cadence terminates the Exposition section.

The Midsection begins abruptly with a sudden, starkly unharmonized E♭, sounded in strings and brasses, which serves to negate the foregoing F cadence and set the new section into motion. A long portion (meas. 87–146) enlarges on the sixteenth-note motives of Themes 1 and 2, with added interest stemming from a new rhythmic motive  that enters at measure 121. At measure 147, the movement departs strikingly from the conventional sonata-allegro design: a distinctive new element, Theme 3 (Ex. 4-4), is introduced in the key of F major, the second key level of the Exposition section. The interpolation of a new theme into the Midsection is not of itself extraordinary, but Schumann's plan for Theme 3 is unique. It is reiterated four times within the next 150 measures, in each instance at a fresh key level, as follows:

Meas. 147—F major

159—A major

221—A-flat major

233—C major

297—D Major (this entry is expanded to intersect the re-entry of Theme 1).

EXAMPLE 4-4   Schumann, Symphony No. 4/I, meas. 147–54, Theme 3

To terminate this extended hybrid movement, Schumann recalls Theme 1 at the parallel level of D major (meas. 337) but cadences summarily and unconvincingly only 22 measures later. This deliberate truncation aids the first movement in intersecting the second with only a token pause between them.

SECOND MOVEMENT: *Romanza—Ziemlich langsam*

THIRD MOVEMENT: *Scherzo—Lebhaft, with Trio*

The second movement is totally hybrid in form, and ambivalent in its key inference. Theme 1, which begins with a querulous little air given out by oboe and cellos doubled, is in a miniature ternary design (ABA′) in which the contrasting *B* portion recalls the *X*-motive in the key of A; the reprise (A′) is token, occupying only 4 measures. Next, a section in D major uses a motive based on the first four notes of the *X*-motive; the strings carry the lines deriving from this material, but a solo violin both softens and disguises these parts with its persistent triplet embellishment. A token reprise of the opening material (meas. 43) begins in D minor but soon turns toward A; the concluding cadence, in A major, leaves the enigma of what is the principal key unsolved.

The compressed plan of this little piece is a deliberate means of effecting closer conjunction with the Scherzo, which ensues without break. This third movement is a routine affair, its Trio establishing a very tenuous link with the X-motive: the first violin part derives from the solo violin line in the middle of the Romanza, which, in turn, embellishes lines derived from the X-motive.

FOURTH MOVEMENT: *Langsam/Lebhaft*

The X-motive germinates the entire 16-measure introduction (*Langsam*). The sonata-allegro design that follows (*Lebhaft*) has some unusual features, but it is more full-fledged than that of the first movement—for the obvious reason that this movement must round off and conclude the symphony.

Area I of the Exposition, in D major, has two sections strikingly contrasted to each other. The first (meas. 17–26) is structured from chordal motives in full orchestra except for the low strings, which underlay X-derived material recalled from Theme 1 of the first movement. The second section (meas. 27–38) has a new Theme 1b in first violins, of considerable importance because it has a special role in the conjunction between the Midsection and the Recapitulation.

Area II, in A major, begins with its own distinctive Theme 2 (meas. 39), which has a strong, lyric quality and is related, perhaps inadvertently, to the theme of the Larghetto of Beethoven's Second Symphony.

The discursive scale passages that conclude the Exposition recall similar passages in the first movement, mostly through the sparse, awkward scoring; and a strong A cadence precedes the double bar.

When the Midsection begins on a stark G♮, it, too, recalls a parallel point in the first movement; for G♮ is a somewhat abrupt negation of the key of A major, as the E♭ at the start of the Midsection of the first movement was a negation of the F cadence that had preceded it.

The Recapitulation section is the only part of this sonata-allegro design to show significant mutations. Strictly speaking, Recapitulation is deferred until Theme 2 enters, in D major, at measure 129. But the distinctive Theme Ib enters at measure 115 to climax the Midsection and is expanded to occupy 14 measures, thus generating an illusory Recapitulation of part of Area I.

From measure 172, the Finale expands into a fantasia that alternates new and recalled materials as follows:

Meas. 172–87	Closing Theme in clarinets, bassoons, and violas
188–210	*Schneller* (Faster)—orchestral tutti based loosely on X-motive
211–end	*Presto*—begins with fugal scale entries, enlarges to routine close

Schumann wrote two symphonies, his third and fourth in proper compositional sequence, after the B-flat and the D minor. They are known today as Symphony No. 2, in C major, Op. 61; and Symphony No. 3, in E-flat major (the "Rhenish"), Op. 97. Both were published before the D minor, which bears the confusing designation Opus 120, for reasons that have already been indicated.

Schumann's "Rhenish" could be grouped with Mendelssohn's "Italian" and "Scottish" symphonies as a piece inspired by a journey. One of the last serene and happy times Clara and Robert Schumann were to have together was a pilgrimage to the Rhineland, which is commemorated in Schumann's final symphony, completed late in the autumn of 1850. The central key is E-flat, and it is probably indicative of a kind of accord in the nineteenth-century aesthetic of key that Wagner also chose E-flat for his Rhenish opera, *Das Rheingold*, which was completed some three years after Schumann's symphony. Aside from the majestic river itself, the Cathedral at Cologne seems to have most impressed the travelers. A ceremony they witnessed there may have suggested the fourth movement of the "Rhenish" Symphony, marked *Feierlich* (Ceremonious). A few comments about the five movements of the "Rhenish" Symphony follow.

FIRST MOVEMENT: *Lebhaft (Lively)*

The pervasive trait of this movement is the metric complexity *hemiola*, which involves the ratio of 2:3 within a given time span. During Area I (meas. 1–82), hemiola gives Theme 1 its characteristic sound and is present during much of the expansive and transitional material as well. As expressed at the opening, two measures of 3/4 time equal one (hypothetical) measure of 3/2, as follows:

During Area II (meas. 95–183), a new, more lyric theme in G minor/B-flat major is conspicuously "on-the-beat"; but hemiola returns for transitional sections. The Exposition cadence confirms B-flat as the true second key in the traditional sonata-allegro tonal dualism.

During the Midsection, the key of B major (meas. 281–93) proposes for the first time a key relationship that is recurrent in subsequent movements. To E-flat major, B major (C-flat major) is the submediant of the parallel minor expressed enharmonically.

SECOND MOVEMENT: *Scherzo*

C major, the "submediant-made-major" of the central key of E-flat, brightens the movement. One or the other of two principal thematic ideas (measures 1 and 17 respectively) is present almost constantly during the movement; often they combine with each other. Even when contrasting material is introduced (meas. 41ff.), it is underlaid with the running sixteenth notes of the second principal idea, and the entire design suffers from unclear delineation.

THIRD MOVEMENT: *Nicht schnell (Not fast)*

Like its predecessor, this movement lacks contrast in material and, most of all, in instrumentation. The lyric ideas are beautifully shaped, however, and brevity makes want of diversity a less serious circumstance.

FOURTH MOVEMENT: *Feierlich*

By tradition, this movement is Schumann's salute to the great cathedral at Cologne. The orchestral texture throughout, which stresses brass (horns, trumpets, trombones) and woodwind choirs, is planned to suggest the organ. A motive in which the interval of a rising fourth is conspicuous is enunciated first by trombones and horns; it is the source of most subsequent material. The prevailing key is E-flat minor, although the signature for the major mode (three flats) appears, with Gb, Cb, and Db imposed consistently as accidentals. After measure 23, the orchestral texture is lightened with a series of imitative entries based on the opening motive. This portion achieves climax just before the key of B major (meas. 52), which establishes palpable contact with the first movement.

FIFTH MOVEMENT: *Lebhaft*

The free sonata-allegro design of this movement has one or two points of interest. For example, Area II and its Theme 2 (meas. 57ff.) progress and dissolve without definitive cadence into a developmental Midsection: by measure 98, the key is F-sharp minor (really G-flat minor, a derivative of E-flat minor) and sharp keys predominate until the impulse toward Recapitulation (meas. 153) begins. The pervasive enharmonic inference of this middle section is one of the most advanced traits of the "Rhenish" Symphony. A fugal section, followed by a coda (*Schneller*) brings the symphony to a firm close.

Within two years of the completion of his E-flat Symphony, Schumann's emotional difficulties had progressed into serious mental illness. His musical heir was a young man whose career had barely begun as Schumann's was ending. Johannes Brahms was to adopt and make plausible many of the musical ideas that Schumann had proposed, most notably pervasive enharmonicism and polyrhythmic complexity.

5

Brahms: A Great Mediator
Of Classical and
Romantic Styles

More than chronological logic suggests moving from Schumann to Brahms, for the unfortunate older composer was the first to recognize the young Brahms' extraordinary talent and to draw him to the attention of leading musicians of the mid-nineteenth century. Johannes Brahms (1833–1897) was eking out a dismal and precarious existence indeed before Schumann cited him as a voice of the future in the famous and prophetic essay *Neue Bahnen* ("New Paths"). This was published on October 28, 1853, in the *Neue Zeitschrift für Musik* (*New Journal for Music*), which Schumann himself had founded a number of years earlier. Writing the essay was one of Schumann's last lucid acts, and so great was his prestige at the time that the obscure young artist from Hamburg found himself a celebrity almost overnight. But the effect of this laudatory article was not totally fortunate: Brahms was inhibited for several years by the fear that he might not prove worthy of Schumann's confidence.

As is the case with so many major artists, Brahms appeared at a propitious time. By the 1850s, when he began his career, the extreme radicalism of the thirties was tempered, and more conservative taste was evident in many quarters. Brahms' own compositions run the full gamut, from the passionate effusiveness of such early works as the first piano sonatas and the Piano Trio in B major to the chaste, elegant restraint of the magnificent clarinet sonatas of Op. 120, written four decades later. In a broad sense, Brahms' four symphonies capsulate this whole stylistic compass: the first movement of his First Symphony is marked by the sullen ardor so admired by Romantic composers; whereas the entire Fourth Symphony is characterized by clarity, elegance, and, as a source of added interest, recourse to earlier forms and devices. Once the First Symphony had been achieved and performed (in 1876–77), Brahms' modesty about essaying the form that Beethoven had brought to such splendor was overcome; his Second Symphony followed within the year (1877), and the Third and Fourth within less than ten years (1883–85). All four of Brahms' symphonies are splendid, major works; they crown the symphonic writing of the nineteenth century; at the same time they reconcile, in superbly convincing guise, the progressive and the conservative strains in nineteenth-century taste.

Brahms completed his First Symphony when he was 43 years old, although he had sketched the first movement almost twenty years prior to that time. During a period of several years before he resumed active work on the symphony, Brahms was occupied intermittently with three compositions that honed his ability to write for instrumental ensemble. The first two, the Serenade in D major, Op. 11 (1857–58), and the Serenade in A major, Op. 16 (1857–60), are delightful examples of a type of music found in abundance among works of eighteenth-century masters. The instrumentation in each case is specialized, however, and the two Serenades served principally to acquaint Brahms with the unique capacities of wind and brass instruments.

That the lesson was learned well is attested by Brahms' next orchestral work, which may be regarded as the real progenitor of the First Symphony: *Variations on a Theme by Haydn*, Op. 56A. The theme upon which the Variations are based is designated "St. Anthony Chorale" and probably originated as a pilgrims' song of the Burgenland region. Brahms received the theme from Karl Ferdinand Pohl, a major Haydn biographer, who pointed out its presence in the second movement of Haydn's[1] unpublished *Feldpartita* (or Divertimento) in B-flat major. Brahms copied the engaging tune in his sketchbook and during the summer of 1873 used it as the subject of the masterly orchestral work.

The Variations were probably completed first in the version for two pianos, although the orchestral composition was planned from the start as the ultimate guise of the piece. The composition consists of the theme itself cast as a three-part form with repetitions (|= a =|= b a =|), followed by eight variations, in which the melodic integrity of the theme is never lost. The Finale, which follows the eighth variation, commences with a set of imitative entries based on a head-motive $\underset{\text{(B♭}}{}\overset{\text{E♭}}{\diagup}\underset{\text{D)}}{\diagdown}$ that prefigures the principal theme of the Finale of the First Symphony (see Ex. 5-11c). The Variations were first performed, from manuscript, on November 1, 1873. Their immediate success must have been a stimulus, for Brahms soon resumed work on his First Symphony, this time pushing on to complete it.

Characteristics of the Symphonies of Brahms

In their more obvious traits, all Brahms' symphonies stem from Classical models, for each is a work of four movements arranged in the traditional sequence of a sonata-allegro first movement, a slower episode, a scherzo- or intermezzo-like

---

[1]Certain historians now attribute the tune to Pleyel.

third movement, and a massive finale. None of the symphonies employs the ruses for intermovemental unity found in the symphonies of many of Brahms' contemporaries (Schumann, for example), although Brahms' use of a "basic motive" in three of the first movements is an allied device.

Certain idiomatic traits found in almost any of Brahms' large, mature works are repeatedly evident in the symphonies. We shall cite a number of them before discussing the symphonies individually.

Variant Means of Key Confirmation

For at least two centuries before Brahms' time, the traditional means of confirming a key or tonal center had been the harmonic succession known as the authentic cadence: the progression V–I. While the effect of this progression had acquired the weakness of a cliché long before Brahms' day, composers were loath to relinquish it, fearing that to do so would be to cloud the tonal language that had served their forebears so well.

In his symphonies, Brahms makes frequent and effective use of nondominant progressions at even the most important points of key affirmation—namely, the conjunction of the close of the Midsection with the beginning of the Recapitulation in a sonata-allegro design, and the final cadence in any type of movement. A majority of these progressions are variants of the time-honored plagal cadence (IV–I) and show bass movement of a rising fifth—or descending fourth—in contrast to the descending fifth of the authentic progression.

In the First Symphony, in C minor, three of the four movements have plagal-type final cadences. In the first movement (Ex. 5-1), the bass movement of F to C (meas. 503) marks the cadence as essentially plagal, although the upper parts resolve linearly and need not be construed as producing any particular harmony.

In the second movement (Ex. 5-2), which is in E major, the bass movement of A to E (meas. 123–24) again signals a plagal-type close, but the supporting harmony is II^6 (F♯-A-C♮), a subdominant-type chord.

EXAMPLE 5-1   Brahms, Symphony No. 1/I, meas. 501–end, final cadence

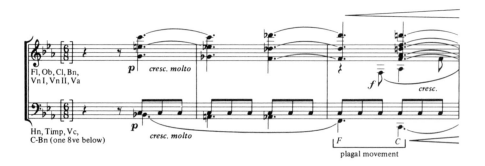

EXAMPLE 5-2   ₋Brahms, Symphony No. 1/II, meas. 123–end, final cadence

In the Finale, a simple plagal cadence is taken and reiterated.

In the first movement of the Third Symphony, the key of F, required for the Recapitulation, must be established twice, since Theme 1 is comprised of two elements—its preliminary "basic motive" and its essential melodic component, each of them beginning on F (Ex. 5-3). The approach to the basic motive (meas.

118–19) is accomplished in linear fashion but over an F pedal point in the timpani, which anticipates the pitch of the start of the basic motive. The immediate approach to Theme 1, 4 measures later, is through the diminished-seventh chord on the raised fourth degree of F major—B♮-D-F-A♭—which recalls the original approach to this theme, in measure 2.

EXAMPLE 5-3   Brahms, Symphony No. 3/I, meas. 118–24,
                                Retransition and Recapitulation

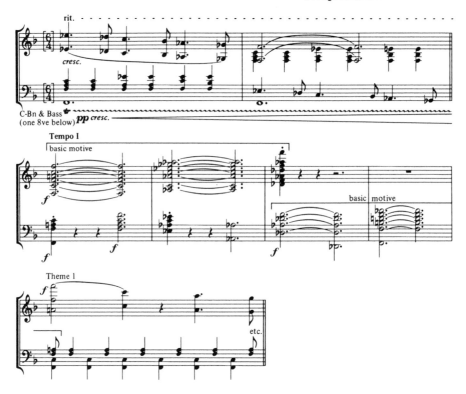

The second movement of the Third Symphony, a large ternary design in C major, has an extremely passive Retransition leading to reprise of the first subject: changing harmonies overlie the tonic pedal point, C; the release of these shifting harmonies into a simple C major triad is the final gesture of reprise (Ex. 5-4). This same movement closes with a plagal cadence (meas. 129–34), the progression being enlivened with inflections borrowed from the opposite mode—C minor.

A final example, drawn from the second movement of the Fourth Symphony, is the most prophetic of all: the opening motto (Ex. 5-5) uses melodic symmetry and a sense of concentricity to establish E as tonal center. As may be seen, the motto, unharmonized, rises to a third above E, then descends to a third below it: C E G. This kind of "mirror" relationship among pitches became more and more important for composers of the generation following Brahms.

EXAMPLE 5-4   Brahms, Symphony No. 3/II, meas. 80–85,
Retransition and Recapitulation

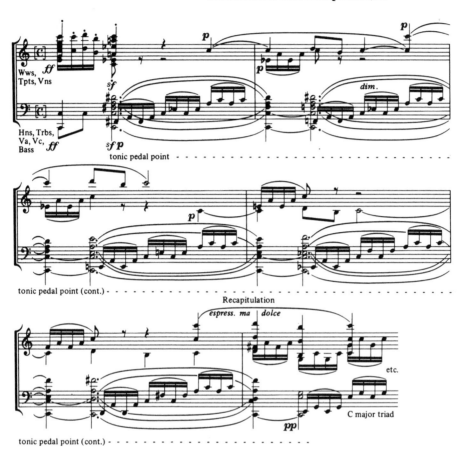

EXAMPLE 5-5   Brahms, Symphony No. 4/II, opening motto

Flexibility through Mixed Mode (Bimodality)

Although composers from Haydn onward made occasional use of the mixed mode, the quality of "bimodality" is pervasive in most of Brahms' music. Brahms conceives any key as having implicitly flexible inflections for the third, sixth, and seventh scale degrees, the lower inflections stemming from the minor mode, the higher from the major. Theme 1 of the first movement of the First Symphony (Ex. 5-6) serves to illustrate how such a bimodal resource gives flexibility to a linear structure: all three variables in the key of C bimodally realized (E♭-E♮, A♭-A♮, B♭-B♮) appear in this powerful subject.

EXAMPLE 5-6   Brahms, Symphony No. 1/I, meas. 42–51, Theme 1

Theme 1 of the first movement of the Third Symphony, in F, is also bimodal, as may be observed in Ex. 5-7.

EXAMPLE 5-7   Brahms, Symphony No. 3/I, meas. 1–6,
                              basic motive and Theme 1

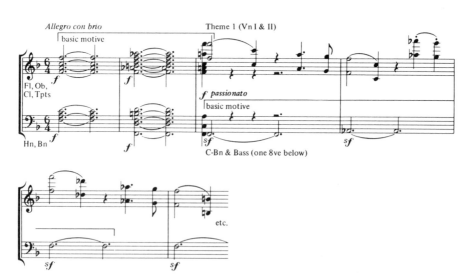

In the second movement of the Fourth Symphony, Theme I, which immediately follows the opening motto shown in Ex. 5-5, is in the key of E realized as a mixed mode; the major mode inflection of the scale third—G♯—is used, along with C♮ from the minor mode, and D♯/D♮ in free alternation. The total effect is whimsical and a little exotic.

New Textures

Brahms was the first major composer to use what might well be called "stratified texture." The clearest examples lie in passages that are genuinely bitonal (in two keys)—a very forward-looking texture indeed. Such a passage occurs during preparation for Recapitulation in the fourth movement of the First Symphony. Beginning at measure 168 (Ex. 5-8), violins, cellos and string basses, trumpets, timpani, and contrabassoon have figures suggesting the key of C; simultaneously the woodwinds, horns, and violas are equally suggestive of E minor. These two keys, used simultaneously or in alternation, are kept in equipoise for 16 measures; the riddle of which key is to prevail is solved finally with the entrance of Theme 1 in C major.

EXAMPLE 5-8   Brahms, Symphony No. 1/IV, meas. 168–69,
                              bitonal texture during Retransition

An even more striking instance of stratified (and bitonal) texture occurs in connection with the second subject in the second movement of the Third Symphony. The movement commences in C major, and the expected dominant key of G is prepared, then obscured, during measures 27 to 40. Theme 2 (Ex. 5-9) maintains the expected key of G in the harmony of the accompaniment in the strings, but the theme itself, in clarinet and bassoon, is clearly in A minor.

Variations in Classical Forms

Each of the movements of Brahms' four symphonies clearly reflects one or another of the Classical forms, most often the sonata-allegro. All four first movements use a fairly orthodox sonata-allegro design. Subsequent movements, however, are likely to show interesting mutations: most of them eliminate the traditional Midsection and interpolate a significant section of development at

EXAMPLE 5-9   Brahms, Symphony No. 3/II, meas. 41–45,
                                               bitonal texture during Theme 2

some other point in the design. The variant design encountered most frequently
is this:

Exposition

Theme 1   Theme 2   Extension
tonic key   deviant key   and Retransition

Recapitulation   *Coda*

              Sizable
Theme 1   section   Theme 2
tonic key   of   tonic key
              development

The following movements use such a mutation of the sonata-allegro design:
Symphonies No. 1/IV, No. 3/IV, No. 4/II, No. 4/III.

Another mutation of the sonata-allegro design is found in Symphony No. 2/IV;
this plan provides the illusion of a three-part design, since each of the three

portions begins with Theme 1 in the tonic key of D major. This is the skeleton of the design, with measure clues for this specific movement:

Exposition		*Midsection*	
Theme 1	Theme 2	Theme 1	Fantasie-Development
D Major	A major	D major	
	(meas. 78)	(meas. 155)	

Recapitulation	
Theme 1	Theme 2
D major	D major
(meas. 244)	(meas. 281)

An additional and characteristic formal device for Brahms is the use of note-worthy materials in addition to the prescribed thematic components. Generally these added materials are brief but distinctive, and often they could be given such a descriptive title as "transition motive," "disruptive motive," or "framing motive." A number of these will be pointed out in discussions of the individual movements.

Three compositional techniques are encountered so often in all Brahms' music that they become near-clichés for him. These are the pedal point in all its forms and ramifications; the metric device of hemiola (see p. 102), and the use of the diminished-seventh chord as a "free agent" tonally speaking—a neutral harmony to be used as needed.

Analyses of the Symphonies of Brahms

Symphony No. 1 in C Minor, Op. 68

FIRST MOVEMENT: *Un poco sostenuto/Allegro*

The prefatory *Un poco sostenuto* prefigures three essential components of the Allegro that follows. The first of these is the "basic motive"—the three-note chromatic succession C-C♯-D, which occurs in violins and cellos at the beginning. The second is the suggestion of Theme 1 in the broken triads of measures 21 to 24. A third is the rhythm ♩♪♪♪ and its augmentation ♩. ♪♪♪ , which are diffused in most parts of the movement. The turgid orchestration for this Intro-duction is largely responsible for the dour effect.

The Allegro is cast in a lengthy, but quite conventional, sonata-allegro design. There are, however, two points of paramount interest. The first is the wonderful malleableness of the basic motive, which is as useful in inversion (descending form) as in its original guise and which permeates most sections of the movement. The beginning of the Allegro (Ex. 5–10) illustrates how adaptable this central structural element is: the basic motive appears first in woodwinds as a preface for Theme 1; 4 measures later, it appears in cellos as counterpoint for the first statement of Theme 1, in first violins.

EXAMPLE 5-10   Brahms, Symphony No. 1/I, meas. 38–46,
                                                          opening of Allegro

The second point of interest is that Area II and its Theme 2 (meas. 121ff.) are developed by simply inverting in position the two essential materials of Theme 1 as seen above: the basic motive, in woodwinds, is on top, and this is underlaid with the triadic theme in cellos—both in the relative major key of E-flat.

A supplementary material of the type cited earlier occurs at measure 157, when the easy-moving 6/8 rhythm is interrupted abruptly by the figure $\frac{6}{8}$ ♩♩♩ 𝄾 ♪ | in violas, made very incisive by the accompanying pizzicato chord. This might be termed a "disruptive motive," one that suddenly terminates Theme 1 but later evolves into a section of closure for the Exposition.

SECOND MOVEMENT: *Andante sostenuto*

This slow movement opens in such striking contrast to its dour predecessor that it emphasizes the considerable time intervening between the writing of the two portions. The key, E major, is startlingly remote from C minor and consequently sounds even brighter than usual. It instigates a "mirror" scheme of key relationship for the four movements of the symphony, since the third movement is in A-flat, whereas the Finale returns to C:

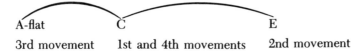

A-flat	C	E
3rd movement	1st and 4th movements	2nd movement

This *Andante sostenuto* is in a ternary design (ABA'), with the deviant section in the key of C-sharp minor. All the materials are beautifully lyric, the products of a composer who was a distinguished writer of *Lieder*. The reprise of the first strain (A') is lavishly embellished (meas. 67ff.), and the use of an obbligato solo violin is a special romantic gesture.

THIRD MOVEMENT: Un poco Allegretto e grazioso

This intermezzo-type movement is cast in a rondo design, with the principal components as follows:

A	B	A'	C	A''
A-flat major	F minor	A-flat	B major	A-flat
	(meas. 46ff.)	(meas. 62ff.)	(meas. 71ff.)	(meas. 115ff.)

The key scheme of this somewhat pedestrian movement is another "mirror," reflecting the more pervasive mirror scheme of the entire symphony:

F minor	A-flat	B major (C-flat)

In this case, the deviant keys, F minor and B (C-flat) major are a minor third on either side of the central key, A-flat major.

FOURTH MOVEMENT: Adagio/Piu Andante/Allegro
non troppo ma con brio

This fourth movement is by far the finest part of the First Symphony. It presents in the introduction two of the noblest orchestral subjects Brahms ever devised, in the horn theme and the chorale.

The preliminary portion comprises two parts: the Adagio, which prefigures Theme 1 of the *Allegro non troppo,* then is diffused in extensive transitional material; and the *Piu Andante,* which is a small three-part design in itself. The majestic horn solo in C major occupies the greater part of this *Piu Andante;* but the wonderful brief (4-measure) chorale that intervenes between the two statements of the horn theme is so distinctive—beginning, as it does, abruptly on the A major triad—that it creates an indelible effect. Both these materials are incorporated into the sonata-allegro design that follows, the horn theme

acting as a precursor of Theme 2. The four principal materials of this Finale
are shown in Ex. 5-11.

EXAMPLE 5-11   Brahms, Symphony No. 1/IV,
                                                            principal thematic components

a) Horn Theme in Introduction

b) Chorale Theme in Introduction

c) Theme 1

d) Theme 2

   The materials in the sonata-allegro design unfold conventionally up to the close
of the Exposition, which is prolonged to climax in the bitonal passage cited in
Ex. 5-8. Once Theme 1 has been restated for the beginning of the Recapitulation
(meas. 186ff.), this portion evolves into a section of extended development, with
the excursions to various keys and thematic fragmentation that often characterize
such sections. The apex, however, is a recall of the noble horn theme from the

Introduction, which acts here as a prologue to the Recapitulation of Theme 2 in the prescribed key of C major (meas. 302ff.). The climax of the movement occurs early in the Coda (*Piu Allegro*), when the chorale is heard again for the first time since the Introduction. A plagal cadence brings an intense, powerful symphony to a reposeful close.

Symphony No. 2 in D Major, Op. 73

Brahms' blithe Second Symphony contrasts strikingly with his somber First, which it followed so closely; this difference is not unlike that found between Beethoven's Fifth and Sixth symphonies, or even Mozart's G minor and his "Jupiter." But the D major Symphony does reveal several similarities to its predecessor. The most immediate is the presentation, in the very first measure, of a basic motive that subsequently permeates or germinates much of the later texture. This basic motive is the auxiliary-note figure D-C♯-D, which might even be seen as derived from the first figure of Theme 1 in the Finale of the First Symphony (see Ex. 5-11c).

FIRST MOVEMENT: *Allegro non troppo*

After the terse statement of the basic motive in cellos and string basses, Theme 1 is presented in simple grandeur—the first phrase in horns and the consequent phrase in woodwinds. Even during this initial statement, the three-note basic motive is an integral component of the supporting part in low strings (meas. 5, 9, 13, etc.); and it is present frequently in the transition bridge leading to the second element of Theme 1 (Theme 1b) at measure 44. This Theme 1b is initiated with the figure A–G♯–A, also deriving from the basic motive.

Area II of the Exposition section is especially interesting, since it employs still another ruse for augmenting the sonata-allegro design. Theme 2, in F-sharp minor and A major (meas. 82ff.), is stated twice, then dissipated with rhythmically energetic new material (meas. 118ff.), which gives way to a massive section of Retransition (meas. 135–55), based largely on a dominant pedal point with rhythmic activity in horns, violas, and clarinets. The outcome of this impressive Retransition is a complete restatement of Theme 2. Area II occupies a full one hundred measures, so that unusual emphasis is given its Theme 2.

The Midsection is routine, but, perhaps predictably, it is well laced with reminiscences of the basic motive; a portion commencing at measure 246 is interesting since it employs the basic motive in diminution (halved rhythmic values) and in continuing sequences. The portion of Retransition culminating the Midsection is masterly: plotted over a long dominant pedal point A in timpani, the active upper parts recall various earlier materials but climax with recall of the first two notes of Theme 1 in full orchestra (meas. 282). This brief figure of a rising third builds still more tension as the device of hemiola is invoked, so that the following rhythmic pattern develops and is reiterated:

The orthodox Recapitulation is followed by a powerful coda that uses all manner of developmental techniques (meas. 447–end).

SECOND MOVEMENT: *Adagio non troppo*

This is one of Brahms' numerous *Lied*-inspired movements; it opens in B major with a legato subject in cellos, accompanied by woodwinds. As the subject is repeated and extended, high strings and horns have important roles. The design of the movement becomes essentially ternary (ABA′) when a contrasting section in 12/8 time passes through the keys of F-sharp and B minor, ahead of the recall of the initial idea first in G, then in E major, before reverting to the tonic key of B major. The effect of the brief movement is that of a lyric fantasia.

THIRD MOVEMENT: *Allegretto grazioso*

This is a faintly exotic, intermezzo-like piece such as Brahms included in so many of his multimovement works. The exotic quality at the start stems from a mildly bitonal conflict, for the melody in the oboe sounds in E minor, while the supporting accompaniment is clearly in G major (Ex. 5–12).

EXAMPLE 5-12   Brahms, Symphony No. 2/III, opening theme

A first contrasting section, *Presto ma non assai*, uses the oboe subject of the opening but casts it in 2/4 meter; eventually the original theme returns (meas. 107). A second contrasting section, also marked *Presto ma non assai*, is in 3/8 meter and uses contrasting melodic material in the keys of A minor and C major. When the original theme and tempo are restored at measure 194, a five-part form (ABA′CA″) is achieved, although the key of G is withheld to measure 207.

FOURTH MOVEMENT: *Allegro con spirito*

This movement has been discussed under the heading "Variations in Classical Forms," pages 111ff.

Symphony No. 3 in F Major, Op. 90

FIRST MOVEMENT: *Allegro con brio*

The basic motive for this excellent design is again stated at the very outset—in measures 1 and 2—in woodwinds and brasses. Essentially, this basic motive is the interval of the minor third, here F to A♭, although often the octave of the initial note is added. This initial presentation of the basic motive discloses two important components of the movement: mixed mode and use of the neutralizing diminished-seventh chord (see Ex. 5-7). This proves to be the most tractable of all Brahms' basic motives; the following places in the first movement employ it, in each case with a new, vital harmonic context: measures 3 and 4 (string basses); 19 and 20 (string basses); 21 and 22 (upper winds and first violins); 27 and 28 (string basses); 49 to 51 and following (oboe, then strings); 101 to 102 (horn, which uses the basic motive as the germ of a "midtheme"); 120 to 124 (upper woodwinds, then horn and trombone); and so on, through parallel instances in the Recapitulation.

The pervasive quality of the basic motive is the most important attribute of this movement, which shows a quite conventional sonata-allegro design. Several other interesting characteristics of the movement were mentioned in the general discussion at the beginning of this chapter. It remains, however, to cite the splendid metric flexibility, the chief source of vitality in so many portions, beginning with the first statement of Theme 1 (see Ex. 5-7), which incorporates hemiola before the movement is three measures along. The rhythm of this Theme 1 was almost surely suggested by the opening of Schumann's "Rhenish" Symphony. A comparison of the two subjects will disclose how Brahms clarified and delineated Schumann's idea, most importantly through use of the double measure (6/4). Other points of metric interest occur at measures 51ff. (subverted measure bars), 87ff. (hemiola), and 187ff. (cross-rhythms).

SECOND MOVEMENT: *Andante*

This movement was also discussed in the opening of this chapter: see especially Ex. 5-4 and Ex. 5-9. Aside from the stratified, bitonal second theme (Ex. 5-9), a principal point of interest lies in two passages of intervention, when a key is carefully prepared by conventional means, only to be dissipated by a nontonal passage constructed through melodic sequence. The first of these passages occurs between measures 33 and 40, just prior to the presentation of the bitonal second theme. The second passage, occurring between measures 57 and 62, dissipates the light G-cadence of measure 56 and provides justification for the extended cadential passage in G that follows (meas. 63ff.).

While the basic key relationship of this ternary design appears to be simple enough—C-G-C for the three large sections—the extraordinary deviousness of the G-major portion approaches the nontonal (without key) writing of later composers.

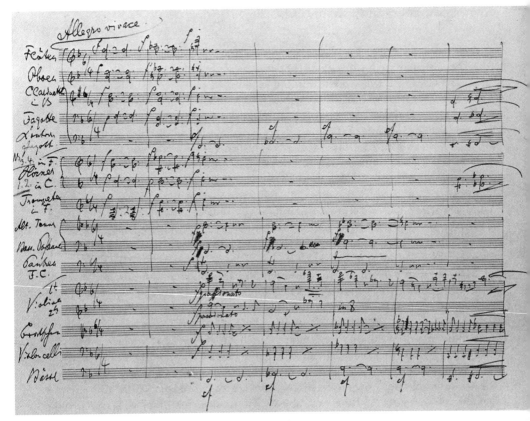

A manuscript page from Brahms' Third Symphony.

THIRD MOVEMENT: *Poco Allegretto*

This piece in C minor has the most exotic harmonic coloring of any movement of the four symphonies, yet its setting is essentially very simple. Like the Andante, it shows a sizable ternary design; the additional length derives from two interpolated sections of development, which digress significantly from the essential key plan. This is the basic plan of the *Poco Allegretto:*

Part I, in C minor
Theme 1 is stated (meas. 1–13), then restated (meas. 13–24) and extended; about measure 30, the key veers away from C, initiating the first of the developmental episodes. Theme 1 returns for a third statement, at measures 40–52.

Part II, in A-flat major and B major
A very simple Theme 2 (meas. 54ff.), assigned to woodwinds with flute and clarinet on the "tune," soon dissipates into a second idea (meas. 70ff.) in B major; then Theme 2 is recalled (meas. 78ff.).

Part III, in C minor, with developmental episode

Theme 1 has an uncomplicated restatement (meas. 99–122); at this point, another modulatory episode occurs until Theme 1 and the key of C minor are restored at measure 139. The remaining measures are devoted to the closure.

This ternary design, as is readily apparent, has acquired much of the compositional sophistication more generally associated with the sonata-type designs.

FOURTH MOVEMENT: Allegro, in F minor/major

As has been remarked, this movement has a sonata-allegro design with virtually no Midsection, but with a sizable developmental episode intervening between Theme 1 and Theme II in Recapitulation.

Area I of the design embraces two contrasting portions: Theme 1a at the outset and Theme 1b beginning at measure 20. Theme 1b is related to Theme 2 of the second movement (Ex. 5-9), most conspicuously through its rhythm:

etc. Theme 2, in C major (meas. 52ff.), is stated in horn reinforced by cellos and is characterized by its triplet rhythms. This robust theme is expanded, reaching a full orchestral tutti around measure 66; a closing motive beginning at measure 75 spins out into a massive codetta. The inception of a Midsection is suggested at measure 96, when Theme 1a is recalled in B minor; but this is truncated after only 2 measures, and an impulse toward Recapitulation in F minor begins to build at measure 102. The interpolated section of development, which starts around measure 130, includes an interesting and daring mutation of Theme 1b (meas. 149ff.). A fantasia-like coda begins in B-flat minor at measure 246 and climaxes in some brilliant contrapuntal writing.

Symphony No. 4 in E Minor, Op. 98

In his final symphony, Brahms departs strikingly from the style of the three preceding works. The harmonic language is at once simpler and subtler, invoking sounds and progressions from a quite distant past. The formal designs are less devious, and the serene, confident mood of this Fourth Symphony prefigures that of some of Brahms' wonderful chamber works written during the final four or five years of his life.

The intermovemental key plan has become progressively simpler with each symphony; the fourth is simplest of all: three movements in E, with the third (*Allegro giocoso*) in the submediant key of C major. The first and third movements are organized within orthodox key schemes. The second and fourth, however, derive added color when they employ progressions that characterized the Phrygian mode of earlier times.

FIRST MOVEMENT: Allegro non troppo

No basic motive is used in this movement, and Theme 1 begins nobly and openly in the first measure. The clear, "well-ventilated" scoring is an immediate indication of Brahms' new mastery of the orchestra. Theme 1 is stated twice, the second time, with mutations beginning at measure 19. An interesting point of both relationship and contrast between the two statements is found in the chromatic bass line that underlies the second segment of Theme 1: during measures 9 to 14, the line ascends from D♯ to A, whereas at a parallel point, measures 27 to 31, the line descends from D♯ to B. An important supplement is the transitional motive beginning at measure 45, which leads directly to Area II, in the key of B minor, then B major.

Theme 2a, beginning in cellos at measure 57, is preceded and followed by another supplementary material (perhaps suitably designated "framing motive") that proves to be the most individual and pervasive element of the entire first movement (Ex. 5-13).

EXAMPLE 5-13   Brahms, Symphony No. 4/I, meas. 53–63,
                                      "framing motive" and Theme 2a

At measure 95, Theme 2b, in the key of B major, appears; the melodic part, assigned to flute, clarinet, and horn, is doubled in three octaves for the statement. The framing motive, enlarged and developed, has a major role in the closing episode of the Exposition section (meas. 110–37), which concludes without the customary double bar, but with a firm cadence in B major, the second key level. A short (7-measure) bridge leads to the Midsection (meas. 145), which starts with a recall of Theme 1 at the original level of E minor.

This section of development is kept lively by frequent use of two incisive rhythms: ₵ ♩· ♫ ♫ from the framing motive, and the pervasive triplets of Theme 2b. The section of Retransition leading to Recapitulation is one of Brahms' finest, for it is based on extremely free, sequential dispersion of the continuous figure ♩ ♫♫, which is derived from Theme 1. The dominant of the approaching key, E minor, is withheld until the moment of juncture with Recapitulation (meas. 245–46).

The remainder of this sonata-allegro design is unwontedly orthodox, with all principal materials presented at the prescribed tonic level.

SECOND MOVEMENT: *Andante moderato*

The opening motto of this movement has been shown and discussed (Ex. 5-5). The motto itself centers on the pitch E but is not tonal in the usual sense; the E major triad is heard only when the clarinets enter in the second half of measure 4, setting the key of E for Theme 1, which follows immediately. Theme 1 takes its rhythmic shape from the opening motto and, as has been remarked, derives exotic color from use of the mixed mode on E. By contrast, Theme 2 (Ex. 5-14) is lush, lovely, romantic, and unabashedly in the key of B major.

EXAMPLE 5-14   Brahms, Symphony No. 4/II, meas. 41–44, Theme 2

After a Recapitulation with a sizable episode of development, recall of Theme 1 at the subdominant level of A major (meas. 103ff.) initiates a coda that lays great stress on the more passive harmonies of IV and VI. The final cadence is from VI to I, a variant of the plagal cadence.

THIRD MOVEMENT: *Allegro giocoso*

This robust C major movement is the only one of true scherzo-like quality among all the inner movements of Brahms' symphonies. Although the movement actually uses one of the composer's favorite variants of the sonata-allegro design (see above), the superficial effect is that of a rondo form, through the frequent reprise of Theme 1. This initial idea is designed to bear repetition without undue monotony because it has two melodic components—the highest and lowest parts as first stated (Ex. 5-15), which can be inverted in position with good effect.

EXAMPLE 5-15   Brahms, Symphony No. 4/III, Theme 1

Brahms uses such a change of position with the reprise of Theme 1 at measure 35; at some other points of recall, the upper element appears without its associate part.

The principal developmental interlude, which evolves out of the recall of Theme 1 at measure 89, is set into motion with a section of louvered texture in which the various choirs of the orchestra engage in bold antiphonal play. Conspicuously longer note values provide agogic stress. A brilliant coda is prepared by a 27-measure dominant pedal point (meas. 282ff.), kept active by the anapestic rhythm ♪♪♩ in timpani.

FOURTH MOVEMENT: *Allegro energico e passionato*

This splendid set of orchestral variations is written in the general style of a *passacaglia* (or perhaps *chaconne*); it is Brahms' tour de force of orchestral technique. The theme, a chorale-like phrase of eight measures, is stated at the beginning in woodwinds and brasses (Ex. 5-16). While the key is fundamentally E minor/major, the Phrygian mode is suggested in the strong A minor flavor and through the F♮ of the bass in the final cadence, which imitates the lowered second degree of the Phrygian mode. In this initial statement of the theme, Brahms has been adroit in providing built-in linkage, for the theme opens on the A minor triad and closes on the E major one, which progresses to the start of the first variation with a sense of V moving to I.

EXAMPLE 5-16   Brahms, Symphony No. 4/IV, passacaglia theme

Viewed as a whole, this Finale comprises thirty masterly variations, each maintaining close contact with the passacaglia theme, plus a massive coda (meas. 253–311). Two concepts of design seem to transcend the mere idea of successive variations and give the Finale dynamic shape. Within the first concept, the theme in its essential long-note guise appears three times, each time with progressively fuller instrumentation and more complicated harmony:

Meas.   1–8   Brass, woodwinds, timpani. E minor is the key, with Phrygian inflections.

129–36   Same instrumentation at the beginning, but with strings added from fourth measure. The harmony leans toward B minor through the cadence chord F♯-A♯-C♯-E.

253–72   Full orchestral tutti. Harmony is drastically altered, suggesting G minor through the V–VI progression (meas. 254–55). A sequential extension (meas. 261–72) begins at the first modulation, and the key of E minor is not restored until measure 281, but then is maintained to the close (meas. 311).

As seen above, the segment introduced by each statement of the passacaglia theme is progressively shorter: 128 measures, 124 measures, 59 measures, respectively, which might suggest increasing tension toward the end. This illusion is heightened between measures 297 and 300 when the entire passacaglia theme is compressed into 5 measures; from measure 300 to the close, the E minor harmony is simply maintained, with a final V–I progression as a closing gesture.

In an alternative design concept, the Finale shows an unbalanced ternary design with coda, as follows:

Meas.   1–96   Part I   Includes the first thematic statement plus eleven variations.

97–128   Part II   Provides signal contrast throughout variations 12, 13, 14, and 15, which are included in this part. The changed meter (3/2 as opposed to 3/4) gives twice as long a measure and a sense of slowing down. The major mode from variation 13 on gives brightness.

129–252   Part III   Restores E minor and the 3/4 measure. Variations 16 through 30 are included, maximum tension occurring during the 21st and after the 24th.

253–311   Coda   Provides significant tonal deviation before the final confirmation of E minor.

After the Fourth Symphony, Brahms' only orchestral work was the Double Concerto for Violin, Violoncello, and Orchestra, Op. 102. He turned to chamber works and *Lieder* during the remaining ten years of his life.

6

The End of a Tradition:
Bruckner and Mahler

The Symphonies of Bruckner

In a strictly chronological sense, Bruckner's earlier symphonies antedated those of Brahms, so that to discuss them afterward appears to be an anachronism. But Anton Bruckner (1824–1896) never fully joined the mainstream of Austro-German music in his own lifetime, and the years since his death have scarcely clarified his rightful position. At the present time and for many people, Bruckner remains an earnest, sometimes tedious organist-composer, who succeeded in writing the same number of symphonies as Beethoven. Yet few composers of any generation have been more loftily motivated or have attracted as loyal a cult of admirers; this is small at present, but it includes some very discerning and articulate people.

One problem in comprehending and judging Bruckner's symphonies is that, in many instances, it is not certain which version the composer himself preferred. Bruckner was forever revising his symphonies, and in several cases conductors or zealous editors made still other alterations. In 1932 a collected edition of Bruckner's music was undertaken at the instigation of the Austrian National Library at Vienna (which inherited manuscripts, mostly originals, from the composer) and the International Bruckner Society, founded in 1929. All the symphonies, including the unfinished sketch for the Finale of the Ninth, are now available in this collected edition; but there is still controversy as to whether these or the variant versions published many years earlier represent Bruckner's ultimate intent.

Bruno Walter remarked, sagely if caustically, that Bruckner's "unshakable faith in God and Richard Wagner enabled him to carry out his unwieldy artistic plans despite opposition, intrigue and ridicule."[1] Each of Bruckner's deities seems to have impelled certain aspects of his symphonies: the Almighty probably inspired the spacious hymnlike Adagios and the evocative blasts from the brasses; but Wagner, the deity of Bayreuth, certainly furnished the model for the sensuous chromatic harmony and the melodramatic changes of mood. Bruckner shared his second deity with most composers of the later nineteenth century, but on few did Wagner have so immediate an effect. One of the oddities of the late Romantic symphony is that Wagner, who himself almost totally eschewed the form, left an indelible mark on the symphonies of most of his contemporaries.

Bruckner wrote his nine symphonies between 1867 and 1896. His other major works comprise mostly Masses and the ever popular *Te Deum*. Despite their lack of a text, the symphonies closely resemble these liturgical compositions and even quote passages from them. Probably because Bruckner was an organist—a superb one according to all reports—he realized the orchestra as a composite instrument. Louvered texture and the sense of light and shade that are so vital in works of the best orchestrators are conspicuously rare; Bruckner's crescendos and sudden *forte* passages sound as though he had opened the swell box, or suddenly pulled the *plein jeu* stop.

The almost thirty-year span that separates the writing of Bruckner's First and Ninth symphonies was considerably longer than the interval between Beethoven's First and Ninth. Yet Bruckner's style did not change notably from symphony to symphony, nor even from the first to the last. This circumstance as much as any other marks him as not belonging to the truly elite; for the ability to evolve and grow is a capacity of all major artists.

Because his works from first to last share a number of highly personal traits, it is possible to describe the typical Bruckner symphony. With one exception, the symphonies open with a kind of paleolithic murmur, evoked by strings played tremolo or with rapidly repeated notes. (The exception is No. 6, which starts

with a long ostinato on the rhythm etc.). Out of this haze emerges, characteristically, a theme of triadic derivation in brasses, most often horns, which is extended and manipulated at some length. Eventually, another idea or group of ideas of more suave, lyric quality ensues. This, of course, brings the movement into general conformity with the Classical sonata-allegro design. But each section is likely to be interlaced with episodic materials, in some cases recollections of ideas used in earlier symphonies or in liturgical pieces. Certain rhythmic figures are obvious favorites with Bruckner: alternating duple and triple groups, such as or the reverse; and such "triumphant" brass figures

as etc. The clear dualism of key, which is the basis of most Classical designs from Haydn through Brahms, is often exchanged for a pervasive central key, interspersed with episodes at almost any level, or with vaguely nontonal passages cast in sequential chains that betray their keyboard origin.

[1] In *Gustav Mahler* (New York: Greystone Press, 1941), p. 162.

Bruckner's orchestra is formidable; the brass choir is augmented, in later symphonies, to Wagnerian size. Four horns, three trumpets, three trombones, and a bass tuba are normal requirements, and this imposing brass choir can provide episodes of real grandeur. In the last symphonies, the requirement of a full choir of tubas (after Wagner's model) poses obvious problems of performance for any but the largest orchestras.

Bruckner's slow movements are, on the whole, the finest parts of his symphonies. Melodic inventiveness was a valuable asset for him, and, in lyric surroundings, Bruckner was less tempted to indulge in the prolonged pedal points, sterile sequential episodes, and opaque scoring that often weaken his longer movements.

The young Bruckner was just commencing his activity as a serious composer as Wagner's star was rising, and the impressionable young man became one of Wagner's most ardent devotees. *Die Meistersinger* and *Tristan* were both produced during the 1860s, and Bruckner's First Symphony was finished in 1866. Although Wagner was no symphonist, Bruckner adapted many mannerisms of the Wagner orchestra to his own symphonies. The Fourth Symphony ("Romantic") is typical of all Bruckner's symphonic writing and has examples of his (and Wagner's) mannerisms. The first version of this work was completed in 1874, but the Scherzo and Finale were revised later and the work was given a first performance at Vienna under Richter on February 20, 1881. Brief comment on each of the four movements follows.

FIRST MOVEMENT: *Bewegt, nicht zu schnell* (moving, not too fast)

A horn sounds the first motive of the first theme over string tremolo. Woodwinds are added gradually, then the full brass choir enters for a splendid tutti. The scoring of these opening measures constitutes a typical Bruckner sound. A second idea commences in strings and gradually picks up instrumentation. The many tutti. portions are majestic in sound with gleaming brasses, as were, of course, similar passages in Wagner's operas.

SECOND MOVEMENT: *Andante quasi Allegretto*

Bruckner is often at his best in slow movements, as has been remarked. A theme in cellos with accompaniment in muted upper strings opens the movement. The scoring is refreshingly thin as the piece progresses, with the solo melodic lines passed among various instruments, until the inevitable Bruckner tutti is imposed after the 200th measure. The close features timpani.

THIRD MOVEMENT: *Scherzo—Bewegt*

The Scherzo opens with a hunting motive in horns over the inevitable string tremolo. The material of this opening is the source of the entire first statement of the Scherzo. A new idea marked "etwas langsamer" (somewhat slower) intervenes, then the hunting theme returns, scored fully up to its close. The Trio section offers the strings the first opportunity for prominence with a curious combination of bowed and pizzicato notes in all parts. The *da capo* is literal.

FOURTH MOVEMENT: *Bewegt, doch night zu schnell*

The frequent passages of full orchestral sound are truly formidable. The rhythmic contours of many parts, especially those with alternating two and three rhythmic groups, remind one of the first and third movements. The closely juxtaposed succession of contrasting materials provides stimulating surprise throughout.

The Seventh Symphony seems to be the best liked in the United States, not surprisingly since it is one of Bruckner's strongest works. The first movement, in E major, exhibits virtually every characteristic described in the foregoing paragraphs, but the tonic-dominant dualism (E-B) between the two areas of the Exposition is clearer than usual. The interval of a fourth, either ascending or falling, initiates many ideas, for example: Theme 1 (meas. 3ff.); the bridge passage (meas. 67ff.); the climax of Area I (meas. 141ff.); Theme 2 (meas. 165ff., clarinet); and so on. The same interval initiates the opening theme of the Adagio and thus serves to link the first two movements. The first movement closes over a 53-measure tonic pedal point, Bruckner's habitual safe haven.

The second movement of the Seventh Symphony, marked Adagio but also *Sehr feierlich und langsam* (Very solemn and slow), begins with a typical chorale-like phrase scored for five tubas—two tenor, two bass, and a contrabass. The next phrase is scored for strings, and a dialogue between these two choirs offers an example of Bruckner's less opaque scoring. The key is C-sharp minor, and the movement's elegiac mood is traditionally associated with Bruckner's premonition of the death of his idol, Richard Wagner, which did, indeed, take place soon after the writing of this Adagio (February 13, 1883). A less melancholy strain, mostly in F-sharp minor, intervenes at measure 37 and is followed by a reprise of the opening chorale, extended and developed through 56 measures. Both strains return still again, with much elaboration, and a tranquil coda in C-sharp major concludes the movement. The manner of alternating these contrasting materials has caused the movement to be compared to the Adagio of Beethoven's Ninth Symphony.

Wagner's impending end probably inspired the quotation of the melody of "Non confundar in aeternum" from the closing of Bruckner's own *Te Deum* (meas. 118ff.). The entire closing line of the *Te Deum* is "In te Domine speravi, non confundar in aeternum" ("In thou Lord have I trusted, let me never be confounded"); Bruckner, a very devout man, must have spoken for himself as well as for Wagner. Such covert symbolism was a commonplace of late medieval art, when hidden meanings abounded; and the Cecilian Movement (a nineteenth-century Catholic renewal) may have suggested this comparable gesture.

The third movement—Scherzo—is unusually close-knit, since three elemental rhythmic figures generate most of the material, even in the Trio. A 4-measure, widely spaced motive in the opening is scored for the low register of the F trumpet, which imparts a kind of macabre quality, especially when the motive occurs later in the midst of a full orchestral tutti.

The Finale, marked *Bewegt, doch nicht schnell* (Activated, but not quick), is in a classic Bruckner pattern: it is serious, quite long, and utilizes material from previous portions, in this case mostly the Adagio. The movement is kept colorful through several bold juxtapositions of unrelated key levels. Some of these are: measures 198–99 (A-flat or E-flat to A minor); measures 208–09 (F-sharp minor to D minor); and measures 50–51 (A-flat minor to C minor). For stabilization, the closing section is taken over a 24-measure tonic (E) pedal point.

The Symphonies of Mahler

Mahler's name is generally linked with Bruckner's in one of those convenient pairings that seem to abound in the annals of Western music. This link has little to support it, except that both men were often in Vienna, wrote uncommonly long symphonies, and were admirers of Richard Wagner. Gustav Mahler (1860–1911) was an intensely practical musician, for he spent his entire life as a conductor. His ten-year (1897–1907) tenure as artistic director at the Vienna Court Opera (now the Austrian State Opera) is still remembered as a legendary era for that great house, a time when incomparable performances of works by Wagner, to be sure, but also by Mozart and Beethoven, were given. During that same period, he often conducted the Vienna Philharmonic, not always without controversy since he was known to "touch up" the orchestration of Beethoven's Ninth Symphony and even gave a performance of Beethoven's F Minor String Quartet, Op. 95, with full string orchestra.

Mahler was volatile, pragmatic, bold—and ruthless in his attitude toward people he considered stupid. In most respects, he was the exact opposite of the reticent, scrupulous, irresolute Bruckner. The attitudes of the two men toward Richard Wagner epitomize their differences of temperament. Bruckner worshiped from afar and reflected some of Wagner's more obvious qualities in his own music; Mahler's regard for Wagner inspired him to give Wagner's music the most vigorous, meticulous, lavish performance possible. In the end, Wagner's effect on Mahler's own music was of a more practical, salutary kind than on Bruckner's.

In the United States especially, Mahler's music was somewhat neglected for half a century after his death, often disparaged in the general rejection of the whole post-Romantic German tradition. This was occasioned partly by the interest in new systems and cacophony espoused by the generation between the two World Wars. The present Mahler "renaissance" was instigated by Leonard Bernstein when he played, recorded, and championed all Mahler's symphonies.

Compared to his later symphonies, Mahler's First could be described as terse, even modest. But compared to much of the music of his time, even the imposing symphonies of Brahms, it emerges as of heroic proportions. Writing the First Symphony occupied Mahler at intervals between 1885 and 1888. (The fifty-two-year-old Brahms was just finishing his Fourth and last symphony as Mahler undertook his First.)

Mahler's First Symphony had its première at Budapest in 1889, titled then as a symphonic poem in two parts. Five years later, played at Weimar, the same composition was programmed as a symphony subtitled "Titan," probably after Paul

Richter's romantic novel of the same name. In subsequent publication of the work, there were no programmatic titles affixed to subsections of the piece; but the labels associated with them by several of Mahler's biographers indicate that the symphony may have certain autobiographical connotations.

The first part, often entitled "From the Days of Youth," opens slowly with an extended prelude in which the strings sound a multiple note *A*, while the woodwinds have a series of intervals of the fourth that soon generate a theme. The second and principal portion of the part borrows the melody of a lied, "As I Walked Abroad This Morn." The third and closing section becomes a turbulent Scherzo in A major with a Trio in the vividly contrasting key of F major.

The second large portion was originally called *Commedia umana* (human comedy), its two subsections "The Hunter's Funeral Procession" and "Dall' Inferno al Paradiso." The first section combines the old French canon "Frère Jacques" with a gypsy-like melody in the wind choir. Another borrowed Mahler lied, "My Darling's Blue Eyes," intervenes before a return of "Frère Jacques" and a quiet closure.

A cymbal crash followed by a stormy tutti signals the opening of the final section as new ideas appear, followed by recall of principal motives from previous sections. (This recall of earlier materials as a means of unity is a favorite device of many nineteenth-century composers.) A triumphant climax apparently signals the approach to "Paradiso."

Many of the tendencies that were later to dismantle the 200-year-old tonal system and leave serious music without its firm anchor may be observed already in Mahler's music. It should be recalled, though, that Arnold Schoenberg and Béla Bartók, who were to be instrumental in bringing some order and plausibleness into the resultant disarray, were composing their earliest pieces while Mahler wrote his symphonies. An important compositional premise had long been the cyclic concept of tonality—the notion that, in a multimovement work, the last movement would return to and corroborate the key of the beginning. Even Brahms, who made some extremely venturesome tonal excursions in one or another of his symphonic movements, clung fast to this idea of the tonal cycle. (However, C. P. E. Bach, writing as early as the 1750s, did experiment in his "Essay Sonatas"—often concluding a final movement in another key than the first). Mahler's Symphony No. 4, which is probably the most readily comprehensible and attractive of his nine, makes striking departures from the tradition of cyclic tonality. The openings of the four movements are related in prescribed fashion, but not necessarily their conclusions, as can be seen below.

Key Plan of Mahler's Symphony No. 4

Movement	Initial Key	Concluding Key
I	G	G
II	C minor/major	C
III	G	G (cadence on V)
IV	G	E

Mahler continued to experiment with such progressive key plans, and they evolve as quite revolutionary in the last three symphonies. As has been remarked, however, Mahler was a very practical musician, and he judiciously compensated for tonal disparity with other unifying factors. The Fourth Symphony, cited above, offers an excellent opportunity for viewing some of them.

In the first movement, a chirping, birdlike motive opens, given out by two flutes with sleighbells (Ex. 6-1); in subsequent portions, this unmistakable motive replaces a central key as a point of return, after the fashion of the ritornello in Baroque music.

EXAMPLE 6-1   Mahler, Symphony No. 4/1, opening motive

The principal points of return and key levels for this motive are as follows: measure 1—G (B minor); measure 72—G (B minor); measure 102—B minor; measure 155—E-flat minor; measure 298—G (E minor). Although the movement as a whole shows a large sonata-allegro design, this ritornello motive is the most audible organizing factor. It will be noted, also, that the first and last occurrences of the motive (meas. 1 and 298) have a mirror relationship to G, the principal key, but have dominant-tonic relationship to each other:

E	G	B minor
motive level	central	motive level
at meas. 298	key	at meas. 1

In this first movement, the first and second principal themes (meas. 4 and 38) are strongly tonal (G and D major). When either theme is recalled in subsequent portions of the design, it tends to create a "tonal island" in the midst of more chromatic texture.

Mahler's orchestration is magnificent, as could be expected from a composer who literally spent his life on the podium. In his rapport with the orchestra, Mahler is the only rival of Berlioz, of whom more will be said presently. Virtually any movement provides evidence of Mahler's skill, none more convincingly than the first movement of the Fourth Symphony. The orchestra is as large as Bruckner's; but in Mahler's case the woodwind and percussion choirs rather than the brass are augmented, so that the total timbre in a tutti is at once lighter and brighter. Required are four flutes, three oboes, three clarinets, and three bassoons; the kettledrums are supplemented in the percussion by a varied batterie. Any score page, opened at random, will demonstrate Mahler's active, louvered texture, for instruments or choirs are in and out, constantly on the move, with the result that the mass of sound never congeals. The full tutti is the more effective because it is used so sparingly. The dispersion of instruments in the

Caricature of Gustav Mahler

tutti is often made in the French fashion, with each choir maintaining auton-
omy—as opposed to the mixed scoring (typically with a woodwind instrument
and a string choir doubled on the same part) favored by the Germans. Because
instruments are generally assigned to play the kind of part they do best, Mahler's
scores are a pleasure to perform, despite their rigorous requirements.

The second movement of the Fourth Symphony is one of Mahler's most
imaginative, not to say bizarre, pieces—a macabre serenade that the composer
himself is said to have dubbed "Freund Hein spielt auf" ("Death plays a tune").
"Freund Hein" is represented by a solo violin "mistuned" a whole tone too high
(such altered tuning is called *scordatura*), with the four open strings, from the
lowest, sounding A, E, B, F♯. This tuning exerts great tension on the strings and
causes the violin to produce a raucous, unpleasant sound reminiscent of the tone
of the medieval *Fidel*. Since the rest of the string choir plays with mutes, the
sound of the solo violin is especially distinctive and extrusive. The line assigned
to this mistuned violin is recurrent throughout the movement and is always an
elaboration or variant of its 4-measure initial phrase (Ex. 6-2).

EXAMPLE 6-2   Mahler, Symphony No. 4/II, meas. 6–10
                                        (shown at sounding pitch), part for
                                        solo violin in *scordatura*

This movement acquires even more exotic flavor through the continual repetition of other extremely simple materials, which is a characteristic of much non-Western music. The two most distinctive of these materials are the tune introduced by the horn at the very first measure, which acts as a kind of free ostinato in many portions, and the quiet, contrasting strain assigned to clarinets and bassoons beginning at measure 72. The string parts throughout are a veritable catalogue of special effects: parts played very high on the G string of the violin; intricately divided string sections, sometimes dwindling to one desk (cello at meas. 109) to achieve the dynamic *pppp;* pizzicato and *arco* in quick alternation; and use of the glissando, a slide between two tones that sounds all intervening notes in quick succession (violins, meas. 276–80 and elsewhere, and cellos in the final cadence).

The third movement is a free set of variations, and the fourth movement adds a woman's voice to the orchestral forces. The part assigned to the voice is "Das himmlische Leben" ("The Heavenly Life") from the folk song collection *Des Knaben Wunderhorn* (*The Youth's Magic Horn*), which furnished texts for Mahler's Third Symphony as well. The movement soon develops into one of the fantasies of recollection that nineteenth-century composers found so attractive. In this case, quotations from prior movements of this symphony are supplemented by at least one from Mahler's Third, to which it is related: at measure 36, the tune for "Sankt Peter im Himmel sieht zu!" ("St. Peter in Heaven Is Watching!") derives from measures 58 to 62 of the fifth movement of the earlier work, with the single substitution of F♯ for F♮. Seven measures before the end, the English horn with only harp accompaniment rounds out the entire composition by recalling the birdlike ritornello motive of the first movement, but with augmented values (half notes).

The next four symphonies after the Fourth are progressively more grandiose, both in orchestral forces and design. Each poses menacing problems of performance; and fortunate is the music lover who has heard even one fine, comprehensive performance of any of them. During his final ten years, Mahler composed for performance with the ideal conductor in mind—one with his own unique combination of musicianship and zeal. These have never been plentiful.

The Eighth Symphony, composed in eight weeks during the summer of 1906, typifies these transcendent last works. The orchestra is enormous; the percussion choir especially has grown to truly heroic size: three timpani, bass drum, cymbals, gong, triangle, and tubular chimes—along with celesta, piano, harmonium, organ, two harps, and mandolin as chordal instruments. The vocal complement includes eight soloists and two choirs, one subdivided.

The symphony is cast in two large parts, with the text of each indicating the epic nature of the work: the ancient hymn "Veni creator spiritus" ("Come Holy Spirit") for Part I and the closing scenes from Goethe's *Faust* for Part II. The first movement's spacious sonata-allegro design at once epitomizes and exceeds this most useful of forms. The many thematic components are almost as clear and succinct as in the early symphonies; but their realization in sections of development is often complex and contrapuntal. This is not surprising, because each major composer seems to have reverted to linear texture as his style matured. Many sections show the general influence of the concerted style; that is, voices are opposed to instruments, one instrumental choir to another, or a soloist counters a group texture of some kind.

Although the movement might seem discursive, it is unified by reason of the text. The first part of the symphony closes with a slight paraphrase of the closing verse of the Pentecost hymn: "Deo patri sit gloria . . . in saeculorum saecula, Amen" ("Glory Be to God the Father, World Without End, Amen") set to a glorious conclusion that positions trumpets and trombones above the orchestra. Part II, using the closing *Faust* scenes, includes portions that suggest the traditional Adagio, Scherzo, and Finale; but they share materials and are played without pause. Music had, with Mahler, come full cycle: the rise of Classical forms such as the sonata and da capo designs of the eighteenth century permitted instrumental music to emerge and thrive under purely musical precepts; with Mahler's Eighth Symphony (and allied works) the mainstream of musical style returned to reliance on a text for its validity.

During most of his life, Mahler was fascinated with the mystery of death, as shown by his many compositions inspired by it. When, in 1907, he received a disturbing report of his own physical condition, this fascination became an obsession which climaxed three years later with his last two completed works: *Das Lied von der Erde* (Song of the Earth) and the Ninth Symphony. Both were written between 1907 and 1910, and neither was performed before Mahler's untimely death. *Das Lied* bids the earth farewell in text, instruments, and solo voices, set to poetry from the Chinese. Quite justafiably, the composer considered this work a symphony, although he did not number it as such. His Ninth Symphony, written almost concurrently, continues the tragic mood of *Das Lied*, but uses only the orchestra. The inference is that, for Mahler, abstract music—without text or voices—was the consummate means of human expression.

The first movement of the Ninth Symphony, often called Mahler's "Farewell Symphony," commences with nebulous sounds from low in the orchestra and gradually rises to impassioned, ecstatically tragic melody, finally confirmed by the entry of the brasses. The entire first movement is a near-paraphrase of the Farewell motive at the start of Beethoven's Piano Sonata Op. 81a: the German word *Le-be-wohl* (farewell) is set to a simple motive of scale degrees 3-2-1. Mahler employs this motive in many contexts and many harmonic settings. It is both the amalgam and the inspiration of this movement, Mahler's farewell to earth and her delights.

The second movement, *Im Tempo eines gemachlichen Länders* (In an easy-going ländler tempo), is based on the rhythms and the related mood of the Austrian ländler, a somewhat rustic predecessor of the waltz. The movement starts gently with a simple tune in bassoon, progresses to a heavier tune in strong three time, but returns to more relaxed music for the close.

The third movement, Rondo-Burleska, speaks for itself, since it is a piece rude but jocose in mood. The orchestration is especially brilliant. The finale, *Adagio*, forsakes the recall of happy times as suggested by the middle two movements and returns to the mournful mood of the opening. The *Le-be-wohl* motive is even more pervasive than in the first movement, again in many and varied contexts. Perhaps the closing of *Das Lied von der Erde* best sums up the message of the entire symphony:

> Fate was not kind to me in this world. Whither do I go? — My heart is serene and awaits its final hour — Forever, forever —

Mahler's last completed symphony, No. 9, is less ebullient than the mighty Eighth. The mood is mostly contemplative, and the string parts are especially beautiful. The work, which uses only instrumental forces, is closer to the works of Brahms than any other of Mahler's symphonies.

A Tenth Symphony was planned by Mahler, but he died before progressing beyond the preliminary sketches of the full score. While attempts have been made to "complete" certain of the movements and bring them to performance, these experiments have had only limited success.

The mainline of the Austro-German symphony, which began with Haydn, ended with Mahler. Austro-German composers of the twentieth century are discussed in the last chapter of this book. At this point in the narrative of the symphony, we shall return to the late eighteenth century, to France of Revolutionary times.

PART TWO

Tributary Streams of Symphonic Development: 1780–1914

7

The Symphony in France

We have seen with what consistency and success six generations of Austro-German composers cultivated the symphony. In their hands, this musical type evolved from an undistinguished genre into one of the greatest art forms yet produced by Western composers. Without such coherent and logical expansion, the symphony could never have attained its splendid maturity; the bulk of our symphonic repertoire even today is drawn from the Austro-German legacy. But that mainstream of symphonic progress might have become stagnant and lusterless were it not for the vitality derived periodically from certain tributary currents, most notably those emanating from France at intervals during the nineteenth century.

France, especially Paris, was the musical Mecca of Europe for most of the eighteenth century. The foundations devoted to the public performance of music (Le Concert Spirituel and Le Concert des Amateurs especially) were the most lavish anywhere and enjoyed the patronage of the French court up to the time of the Revolution. French literature, theater, manners had become the models for the rest of Europe, and a musician could scarcely "arrive" without a French pilgrimage. Many foreign musicians made Paris their residence during the three or four decades before the Revolution and contributed significantly to Parisian musical life. Gluck, a Bavarian, was the most important; others were Piccinni, Cherubini, and Spontini, all of them active primarily in the field of opera. The presence of so many foreign artists gave the French capital an international atmosphere and, in the longer view, served to make France a friendly place for the projection of fresh musical ideas.

France had also its own native group of distinguished and gifted composers, active throughout the eighteenth century. Regrettably, their music is not well known in the United States, which has tended to cultivate German music almost to the exclusion of other portions of the repertory. One of those neglected composers is François-Joseph Gossec (1734–1829), a Belgian who resided in Paris after 1751. He was writing his first symphonies at about the same time (the 1750s) that Haydn began his experiments with the form. Fifty-four of Gossec's symphonies survive, some in manuscript copies; and they are of a quality to rival any but the final, consummate works of Haydn and Mozart. That these Gossec symphonies show many of the same traits as the experimental Austro-German works of the same period only emphasizes how Pan-European were musical style and taste during the second half of the eighteenth century.

Gossec had a number of gifted French contemporaries—André Grétry (1741–1813), Jean François Lesueur (1760–1837), and Étienne-Nicolas Méhul (1763–1817), among others. The collaborative activities of these native Frenchmen and their foreign colleagues created an extraordinarily rich milieu in the French capital, and we need only recall Haydn's and Mozart's connections with Parisian publishers and performing groups to comprehend the breadth of French influence during the 1770s and 1780s.

When, in 1789, the French Revolution struck, all the old musical life was swept away, along with most other things tainted by connection with the hated Bourbon regime. Several bleak years must have ensued as musicians watched all the institutions that had furnished their livelihood collapse. The new revolutionary leaders were not antimusical, however, and they soon found new occupations for Gossec, Lesueur, Cherubini, and others from the formidable array of composers and conductors who resided at Paris. Music, these leaders contended, could be a useful instrument of propaganda and might well serve Republican goals. Almost all the French-based composers proved to be surprisingly adaptable. They turned, apparently with a minimum of regret, to writing revolutionary hymns and conducting enormous citizens' choruses in the public parks.

The new regime gave its strongest evidence of concern for music by founding, in 1795, the Paris Conservatoire. Most of the illustrious musicians who had flourished before the Revolution came to be connected with this national conservatory of music; and the nature of French music during the next century was molded by the special circumstances of its establishment. One might expect that a school fostered by a revolutionary government would be especially open-minded to yeasty ideas and would prove fertile ground for developing the new democratic tenet that music is for all men, not for a privileged few. Alas, such lofty ideals are difficult to maintain, and the fiery revolutionist-musicians of the turn of the century had become staunch guardians of the status quo by the 1820s, when the Conservatoire's most famous student turned up in Paris.

Cartoon of Berlioz conducting, by Andreas Geiger, after a cartoon by Grandville, 1846.

The Symphonies of Berlioz

Hector Berlioz (1803–1869) was perhaps the most genuinely radical musician of a century that produced such spectacular revolutionaries as Liszt and Wagner. He was a true child of the French Revolution, one who should have found sympathy and understanding from those old Republicans Lesueur and Cherubini, who were guiding the studies of neophyte composers at the Conservatoire. Unfortunately, this was not necessarily the case, as Berlioz himself reveals in his *Memoirs;* his days at the Conservatoire prefigured the turmoil of his whole creative life. Berlioz, like so many of his musician-contemporaries, was almost as articulate with words as with notes. In his numerous essays and books, he has left a vivid, highly personal, and undeniably biased account of the circumstances surrounding the composition of most of his works.

Berlioz arrived in Paris in 1821 to study medicine. By his own account, he found medical studies disgusting and was soon spending more time at the Opéra and in the library of the Conservatoire than in the dissecting room. After several months, he abandoned medicine and spent the next few years in avid study of orchestral scores, which the Conservatoire library held in abundance. Berlioz was a great pioneer in the art of orchestration, and we shall learn much by reading his own account of how his mastery was acquired:

> By a careful comparison .of the means used with the effects produced, I perceived the subtle connection which subsists between musical expression and the special art of instrumentation; but no one ever pointed this out to me. It was by studying the methods of the three modern masters, Beethoven, Weber, and Spontini; by an impartial examination of the regular forms of instrumentation and of *unusual* forms and combinations; partly by listening to artists and getting them to make experiments for me on their instruments, and partly by instinct, that I acquired the knowledge I possess.[1]

Although Berlioz wrote his *Memoirs* in 1848, the passage of a quarter century had scarcely dulled his recollection of those precious hours spent in the Conservatoire library with the scores of the masters. In 1826 Berlioz was admitted to the composition class at the Conservatoire, and he even carried off the Prix de Rome; but in a very specific sense he was self-taught.

Berlioz composed incessantly between 1823 and 1829, writing for many mediums but turning out no works of moment. The catalyst for his first work of distinction, the *Symphonie fantastique,* was Goethe's *Faust,* which he read in a French translation about 1827. "I was fascinated by it instantly," he writes, "and always carried it about with me, reading it anywhere and everywhere—at dinner, in the theater, even in the streets." He set some of the versified fragments to music and published them at his own expense as *Huit Scènes de Faust.* This music was full of defects, as Berlioz himself admits, but some of the ideas turned up later in his *Le Damnation de Faust* and other works.

Few compositions have acquired an aura to compare with that surrounding the *Symphonie fantastique*—from the very moment of its completion. Berlioz assembled the work while he was still captivated by *Faust,* and it is probable that at least one portion—"Ronde du sabbat" ("Witches' Sabbath")—was derived from the "Walpurgis Night" episode of his *Faust Scènes.* Other portions came from the same source, or perhaps from other earlier pieces. The familiar program of the *Symphonie fantastique*—a series of dream episodes "from the life of an artist"—is traditionally linked with Berlioz's tempestuous affair with a second-rate Irish actress whom he eventually married. This program was apparently overlaid on music Berlioz selected from a mélange of earlier pieces; these episodes were rearranged for the composite work, and the five movements were linked by the new "Estelle" theme—the *ideé fixe* (recurrent motive) that occurs in each of the episodes. It is extraordinary that a composition consisting merely of a medley of previously written pieces loosely joined around a bizarre program should have so profoundly influenced the course of European music. Certain traits of the *Symphonie fantastique,* notably the use of an *ideé fixe* and the reliance on a program or narrative to supply continuity, appear again and again in works of composers of the three generations after Berlioz.

The composer himself prepared no less than four sets of program notes, but

---

[1] *Memoirs*, transl. Ernest Newman (New York, 1935), chapter 13.

he said that these were not essential for concert performances. When stripped of the programmatic trappings, each of the movements proves to be shaped as a free variant of a design used consistently by previous generations of composers. Even the idea of a recurrent theme is very old in Western music: the sixteenth-century cyclic Mass, the five movements of which often use the same material, is but one example. The *idée fixe* (Ex. 7-1) is very simple, as it must be if it is to be readily audible in various metamorphoses: the rising intervals of a perfect fourth, then a major sixth are the principal melodic traits.

EXAMPLE 7-1   Berlioz, *Symphonie fantastique*, meas. 72–79, *idée fixe*

Although Berlioz himself stated that the program was unessential to a concert performance, he did specify that the titles of the five movements should be kept intact, and several of the episodes are specifically descriptive. But it might be difficult to account for the joining of such disparate episodes as a ball, a march to the scaffold, and a witches' sabbath save in the dreams of the opium-drugged young artist whom Berlioz describes. A synopsis of each of the five movements follows.

FIRST MOVEMENT:

Reveries. Passions—Largo/Allegro agitato e appassionato assai

This is a quite free sonata-allegro design prefaced by an introduction in slower tempo. The *idée fixe* appears in flute and Violin I eight bars after the start of the Allegro, occupying the place of the conventional Theme 1. It reappears in the dominant key of G toward the end of the Exposition (meas. 150ff.), in lieu of a real Theme 2. Although the Midsection seems, at several points, to be preparing a retransition, genuine repose with the *idée fixe* stated in the tonic key of C does not arrive until 35 measures before the terminal cadence. Here the *idée* turns quickly to the minor mode and is linked with a chromatic line in oboe; it ultimately terminates in a series of plagal cadences (*Religiosamente*).

SECOND MOVEMENT: *A Ball—Valse Allegro non troppo*

In this relaxed and attractive piece, which is in A major (the "submediant-made-major" to the preceding key of C), the *idée fixe* generates the principal contrasting material, in F major (meas. 120, flute and oboe).

THIRD MOVEMENT: *Scenes in the Country—Adagio*

In this movement, the reference to the *idée fixe* is largely indirect and is perceived in the intervals of the fourth and sixth, which are plentiful in most sections. This tranquil episode, in the "bucolic" meter of 6/8, is kept colorful by several bright key juxtapositions, most of them involving the relationship of a third.

FOURTH MOVEMENT: *March to the Scaffold—Allegretto non troppo*

This graphic piece of descriptive music, in G minor, might mean little without the program. Both the opening roll in two timpani tuned to a minor third (G-B♭) and the heavy march theme in cellos and basses are designed to produce an air of foreboding. The drugged young artist dreams he has murdered his beloved, and a final thought of her comes through a single statement of the *idée fixe* 15 bars short of the close; the blow of the axe falls five bars later!

FIFTH MOVEMENT: *Dream of a Witches' Sabbath—Larghetto/Allegro*

As might be expected, Berlioz lavished every facet of his orchestral wizardry on this mad rondo. A glance at any tutti passage will show French-type scoring at its best: choirs are rarely doubled and the brass is carefully louvered; in the strings, such special effects as pizzicato and tremolo are used often to vary the texture.

The *idée fixe* appears at the start of the Allegro: through its transformation, sharpened with pointed grace notes and trills, the beloved is subtly changed into a veritable shrew and partakes in the witches' revels. Toward the close, the strains of the *Dies Irae* ("Day of Wrath"), the Latin sequence in the Mass for the Dead, mix with the sounds of horrid revelry. As has been remarked, this episode has a direct reference to Goethe's *Faust*.

Berlioz himself tells about the fiasco of the projected first performance of *Symphonie fantastique* in 1830 and gives some very practical suggestions to aspiring impresarios as he recounts his troubles:

> He [Bloc] advised me to ask the directors to perform my symphony, and to help me to get up a concert for that purpose. They agreed, because the strange programme of the work struck their fancy, and seemed to them calculated to excite the curiosity of the public. As I wanted a really great performance, I invited eighty other musicians, which, added to Bloc's orchestra, gave us altogether one hundred and thirty performers. There was, of course, no accommodation for such numbers—neither seats nor even music-desks. With the calmness of people who have not realised the extent of a difficulty, the managers replied to all my demands by assuring me that all would be well, and that their machinist might be relied on. But on the day of rehearsal, when my hundred and thirty musicians were assembled, there was no room on the stage for them. The little orchestra below had barely space for the violins, and there was an uproar on the stage which would have maddened a much more equable temper than mine. There was a call for desks, and the carpenters hastily clutched anything which might serve the purpose: the machinist went about swearing and looking for his flies and wings; on one side there were cries for chairs, on another for instruments, on another for candles; the double basses wanted strings; there was no room for the drums, etc., etc. The porter was hopelessly bewildered. Bloc and I did the work of four, sixteen, thirty-two men, but all in vain; order could not be evolved from such chaos, and it turned

into a regular rout—a musical Passage of the Beresina [scene of one of Napoleon's defeats].

Still, in spite of the confusion, Bloc was determined to try two numbers, so as to give the directors "some idea of the symphony"; we went through the *Bal* and the *Marche au Supplice* ["March to the Scaffold"] as well as we could with such a disorganised orchestra, and the latter piece created a perfect *furore* amongst the players. Nevertheless the concert did not take place; the directors were scared by the upset, and withdrew from the enterprise. *They had not realised that a symphony necessitated such elaborate preparations.* And thus my plan fell to the ground for want of a few stools and desks. . . . Since then I have taken the utmost pains about the *matériel* of my concerts, having fully realised the disasters which may ensue from neglect of details.[2]

Later the same year, a performance of the *Symphonie fantastique* did take place; according to the composer, the second, fourth, and fifth movements created a sensation. Liszt was present at the concert and was deeply impressed by the *Symphonie*, as is amply attested by Liszt's later works.

The question of why a work of this sort should have exerted so lasting an effect on the course of nineteenth-century music is an intriguing one. But after Beethoven a certain ennui had definitely settled over the mainstream of European music; and a symphony attached to so lurid and bizarre a program, written by a young man of such delectable unconventionality, seems to have brought clandestine delight to many of the solid, bourgeois Parisians. Outside Paris, it was a shot of musical adrenalin for the tired concert scene; music has not been the same since Berlioz's bold coup.

The composer himself soon contrived to profit from his experiences with the *Symphonie fantastique*, in his *Harold en Italie*, Op. 16, completed and performed in 1834. *Harold* is a finely constructed symphony that retains much of the romantic enchantment of the *Fantastique*, but avoids its dangerous discursiveness.

During Berlioz's stay in Rome under the support of his *prix*, he traveled extensively, mostly on foot, through many of Italy's wonderful mountain regions. His *Harold* is the fruit at once of these excursions, of his acquaintance with Byron's *Childe Harold's Pilgrimage*, and of his meeting with Paganini. Among these, the encounter with Paganini was of the most immediate import, although the legendary violinist's role in inspiring Berlioz's symphony is unclear. The composer himself asserts that Paganini requested a piece that would permit him to use his fine Stradivari viola; but other people have asserted that Berlioz wrote the piece in the hope that Paganini would indeed play it. Whatever its inception, *Harold in Italy* is a symphony in four movements, scored for large orchestra with a solo viola representing Harold, a wanderer who dreams and reminisces on his experiences. The composition is quasi-autobiographical, as are many of Berlioz's works. The successor to the *idée fixe* of the *Symphonie fantastique* is the solo viola's opening subject (Ex. 7-2), which, in various contexts, literally wanders in and out of the four movements of the symphony.

[2] *Memoirs*, chapter 26.

EXAMPLE 7-2   Berlioz, *Harold in Italy*/I, meas. 38–45, "Harold" theme

The four movements of *Harold in Italy* are the following:

FIRST MOVEMENT: *Harold in the Mountains—Adagio/Allegro*

Despite its programmatic implications, this movement is patterned on the familiar first-movement plan of a slow introduction and a substantial fast movement in sonata-allegro design. The Adagio is vividly colored, principally from its profusion of sinuous chromatic tones and lines, especially in the strings. The overlying melodic parts sometimes prefigure the "Harold" theme and are triadic or diatonic. Once the solo viola has entered, its subject dominates the remainder of the Adagio: after the first solo statement of the "Harold" theme, and beginning at measure 73, the viola engages in a spirited dialogue with a valve cornet, a quite novel instrument in Berlioz's time. The scoring for the orchestra, in this Adagio and the remainder of the symphony, is magnificent, replete with the sensitive adjustments and special effects that Berlioz described so graphically in his own great treatise on instrumentation written in 1844.

The Allegro begins as a conventional sonata-allegro design, but the rather brief Exposition is distinguished by some unconventional key relationships, which sound far less bold to our jaded modern ears than they must have sounded to listeners of the 1830s. Area I and its Theme 1 are in G major; but Theme 2 begins abruptly in F major (Ex. 7-3) with no modulation at all. The juncture stresses the pointed cross-relation between F♯ in the dominant chord of G (meas. 165) and F♮ as the bass note of the next 4 measures. As it turns out, this F is V of B-flat major, and a second, sequential modulation brings the key back to G minor before Area II has progressed more than 6 bars.

The remainder of this sonata-allegro design is conventional enough, except that a considerable section of development is added after Theme 2 in Recapitulation (meas. 330–460). This could have been Brahms' model for parallel episodes.

SECOND MOVEMENT: *March of the Pilgrims—Allegretto*

The movement occupies a five-part rondo design (ABA'CA"). The opening material (A) is a simple, cortege-like theme in E major that is generally played by the string choir. The first contrasting section (B) is Harold's theme, in solo viola as usual, but in the key of B major. The cortege theme returns in E major,

EXAMPLE 7-3   Berlioz, *Harold in Italy*/I, meas. 165–72,
                                juncture of Theme 1 and Theme 2

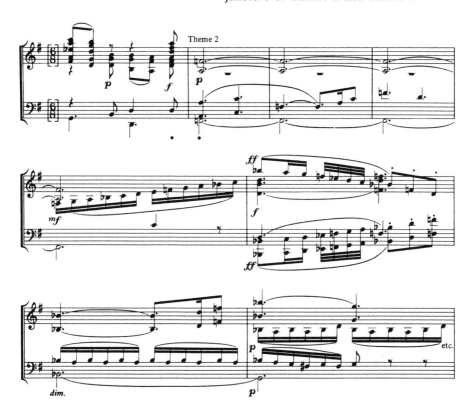

followed by a new contrasting element in C major called *Canto religioso*. The
melodic part of this is negligible, but the solo viola accompanies it with brilliant
arpeggiated chords written to lie easily across the four strings. A brief recall of
the cortege theme closes the movement.

THIRD MOVEMENT:
Serenade, of an Abbruzi mountaineer to his mistress—Allegro assai

This engaging movement—in C major and 6/8 time—has a three-part design
that interpolates a recall of Harold's theme in G major between two episodes
devoted to exploration of the Serenade theme in C major, assigned first to an
English horn (alto oboe). The coda makes use of an interesting metric combination
(Ex. 7-4): the solo viola plays the Serenade theme in the prevalent 6/8 time,
but has an underlying accompaniment in the orchestral violas that is really in
12/8 (6/8 + 6/8), a device called "duple diminution." Simply stated this means
twice as fast, or two measures moving in the time of one.

EXAMPLE 7-4   Berlioz, *Harold in Italy*/III, meas. 166ff.,
                                               cross-rhythms in coda

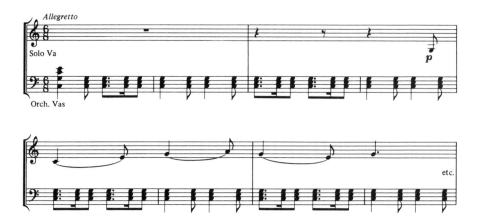

FOURTH MOVEMENT: *Orgy of the Brigands—Allegro frenetico*

The movement probably takes its cue from the Finale of Beethoven's Ninth
Symphony, and it is an early prototype for the fantasia-of-recollections finale
that nineteenth century composers found so useful. The Brigands' motive, which
is stated during the first 11 measures, is the recurrent material in this rondo-
fantasia; alternating with this "malevolent" theme are portions drawn from other
movements including, of course, Harold's own theme.

In 1839, Berlioz finished and brought to performance under his own baton
another major work that he designated a *symphonie dramatique*. This was his
Roméo et Juliette, which calls for major choral forces (chorus, soloists, and a
narrator-singer for the recitatives) as well as a very large orchestra. Berlioz gives
his own concept of this composition in his preface to it. "Even though the voice
is often used," he says, "it is not a concert opera, nor a cantata, but a symphony
with chorus." And he goes on, "If singing occurs near the beginning, it is in
order to prepare the mood of the listener for the dramatic portions in which
the feelings and passions must be expressed by the orchestra."

We are reminded of Berlioz's quickening interest in instrumentation through
the kaleidoscopic variety of special instruments he added to the basic large
orchestra for various movements. The *Prologue* uses a harp, which is employed
in the fashion of the harpsichord in eighteenth-century recitative. *Strophes*
(contralto solo) requires an English horn as well as the harp, while the "Queen
Mab" *Scherzetto* adds piccolo. In the ballroom fête (second movement), a bass
drum, cymbals, triangle, and snare drums augment the percussion—and so on
to the end.

Berlioz's gigantic *symphonie dramatique* underlines the plight of the symphonic composer of the nineteenth century. He was compelled, in effect, to
choose between writing "symphonies" so large, unwieldy, and filled with novelty

as to belie the basic concept of the form; and writing in a more traditional manner, which Beethoven seemed temporarily to have exhausted. Of those who chose the second alternative, only Brahms was completely successful.

After *Romeo and Juliet,* Berlioz's compositions for orchestra were concert overtures, along with a type of composition he called *scène,* a piece that combined voices with instruments but generally on a more modest scale than in *Romeo and Juliet.*

Aside from his compositions, the monumental *Treatise on Instrumentation* (1844) is Berlioz's most important contribution to the progress of music. This is available today in an English translation of the edition prepared in 1904 by Richard Strauss, who speaks somewhat deprecatingly of his own part in preparing the text:

> I thought at first that the masterwork of the great Frenchman did not need such help to be even today a source of enjoyment and stimulation for all musicians. It appeared to me complete in itself and full of ingenious visions, whose realization by Richard Wagner is obvious to every connoisseur.

Strauss then goes on to point out that the citations from Wagner's scores are "the alpha and the omega" of his own additions to Berlioz's treatise. This stresses the final irony of Berlioz's career: this most innovative of modern French musicians found recognition and appreciation mostly outside his native France. Not only Wagner, but Strauss himself and most twentieth-century composers, found inspiration and practical information in Berlioz's *magnum opus.* France was too obsessed with the lyric theater and its operas to pay much heed to purely orchestral music, or to serious musical studies, for that matter.

Later Nineteenth-Century French Symphonists

Several French composers who are best known for their opera scores did, however, write occasional symphonies. The first is Georges Bizet (1838–1875), whose *Carmen* may be the most popular of all French operas. In 1855, when he was only seventeen, Bizet wrote an enchanting Symphony in C Major, which could easily have come from the pen of the young Beethoven. It has almost every trait typical of the late Classical symphony, plus a certain lack of deviousness that is a special French quality. A world premiere of this forgotten symphony was conducted at Basel in 1935, and it is distinctly worthy of more frequent hearings. Bizet's charming little anachronism has somewhat the same relationship to the prevalent nineteenth-century mode as Prokofiev's better-known *Classical Symphony* has to early twentieth-century style.

Camille Saint-Saëns (1835–1921) was a versatile, long-lived musician. His influence as a teacher may have been more important than his activities as a composer, for he defended the French musical tradition when it was in danger of engulfment by the pervasive Wagnerian currents of the late nineteenth century. Saint-Saëns and his gifted pupil Gabriel Fauré (1845–1924), created the uniquely Gallic atmosphere that nourished Claude Debussy (1862–1918), the only Frenchman to rival Berlioz in the originality of his accomplishment.

Samson et Dalila (1877) is Saint-Saëns' contribution to France's lyric theater; but before and after that dramatic work, he wrote symphonies—three of them during his maturity. Only the third of these is known today and needs comment. Saint-Saëns' Symphony No. 3, in C minor (1886), uses organ and two pianos to supplement the conventional orchestral forces. The organ enters mostly at climactic points and serves not only to augment the sound, but also to fuse the various instrumental timbres. The wisdom of this is questionable, for the best French taste in orchestral sound has preferred that the various choirs (woodwinds, brass, strings) preserve their separate identities and not blend in the German fashion. The piano is employed primarily for its percussive effect.

In his Third Symphony, Saint-Saëns joined other nineteenth-century symphonists in experimenting with form. The work shows only two large movements, but this is an optical illusion; for the frequent changes of tempo provide audible partitioning, and certain portions resemble the Scherzo and the Adagio movements of the conventional four-movement symphony. Moreover, the two large movements themselves tend to merge because the close of the first (*Poco adagio*) is nebulous as to key and fails to cadence affirmatively. At best, this symphony is a pleasant novelty.

César Franck (1822–1890) was a Belgian who spent his active musical life in Paris—most of it playing the organ, in the end at the great church of Sainte Clotilde. Franck arrived at the Paris Conservatoire in 1835 in time to study with Reicha during the final year of that venerable teacher's life; thus Franck shared a brief part of his training with Berlioz, who had studied with Reicha five or six years earlier. Reicha's conservative inclinations were less galling to Franck than to Berlioz, for Franck was a "follower" all his life and was one of Wagner's more admiring French disciples.

Franck wrote his Symphony in D minor between 1886 and 1888—which makes it contemporaneous with Brahms' last two symphonies and Saint-Saëns' third. This is Franck's only symphony, although he wrote several orchestral tone poems and compositions using a solo instrument. The Symphony in D minor has maintained a certain popularity through the years and still turns up rather frequently on orchestral programs; hence it merits a brief discussion.

This is, first of all, a symphony of only three movements; but the second fuses the styles of a scherzo and a slow movement, and each of the movements is unusually long. Unfortunately, this perhaps excessive length is generated for the most part by tiresome repetition and interminable sequential procedures. Composers with strong keyboard orientation, particularly organists, seem prone to this kind of writing because in improvisation the temptation is strong to repeat a certain pattern over and over, using it to wander discursively from key to key. The clarity and trenchancy of Franck's harmonic texture are diminished by yet other mannerisms: excessive use of the diminished-seventh chord, along with such "poignant" melodic intervals as the semitone, the diminished fourth, and the diminished third; and fondness for the appoggiatura. The opening measures of the symphony will serve to illustrate all of these (Ex. 7-5).

EXAMPLE 7-5   Franck, Symphony in D minor/I, opening

Franck makes some interesting and successful mutations in the sonata-allegro design. In the first movement, the head-motive of the primary *Lento* (Ex. 7-5, meas. 1) is also the motive for Theme 1 in the *Allegro non troppo* (meas. 29). It may have been suggested by the germ motive of Liszt's *Les Préludes*, which in turn probably derived from Beethoven's "Muss es sein" motive (F major String Quartet, Op. 135, Finale). The key of D minor is maintained through both these portions, and the *Lento/Allegro non troppo* combines as an Area I with two tempos, rather than as an Introduction followed by a movement proper. Both the *Lento* and *Allegro non troppo* portions are duplicated immediately, a third higher, in the key of F minor and with considerable expansion (meas. 49–98). A more lyric Theme 2, in F major, enters at measure 99. But the most powerful idea of the movement comes in the closing theme, toward the conclusion of the Exposition section (Ex. 7-6). This proves to be Franck's cyclic material, since it is used in each of the subsequent movements.

The opening subject of the second movement, *Allegretto*, in B-flat minor, features the English horn. This alto oboe, poignant in tone, came into conspicuous popularity through the forlorn shepherd of Wagner's *Tristan und Isolde* (although Wagner took his cue from Berlioz). It seems especially suited to the cheerless

EXAMPLE 7-6   Franck, Symphony in D minor/I, meas. 129–136,
                              closing theme (also cyclic theme)

mood of much post-Wagnerian music. A contrasting subject derived from the
cyclic theme is followed by a recall of the English horn theme, then still another
contrasting theme in E-flat major (meas. 135). Several briefer recalls of each of
these themes give the movement the general contour of a rondo form.

The Finale (*Allegro non troppo*) begins as a sonata-allegro design, with two
vigorous, contrasting subjects: Theme 1 in D major and Theme 2 (meas. 72) in
B major, which is introduced as a chorale by the brass choir. From this point,
the movement dissolves into a fantasia that recalls most of the symphony's
principal materials, including, needless to say, the cyclic theme.

Vincent d'Indy (1851–1931) might well have been placed among the nationalist
composers of the next chapter, or even with the symphonists of the post–World
War I era, since he lived well into that period. But his only symphony to survive
was written early—in 1886—which suggests its consideration here, after Saint-
Saëns and Franck.

At the close of the Franco-Prussian war in 1871, a group of French musicians,
who feared that the Germans might conquer their country in music as they had
in battle, formed the Société Nationale de Musique. Nationalistic musical activities had been pursued vigorously in other countries since the middle of the
century, and these Frenchmen were following a trend as well as behaving in
a patriotic manner. Vincent d'Indy, who was only twenty at the time, was an
eager participant in the activities of the Société.

D'Indy's best-known work is his *Symphonie sur un chant montagnard français*
(*Symphony on a French Mountain Air*, 1886), which uses a simple tune in the
spirit of a French folk song as cyclic material. This air is given out first in the
opening *Assez lent* by an English horn—a reminder that d'Indy was an admirer
of Franck and that his symphony was written during the same period as Franck's
D minor. The similarity does not go much beyond the conspicuous use of the
English horn, however, and d'Indy's "Mountain" Symphony is a very French
piece, closer in style to Debussy than to Franck.

A solo piano is used in all three of the movements, not as an orchestral
supplement, but in genuinely virtuosic fashion. The brilliant scoring suggests that
d'Indy must have studied Berlioz, for the woodwinds are dispersed in the sensitive, imaginative fashion found in true French pieces, especially those of Debussy
and Ravel, as well as Berlioz.

A trait that takes d'Indy's symphony out of the class of routine works of its period is its metric freedom. In any of the movements, we may discover quick alternation among duple, triple, and quadruple time; and, in several cases, a simple meter in one part is used simultaneously with a compound meter in another, such as 3/4 with 9/8. In the Finale, at *Plus modéré*, the metric signature $\frac{2-3}{4}$ allows some very flexible combinations indeed.

D'Indy outlived not only his contemporaries, but most of his gifted younger compatriots. He saw the French defeat of 1871 reversed in World War I, and he celebrated this with a *Sinfonia brevis* (*de bello gallico*) of 1918. By this time, though, new musical winds were blowing, and this little symphony is forgotten, along with most of d'Indy's other compositions.

We have considered in this chapter the developments in France that nourished and enlivened the Austro-German mainstream of symphonic development. In the next chapter, we shall see how other countries also had a share in the late–nineteenth-century metamorphosis in symphonic music.

8

The Symphonies of Tchaikovsky, Dvořák, Sibelius, and Ives

After the middle of the nineteenth century, composers in several regions bordering on Western Europe began to cultivate the symphony. Often these composers worked in situations where a militant nationalist movement was apparent; but nationalism affected the symphony itself only in tangential ways, for this highly cultivated and organized product of Western musical culture did not respond easily to stimuli from such exotic materials as folk song. The major symphonic composers in these outlying regions were Tchaikovsky, Dvořák, and Sibelius, representing Russia, Czechoslovakia, and Finland. Charles Ives, working in the United States, seems to belong to this group.

The Symphonies of Tchaikovsky

Russia was a pioneer in organizing a nationalist cult. Russia had developed quite a rich musical life during the eighteenth century, but it was court-oriented and scarcely touched any except the great cities of that vast country. Russia had depended, furthermore, on foreign artists—German, Italian, and French—to make its musical life possible. As a result, Russia was thoroughly inculcated with German ideals for instrumental music and Italian and French taste in opera. During the 1830s all this began to change, as certain Russians became keenly aware of their country's rich heritage in folk materials; Glinka's opera *A Life for the Czar* (1836) is usually regarded as marking the beginning of the Russian nationalist movement. The most important purveyors of nationalist attitudes in music, the so-called Great Five, will be discussed among the composers of

154

symphonic poems in the next chapter; only Alexander Borodin (1833–1887) among them wrote compositions that may be designated unequivocally as symphonies. Borodin's Symphony No. 2, in B minor, is an attractive, unpretentious piece, Western in the general framework of its movements but mildly exotic in the flavor of some of its thematic materials.

A contemporary of the Great Five, Peter Ilyich Tchaikovsky (1840–1893), became a major symphonist, however. His compositions, which are essentially based on Western models, served to bring Russia into the mainstream of European musical developments. Tchaikovsky enjoyed considerable acclaim during the later years of his lifetime, and his travels to major musical centers, including New York, Philadelphia, and Baltimore, made his compositions as widely known as those of almost any composer of his day. Not only were Tchaikovsky's symphonies performed frequently in his own time, but they have proved to be surprisingly durable: as recently as the 1960s, Tchaikovsky's Sixth ("Pathétique") Symphony was rivaling Beethoven's Fifth in American polls seeking to identify the best-liked of all symphonies. Although the vagaries of popular taste are not necessarily subject to rational explanations, Tchaikovsky's wide appeal probably stems from his success in bridging the East-West musical gap: he established contact with Western symphonic models at the same time that he imbued his materials with a discreet, pleasantly mysterious exoticism, mixed with a liberal amount of romantic fervor.

Tchaikovsky evinced so much uncertainty about his proper style and manner of writing in his youthful works (before about 1870) that they may be dismissed as largely tentative. But it is significant that for an interval during those formative years Tchaikovsky was in close touch with members of the Great Five group, and he may have leaned at one time toward adoption of their nationalistic dogmas. Ultimately, however, Tchaikovsky went his own way, and his sounder works postdate his decision to work independently. Even so, in his late compositions, reminders of his interest in Russia's native music crop up and bring color to compositions that might otherwise remain bland and undistinctive.

Tchaikovsky's Symphony No. 4, in F minor (1877), is the first to show his more confident posture. The composer set down his own feelings about this work in a letter to Mme. Nadezhka von Meck, the dedicatee of the symphony, with whom he carried on a voluminous and long-term correspondence; but his remarks do little to clarify the music. Essentially, Tchaikovsky asserted that instrumental music is, by its very nature, impervious to analysis. By "analysis," Tchaikovsky apparently meant explanation in verbal terms. He went on, however, to impute subjective meaning to many of his materials, such as "Fate" to the opening motto (recurrent throughout the first movement), "vain striving for happiness" to the tortuous Theme 1 (meas. 27ff.), dreams of joy in a "beloved, radiant creature" to Theme 2 (meas. 116ff.). Such vague, programmatic associations are considered counterproductive at present, and this symphony is best heard as absolute music. The themes are attractive in a romantic fashion and easy to remember, a quality that has doubtless endeared Tchaikovsky to successive generations of concertgoers. The first movement maintains a minimal contact with the sonata-allegro design, although its real adhesive is the recurrent opening motto and, to a lesser extent, the pervasive 9/8 rhythms of Theme 1.

The second movement of the F minor Symphony, *Andantino in modo di canzona*, has an opening theme (Ex. 8-1) that illustrates how certain traits of Russia's folk songs were transferred to otherwise conventional musical materials. The most apparent of this theme's exotic characteristics are these: the frequent recurrence of a small melodic cell, here the first three eighth notes, which occur in transposed position in measure 3, in inversion in measure 4, and so on; the conspicuous use of noncontiguous melodic intervals, such as the fifth and fourth in measures 2 and 3; and a general repetitiousness, a characteristic found in most primitive music.

EXAMPLE 8-1   Tchaikovsky, Symphony No. 4/II, Theme 1

The special qualities of this opening theme are emphasized in subsequent portions of the movement, when they are juxtaposed to more conventional materials.

The Scherzo of Tchaikovsky's Fourth Symphony is one of the most individual of his orchestral movements, since the strings are played pizzicato throughout. The Trio section, *Meno mosso*, is assigned to the winds for a total contrast of timbre.

The Finale, *Allegro con fuoco*, is a brilliant, rousing movement that relies mostly on deft instrumentation to propel it. Fresh thematic ideas are minimal, limited mostly to variants of the folk-like motive introduced at measure 10: ♩ ♫♫♩ ♫♩ |♩ ♩ etc.

Tchaikovsky's Symphony No. 5, in E minor, written eleven years after the Fourth, displays many of the same traits as the earlier work and will not be discussed here. His Symphony No. 6 (the "Pathétique"), however, is this composer's tour de force, the composition on which his place in the history of the symphony relies. Because the "Pathétique" was written during the tragic last year of the composer's life (1893), it has taken on sentimental overtones, such as often attach to an artist's swan song; but the general tone of morbidness and despair is inescapable.

A first, quite general observation is that the "Pathétique" is the most personal and intense of Tchaikovsky's symphonies, but at the same time it is the most coherent and lucidly organized. For it, Tchaikovsky has chosen a conventional intermovemental key plan (B minor, D major, G major, and B minor for the four movements respectively); however, he has altered the traditional sequence of movements by using an *Adagio lamentoso* for the Finale. Each of the principal themes is affective and distinctive; in fact the second theme of the first movement and the permeating theme of the third are probably better known to lay concert-goers than almost any other symphonic subjects. A brief discussion of the four movements follows.

FIRST MOVEMENT: *Adagio/Allegro non troppo*

During the short prelude (Adagio), the bassoon prefigures Theme 1 of the Allegro that follows; this elemental bassoon line is projected over a chromatic line in double basses. At the outset of the *Allegro non troppo*, Theme 1, in B minor, is stated in strings, restated in winds, then expanded into a section that achieves a full tutti just before the bridge to Area II. Theme 2, in D major, derives in its first phrase from a pentatonic (five-tone) scale that omits the fourth and seventh scale degrees. Since much primitive music is similarly pentatonic, the second subject takes on a certain elemental, exotic flavor. The two principal themes are shown in Ex. 8-2.

EXAMPLE 8-2   Tchaikovsky, Symphony No. 6/I, Theme 1 and Theme 2

a) Theme 1, meas. 19–23

b) Theme 2, meas. 89–93

Apparently Tchaikovsky was well aware of the unusual appeal of Theme 2. A lengthy portion (meas. 90–160) in the Exposition section includes several restatements, fragmentation of the material, and embellishment with interesting counter-rhythms. In the Recapitulation, the approach to Theme 2 (in the tonic-major key of B) is stressed with a prolonged pedal point on F♯, the dominant note (meas. 267–304); this becomes even more suspenseful when the tempo slackens and broadens for the final 28 measures of the transition.

SECOND MOVEMENT: *Allegro con grazia*

The principal feature of this intermezzo-like piece, cast in a large ternary design with coda, is its meter: 5/4 throughout, always apportioned in 2 + 3 rhythmic groups. Since Russian folk song often uses alternating meters, especially in uneven groups such as five or seven, the inference is that Tchaikovsky was once more influenced by native materials.

THIRD MOVEMENT: *Allegro molto vivace*

This brilliant piece, which matches the first movement in total length, is a hybrid design that combines scurrying, scherzo-like material with a pervasive march, the rhythm of which eventually dominates the movement. The movement is essentially four-part, as follows:

Section 1 (meas. 1–70) is dominated by the passage-work in triplets that is the essence of the Scherzo. However, the rhythm of the opening segment of the March—♩♪ 𝄾 ♫ ♪ 𝄾 ♪ 𝄾 | ♫ ♩ ♩ ♪ 𝄾 𝄾 |—is prefigured at measure 10 and sporadically thereafter.

Section 2 (meas. 71–138) is dominated by the March, fully realized in a 10-measure passage in E major. The lengthy section, which involves a number of restatements of the March, is punctuated dramatically at three points (meas. 101, 105, 109) by conspicuously longer note values ("agogic" effects).

Section 3 (meas. 139–228) uses the Scherzo material at first, but is gradually invaded by fragments of the March. A transition bridge, devised of new scale passages, leads to the concluding portion.

Section 4 (meas. 229–347) uses only the March, avoiding all reference to the Scherzo.

FOURTH MOVEMENT: *Adagio lamentoso*

The principal subject of this brief movement is so doleful and hopeless in mood that to have prolonged the piece beyond its minimal three-part design would have been intolerable. The unique manner of introducing this principal theme serves to increase its intensity: first and second violins share the statement of what is simply a stepwise descending passage by playing only alternate notes and moving by turns in a wide interval that permits approach to each new thematic note by a leap from below. In Ex. 8-3, the melodic notes are marked with asterisks; in the second half of the example, the passage is shown in its simple linear form, as it appears later (meas. 90) during recall of this material. A more relaxed second theme, in D major (meas. 39ff.), intervenes to relieve the intolerably heavy mood. After the simplified reprise of Theme 1 cited above, the movement ends in a brief coda. This is prefaced by a stroke on the tamtam

EXAMPLE 8-3   Tchaikovsky, Symphony No. 6/IV, Theme 1,
                                     two manners of statement

a) Initial statement, meas. 1–4

b) Subsequent statement, meas. 90–93

(Chinese gong), the orchestra's most portentous timbre. The final measures recall the more lyric second theme, transposed to B minor and projected over a long B pedal point.

The Symphonies of Dvořák

Despite the fact that Bohemia had been part of the Austro-German musical milieu since at least the fifteenth century and had been sending fine professional musicians into Western Europe for many years, this Czech region ultimately developed a strong nationalistic musical movement. Bohemian nationalism was less self-conscious than Russian and produced no music as distinctively exotic as some of that from the Great Five, or even Tchaikovsky. These circumstances relate to Bohemia's less isolated location and the close ties its composers had maintained with the mainstream of European musical developments.

Bedřich Smetana (1824–1886) is regarded as the founder of the Bohemian nationalist movement; but Smetana was not a symphonist and his patriotic tendencies are revealed mostly in opera plots and tone poems. His contemporary and compatriot, Antonin Dvořák (1841–1904), a widely recognized and prolific composer, did write distinctive symphonies, one of which will be discussed here.

By 1889, Dvořák had written four of his symphonies that were to achieve publication. The earliest, now called No. 3, was sketched as early as 1875; but the final version of this, along with the other three, were really products of the 1880s. All four are carefully constructed works, somewhat in the tradition of Schubert and Mendelssohn. While Dvořák was in full sympathy with the Czech patriotic movement in music, only a trace of national flavor is found in these early symphonies, apparent in an overall ingenuousness and in some folk motives that seem rather self-conscious in their conventional contexts.

Dvořák might have remained just another of a rather large group of minor symphonic composers active toward the end of the nineteenth century, if he had not visited the United States. He took that journey in 1892, America's "Columbian" year, for the primary purpose of establishing a National Conservatory of Music in New York City. He did not succeed in establishing a permanent, major institution; but Dvořák was exposed, while in New York, to a kaleidoscopic succession of American experiences. Dvořák had known Longfellow's poem *Hiawatha* in a Czech translation for a number of years. Through it, he had acquired a romantic interest in the American Indian, which quickened when he was taken to see the Indian dancers at Buffalo Bill's Wild West Show. Dvořák also made the acquaintance of Harry T. Burleigh, a black student at the idealistic National Conservatory. On a number of occasions, Burleigh sang spirituals to Dvořák, and the homesick Czech musician probably sensed the universal desolation of all oppressed people in these moving songs. Indian and black materials seem to have merged with Czech tunes in Dvořák's mind; the result, in his most important orchestral piece, is a succession of themes that might be said to exude a kind of pan-primitivism. Dvořák probably hoped that his Symphony No. 9 (originally No. 5), in E minor, "From the New World," reflected the spirit of America; but it does so only in a mannered way, and the composer's central-European orientation is evident.

The attractive, naive themes found in each of the four movements are the elements most people recall when they think of Dvořák's "New World" Symphony. This is inevitable and probably what the composer desired. But only a few people have discovered that the composer has set some of these neo-primitive

The first performance of Dvořák's "New World" Symphony at Carnegie Hall, New York, 16 December 1893. Anton Seidl conducted the New York Philharmonic.

themes in the midst of a texture that is strikingly chromatic, even enharmonic. Dvořák was a far more sophisticated composer than is generally realized, and his carefully prepared dualism—of diatonic substance (themes) versus chromatic or enharmonic environment (transitions and connective materials)—projects the principal ideas in cameo-clear fashion. A discussion of the four movements of the "New World" Symphony follows.

FIRST MOVEMENT: *Adagio/Allegro molto, in E minor*

The brief Adagio prelude serves two purposes: to prefigure some of the elemental rhythms of thematic ideas to come, and to prepare a mildly chromatic approach to Theme I. The chromaticism consists of a 4-measure interpolation (meas. 15-18) of a dominant-ninth chord over B♭, just before B♮ (the dominant of the oncoming key of E minor) is taken for the approach to the main portion of the movement.

The *Allegro molto* has three principal thematic ideas, all presented during the Exposition section and all neo-primitive in character (Ex. 8-4). While none of them is fully pentatonic, all are basically triadic. The "Scotch snap" rhythm

EXAMPLE 8-4   Dvořák, "New World" Symphony/I, principal themes

a) Theme 1, meas. 24–31

b) Theme 2, meas. 91–94

c) Theme 3, meas. 149–56

(short-long), expressed ♪ ♩ , and the repetition of a small cell (in Themes 2 and 3) are definite folk traits.

Theme 1 is realized in E minor throughout; but, as Theme 2 approaches (meas. 75–90), the notes C♮ and C♯ alternate. Theme 2 maintains an initial key of G minor through 20 measures, then veers suddenly to E major and A minor, en route to a restatement in G major (meas. 129ff.). Theme 3 (meas. 149ff.), also in G major, proceeds without connective material out of the restatement of Theme 2. It occupies the position of the Classical closing theme—just ahead of the double bar for the Exposition close.

The Midsection achieves a point of false recapitulation at measure 245 with the appearance of Theme 1 in E minor in bass instruments. This is followed by further development before the arrival of the true Recapitulation (meas. 277ff.), which has a colorful sequence of keys: Theme 1 in E minor/major; Theme 2 in G-sharp minor, followed by a multitonal digression (meas. 336–54), then restatement in A-flat major; Theme 3 in A-flat major, then, in direct juxtaposition, in A major (meas. 401). This permeation of the Recapitulation with conspicuously foreign key levels highlights the restoration of E minor just before the close.

SECOND MOVEMENT: *Largo, in D-flat major*

The English horn theme of this movement is the best known of all the subjects of this symphony. It derives from a pentatonic scale on D♭ and is harmonized in that key. The 4 measures of prefatory harmony, which begin with three vividly posed chromatic chords, furnish an effective setting for the pentatonic English horn theme; together, the colorful chordal preface and the wistful folklike theme constitute the best example of dualism (as cited above) in the symphony (Ex. 8-5).

The Roman numerals shown in Ex. 8-5 suggest a realization of the chords in harmonic analysis. The first three chords are chromatic and remote from the key of this movement (D-flat); but they emphasize an important level of the first movement: E major. The alternation of the notes B♮ and B♭ during the three chords recalls the same variation at the close of the prefatory Adagio in the first movement. Beginning with the fourth chord and continuing to the cadence, the harmonies are in D-flat, mixed mode: the two tonic triads derive from the major mode, the VI (B♭♭-D♭-F♭) and the IV (G♭-B♭♭-D♭) from the minor mode.

In the simple three-part design (ABA′) the English horn subject is the principal material, and a second theme in C-sharp minor (*Un poco piu mosso*) is the contrasting (B) element. The prefatory chords are recalled, but with altered harmony, at measures 22 to 26.

THIRD MOVEMENT: *Scherzo-Molto vivace, in E minor/major*

This Scherzo features the duple rhythm ♫ ♩ in free dispersal within the predominantly triple meter. There are two contrasting sections—*poco sostenuto* in E major and the portion beginning, without designation, at measure 176. The latter section takes off in C minor with the rhythm ♩ ♪ ♩ , continuing up to measure 239 and picking up several new ideas en route.

EXAMPLE 8-5   Dvořák, "New World" Symphony/II, prefatory chords and English horn theme

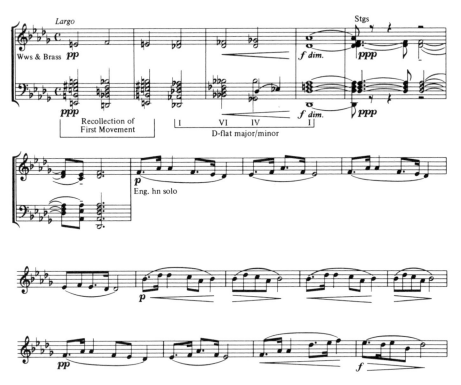

FOURTH MOVEMENT: *Allegro con fuoco, in E minor*

After a brilliant introductory flourish in the full orchestra, a new theme is presented in horns and trumpet (meas. 18ff.). Ultimately, the Finale becomes a fantasia of recollection during which most of the ideas of the previous movements are recalled. All such movements—and they are numerous in late–nineteenth-century symphonic literature—attest to their composers' desire for unity of the total design.

The Symphonies of Sibelius

Jean Sibelius (1865–1957) was the most distinguished symphonist to emerge from the Scandinavian countries during the nineteenth-century period of nationalistic fervor. His devotion to his native country, Finland, and his intense love of nature were dominant personal traits; all his music is steeped in these influences. Except for such works as the popular *Finlandia,* however, his music is remarkably free from folk song quotations and even the vague kind of neo-primitivism found in works of some of his contemporaries.

Sibelius was a superb craftsman, as his seven symphonies firmly attest. Although he is often grouped with the nationalist contingent, this kind of categorizing is deceptive, especially in the case of his symphonies. For these works stand staunchly in the tradition of Beethoven and Brahms—as absolute music; yet they are highly individual pieces that pay scant deference to any particular models. Sibelius may have been born a generation too late to receive the recognition due him as a very skilled symphonist. His decision, after World War I, to spend his life in virtual isolation at his country estate in Finland did little to make his acceptance more widespread.

Sibelius was 34 when, in 1899, he composed his First Symphony; like Beethoven and Brahms before him, he had prepared for this most serious of compositional ventures by writing a great deal of orchestral music before it. He wrote his seventh and last symphony in 1924. Although Sibelius was to live another 33 years, there were to be no more symphonies and very few new compositions of any sort.

General remarks about the entire corpus of Sibelius's symphonies are dangerous and unsuitable. Even the First Symphony is a highly personal work. Certain commentators (Cecil Gray and Gerald Abraham) have cited possible kinship to Borodin's First Symphony in some of his themes, but this seems now to be more a general "northern" flavor than a specific reference. The game of searching out thematic affinities is, at best, inconclusive.

Each symphony of Sibelius's is radically different from its predecessor, so that all must be examined carefully if his symphonic style is to be understood. Those with special interest in these symphonies will do well to consult the detailed analyses included in Gerald Abraham's *The Music of Sibelius* and Cecil Gray's *Sibelius*. Both men present admirably objective critiques of each of the symphonies. Sibelius's Fourth Symphony, written in 1911 and adjudged by many to be his finest, has been chosen for detailed comment here. While it can in no sense be claimed that this work is "typical" of Sibelius, it is unquestionably unique—in its economy of statement and in its ingenious combination of tonal and atonal materials.

FIRST MOVEMENT: *Molto moderato, quasi-adagio*

The first movement is the most cogent of the four, a tight little sonata-allegro design that displays the bare bones of the form in a manner not encountered since the days of the earliest pre-Classical composers. These are the major segments of the design:

Exposition

Meas.	1–6	Introduction
	7–28	Theme 1, in A minor
	29–40	Theme 2 including preparation, on F-sharp
	41–52	Recall of Theme 1 in F-sharp major

Midsection
        54–88

Recapitulation
        89–96   Theme 2, in A major

        97–108   Theme 1, in A major-minor

Concluding cadence (Codetta)
        110–14

The chief interest of the movement, however, lies in relationships other than those generated by the sonata design. The movement might be looked on as an encounter between tonal (meaning "in a key") and atonal factors. The essence of the atonal material is shown in the first 4 measures: the notes C♮ and F♯, constituting the interval of the augmented fourth, are placed in close proximity to each other. The augmented fourth and its inversion, the diminished fifth, constitute the "tritone" (interval containing three whole steps), the *diabolus in musica* ("devil in music") of early times and a difficult interval to reconcile even in later music. Twentieth-century composers were to adopt the tritone rather militantly as a symbolic component in atonal music; Sibelius, consciously or not, seems to have used it in this symphony as the antithesis of the candidly tonal thematic elements. Aside from the interval of the tritone, the 6 introductory measures (Ex. 8–6) yield two other essential ideas: the four-note motive C–D–F♯–E, and an ostinato bass figure produced when F♯ alternates with E. This interval underlies virtually the whole presentation of Theme 1. Since Theme 1 is openly in A minor, the effect is the combination of a "foreign" note (F♯) with a clearly tonal one (E).

With the appearance of Theme 2, in F-sharp major, the previous "foreign" note becomes the tonic of the new key, and the underlying bass combines F♯ and C♯ in a conventional tonic-dominant relationship. The melodic component of Theme 2, in upper strings, is very simple and only 1 measure long; the distinctive feature is its syncopated rhythm. At the recall of Theme 1 (meas. 41), the tritone is again invoked when the triadic motive uses the notes

EXAMPLE 8-6   Sibelius, Symphony No. 4/I, meas. 1–8,
                                     Introduction and start of Theme 1

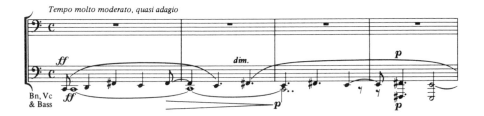

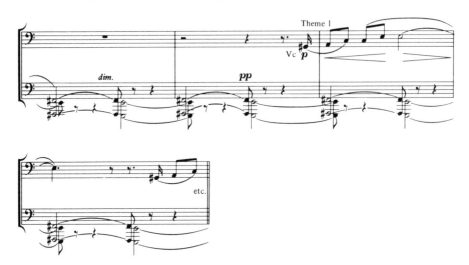

F♯–A♯–C♮. The Midsection explores the syncopated rhythms of Theme 2 and adds a new scale figure (meas. 80ff.) that emphasizes the tritone and might be viewed as prefiguring the opening material of the third movement.

Recapitulation makes contact first with Theme 2; but Theme 1 is not omitted since it occurs after Theme 2, as it did in recall in the Exposition. The final cadence is of major importance in clarifying Sibelius's pitch relationships (see Ex. 8–7).

EXAMPLE 8-7   Sibelius, Symphony No. 4/I, meas. 110–14, final cadence

The essential movement of an authentic (V–I) cadence is implied in the E of the timpani that is followed, in the final measure, by a unison A in the linear parts. Chief interest, however, lies in the activity of these linear parts: the first melodic segment, C♮ to D, is complemented by repeated four-note groups, E–F♯-B♭–A, derived freely from the four-note motive of the Introduction. If the pitches of this cadence group were rearranged as C–F♯–B♭–E–A, they would constitute the so-called "mystic chord" that Scriabin, a Russian contemporary of Sibelius, used to produce the atonal flavor in his later music. Since most of these Scriabin works were written between 1907 and 1910, there seems to be at least a possibility that Sibelius knew this "mystic chord" and was influenced by it in achieving this extraordinary cadence.

SECOND MOVEMENT: *Allegro molto vivace*

This Scherzo seems almost prolix in comparison to the remarkably concise first movement, yet it is of rather modest proportions in comparison to many such episodes of the late nineteenth century. The movement proceeds from first to last without palpable pause, and even the implied Trio section (*Doppio più lento*) simply evolves out of the foregoing texture. The central key is F major, but the tritone interval is so pervasive in the melodic parts that a strong tonal sense is avoided. In its place, a series of pedal points generates concentricity around certain pitches: the first of these is F♯ (meas. 75–81), which moves to E (meas. 82–88) in reminiscence of the F♯-to-E ostinato of the first movement. The entire Scherzo portion is loosely five-part (ABA'CA") in design, with the first digression (*B*) in 2/4 (meas. 49) and the second one (*C*) at *Tranquillo* (meas. 163).

The conventional full da capo of the Scherzo after the Trio is missing; but, 6 bars before the final cadence, the first phrase of the Scherzo, taken in A major but over an F pedal point, gives the merest hint of reprise. The final minicadence in F is sudden and consists of three notes only—E–F–F—which are confirmed by an F pedal point and the three Fs in timpani.

THIRD MOVEMENT: *Il tempo largo*

This concise (101 measures) piece again poses atonal against tonal material, and the design consists of the simple alternation of the two textures in fairly sizable sections. Scale fragments are the most distinctive material in the opening portion, and most of these show the tritone in a prominent location; for example, the first fragment, in flute, shows it in the A-D♯ interval of the first and last notes: A–B–C♮–E–D♯. The contrasting tonal section beginning in measure 38

tritone

emphasizes the interval of the perfect fifth, which is a characteristically tonal interval. This is later replaced by the octave (horns, meas. 56ff.). As usual, the final cadence of the movement is of interest: a tritonal motive, G–A–B–D♮–C♯ is taken in second violin, then cello, and, finally, pizzicato in the double basses; this leads directly to a unison C♯ for the close of the movement.

FOURTH MOVEMENT: *Allegro*

The Finale, the least sophisticated movement of the four, gives the impression of a free fantasia based on a profusion of new motives and short themes. The illusion of a Midsection is generated when unison strings create a conspicuously dense texture from C major scales, so apportioned as to stress pitches C and G of the scale in the various instruments. This 19-measure "core" of the movement suggests that the real design is based on tension: beginning quietly and discursively, the movement becomes more and more concentrated until a climax is reached in the scale passage just cited; the music then relaxes progressively until a quiet authentic cadence in A—the first uncomplicated one of the symphony—is reached in the strings.

In summary, this symphony commences with an atonal "proposition" (Ex. 8-6) but concludes in a candidly tonal authentic cadence. Thus the essence of the entire composition can be seen as the atonal-tonal dualism.

The Symphonies of Ives

The deprecating attitude Americans have traditionally adopted toward their own artists is revealed in the career of Charles Ives (1874–1954). Ives was already writing his First Symphony between 1896 and 1898, while he was still an undergraduate at Yale University. Between 1897 and 1901 he wrote his Symphony No. 2, which we now cite as one of the strong, prophetic works of the waning nineteenth century. Ives' music went totally unperformed and unrecognized for many years, partly because he himself was convinced that, as an American artist who chose not to speak in the prevalent European musical vernacular, he was doomed to be ridiculed and depreciated. His reticence caused him to withdraw into a totally private creative life and it is at least partly responsible for the neglect he suffered.

Some of Ives' earliest music, written even before he entered Yale, utilized sounds and techniques that have long been attributed to the innovative efforts of such Europeans as Schoenberg, Stravinsky, and Debussy. Ives was probably right in concluding that his countrymen were not ready to appreciate his music, but he did not help the cause of American music by his retreat.

Fortunately the situation was reversed within Ives' own lifetime and Americans now seem bent on deifying their neglected genius. The years after the close of World War II saw a series of triumphs for the music Ives had written almost half a century earlier, especially his symphonies. In 1947 his Symphony No. 3 received the Pulitzer prize for music, which Ives shrugged off with the remark: "Prizes are for boys. I'm grown up." Four years later, his Symphony No. 2 also was successfully performed. Despite his public disclaimers, Ives must have derived a certain wry pleasure in the belated plaudits of his countrymen. And the most intriguing question of the many concerning Ives' music is why he wrote it at all. For all the usual motives—acclaim, hopes of immortality, professional accomplishment, execution of a commission—are totally wanting in the circumstances of Ives' activities as a composer. He appears to be the rare Western musician who composed for personal satisfaction alone.

Symphony No. 1 in D Minor—1897–98

Ives' Symphony No. 1 is said to have aroused the ire of Horatio Parker, Ives' teacher in composition at Yale and himself a pioneer American composer—although one thoroughly inculcated with the conventional standards of his German training. Parker insisted on revisions in the first movement, which showed a variety of keys in its opening section and deviated in other ways from academic norms. Ives, although already a man of independent mind, complied, but retained both versions and asserted his continuing preference for the original. In 1910, when Ives was firmly established as a successful New York insurance broker, the composer heard part of this symphony performed for the first time. An acquaintance prevailed upon Walter Damrosch to read through one of the movements at a rehearsal of the New York Symphony Orchestra. Damrosch's unsympathetic attitude and his reported surprise at such devices as polymeter (simultaneous occurrence of, for example, 2/4 and 3/4) and striking dissonance are difficult to credit, because Mahler, Debussy, and Schoenberg were already using similar devices routinely. Whatever the circumstances, Ives withdrew even farther into his self-imposed isolation as the result of the fiasco of this rehearsal.

Symphony No. 2—1897–1901

The composition of his Symphony No. 2 occupied Ives in the first years after his graduation from Yale, although certain portions of it were drawn from earlier compositions. In 1951, Leonard Bernstein conducted a first performance of the piece with the New York Philharmonic Orchestra, in Carnegie Hall. By this time Ives had been "discovered" by his countrymen, and the premiere might easily have become an occasion of excesses. As it was, Ives could not bring himself to attend the performance. His wife and daughter did attend, however, and carried word to the aging composer of the overwhelming ovation accorded the Second Symphony. The critics were almost unanimous in their praise, and Ives was well on his way to becoming an American legend.

Most people who have commented on Ives' Second Symphony have cited its forward-looking traits and its medley of American and other quotations. Equally important, however, are the solid craftsmanship and obvious knowledge of musical traditions revealed in each of the movements, and the sheer beauty of much of its sound. The orchestra is a conventional one for the turn of the century: the work requires a large brass choir (four horns, two trumpets, three trombones, tuba), as did the works of Strauss, Mahler, Franck, and other symphonists who were Ives' contemporaries. The five-movement plan is less extensive than it appears, because the opening *Andante moderato* serves as an introduction to the substantial (382 measures) Allegro, which is numbered as the second movement; and the *Lento maestoso*, designated as the fourth movement, prefaces the final *Allegro molto vivace*. Several brief quotations from Brahms' First Symphony occur during the course of Ives' work; the use of sizable introductions for the first and last movements may be another allusion to that piece, which has substantial preludes for the same two movements.

The opening *Andante moderato* is derived from an earlier organ sonata. The string choir plays continuously throughout the movement, weaving a freely imitative texture with frequent reiteration of certain rhythmic figures, notably that of a pair of eighth notes. An obvious compliance with Classical custom occurs at measure 40, when the opening motive is recalled at the dominant level. At measure 65, a striking deviant passage first heard in measure 20 is recalled entirely intact, this time to serve as preface to the first nonstring timbre of the movement: two horns playing one phrase of "Columbia, the Gem of the Ocean." Measure 79 constitutes a point of major Recapitulation, with the opening motive stated at the original level in first violins, supported by full string harmony. At measure 101, the same motive is recalled in second violins and 6 measures later in oboe, to taper off the *Andante moderato*. The movement cadences only lightly, and a new figure in woodwinds links this portion directly with the oncoming Allegro.

A plan of what might be termed unsystematized recall is the organizing factor in each of the remaining movements of this symphony: Ives is likely to return to certain favored materials at least once, sometimes more often, during the course of a given movement, yet with no regular scheme of alternation such as emerges in the Classical rondo or partite design. Ives' delightfully unpredictable audible recollections in form of quotations from music of every sort are a hallmark of this symphony; they refresh the composition in much the same fashion that more orthodox contrasting sections do in any of the classically organized designs. And if, for example, "Bringing in the Sheaves" seems an odd consort for a fragment of Brahms' First Symphony within the confines of the second movement Allegro, we might recall that Ives was not the first so to associate the serious and the folksy. The German *Liedermesse* ("Song Mass") of the sixteenth century used fragments of popular song in much the same ingenuous manner, and as respected a composer as J. S. Bach based many of his sacred cantatas on chorale melodies that, in turn, had started out as popular songs. Clearly, Ives believed that disparity exists only in the mind, and his free intermingling of all manner of materials testifies to his faith in the innate unity of all matter. This attitude probably accounts for the disarming ease of Ives' key changes: studied modulation must have seemed superfluous, since he clearly conceives the twelve different pitches as belonging to an essentially unified pitch resource. For example, the first 7 bars of the second movement slip easily out of A-flat, through E major/minor, to a very tenuous pause on a chord comprising G-Bb-Db-Fb; the section beginning at measure 130 in the same movement is another excellent illustration.

The final *Allegro molto vivace* is a gay romp of a movement in which the listener can probably find traces of almost anything he chooses to identify. Some of the unmistakable allusions are Stephen Foster tunes, including "Camptown Races" and "Old Black Joe," "Columbia, the Gem of the Ocean," and, just before the final raucous cadence chord, reveille on the trumpet. Although no one seems to have suggested it, Ives may have wished to satirize the kind of "fantasia of recollections" finale often found in the symphonies of several major nineteenth-century composers whose works have been described earlier.

Symphony No. 3, "The Camp Meeting"—1901–04, revised 1911–12

As was pointed out earlier, this symphony was the first of Ives' works to bring him wide acclaim. It was first performed in 1947 by the New York Little

Symphony, with Lou Harrison conducting. The orchestra is notably smaller than that required for the Second Symphony, with the brass limited to two horns and a trombone. As usual, the strings carry the principal burden of statement, with other choirs used for contrast or affirmation. All Ives' orchestral works "sound" because of his skillful deployment of the instruments. In his reversion to essentially a chamber orchestra for his Third Symphony, Ives was again ahead of his time, for composers of the post–World War I era were to seize on the chamber symphony as one antidote for the excesses of the post-Wagner generation of symphonists.

The Third Symphony uses titles for the three movements, all alluding to the overall title of "The Camp Meeting": I. "Old Folks Gatherin'," II. "Children's Day," III. "Communion." The first and third movements are adaptations of earlier organ pieces; the middle Allegro started out as "Children's Day Parade" for string quartet and organ. The quotations, mostly hymn fragments, are less disparate than those in the Second Symphony.

An examination of the opening statement (Ex. 8-8) will provide insights into Ives' advanced and dexterous compositional techniques, which are apparent throughout the movement.

In the first 5 measures, the strings engage in a type of texture designated later as "linear counterpoint." Simply defined, this means that a number of melodic lines moving simultaneously produce a counterpoint of melodic shapes (lines)—as opposed to the more conventional counterpoint based on specific intervallic relationships, often derived from implied harmony. Since each of the four string instruments moves independently in producing its particular line, the relationship among the four parts at any particular spot is unimportant, and constant motility is the objective. At measure 6, the texture becomes suddenly harmonic, as the four instruments join in producing G minor, then E-flat major triads; in the next measure, the three triads—C major, G major, A major, each in root position—are colorful because they are not key-oriented. In the brass-plus-bassoon harmonies of measures 8 through 13, the successive triadic relationships are quite casual and not tonal except for the suggestion of G♭ at measure 10. The first five measures contrast those that follow by posing a dualism of linear versus harmonic texture; the opening measures provide insight into Ives' unpretentious, free use of twelve-tone pitch materials.

"Children's Day" uses a free three-part design, as befits a movement that is primarily a march. During the opening portion, horns and bassoon maintain a steady march rhythm, over which the violins play a very lithe, active part marked by versatile rhythms; the opening phrase is characteristic:

The contrasting section (*Piu allegro*) features some folk rhythms and dispenses with the march-beat background until *Alla marcia*, which begins a section of transition. Recall of the opening linear material, in violas and cellos and in A major (in contrast to the prevalent E-flat), occurs at *Allegro moderato;* but the

EXAMPLE 8-8   Ives, Symphony No. 3/I, meas. 1–14

flat-key orientation is restored before the close, which is taken with a colorful chordal succession: successive major triads on D♭, G♭, and E♭.

In using a Largo for the closing movement, Ives, like Tchaikovsky, anticipated the preference of many later composers for a quiet finale. "Communion" opens with a series of pseudo-imitative entries in strings and proceeds in linear counterpoint to a quiet close that calls for "distant church bells."

Before he ceased to compose, in 1928, Ives produced two other works that may be considered symphonies. In 1913, he assembled a composite work, *A Symphony: Holidays*, by rescoring and rearranging four patriotic pieces composed during the previous ten years. This symphony, which bears no number, has movements entitled: I. "Washington's Birthday" (1909); II. "Decoration Day" (1912); III. "Fourth of July" (1912–13); IV. "Thanksgiving and/or Forefathers' Day" (1904). Ives directed that these pieces might be played separately or "lumped together as a symphony."

Between 1910 and 1916, Ives completed his Symphony No. 4, sometimes called *Symphony with Two Pianos*, or *Symphony for Orchestra and Pianos*. In this amazing and complicated piece, Ives expands on the techniques initiated in his earlier works. Especially important is the expansion of counterpoint to include metric and durational counterpoint in addition to linear counterpoint. Few scores from any composers before the 1950s reveal the incredible mathematical complexity of, for example, the second movement of this symphony. The only counterpart for Ives' unfettered rhythm would seem to be in the music of Ockeghem, the great fifteenth-century contrapuntist.

At the end of his life, Ives was still engaged in adding notes, from time to time, to his *Universal Symphony*. This exists only in fragmentary sketches, and the composer probably intended that it remain uncompleted.

9

A Parasymphonic Type:
The Symphonic Poem

The symphonic form was useful to composers of the Romantic period only in proportion as it was amenable to adjustments and mutations suggested by the changing taste of the times. Berlioz was the first major composer to realize overtly in his music that the time of the Classical symphony was passing. But Berlioz continued to call his large orchestral works symphonies, and, as has been noted, the narrative or verbal aspects of such compositions as the *Symphonie fantastique* and *Harold in Italy* were extraneous, not intrinsic to the music. Berlioz himself made this quite clear. Most of the composers of symphonies in the two or three generations after Berlioz were influenced by his bold ideas, although many of them adhered more closely to the Classical prescription than he had done. But one man, who was Berlioz's junior by only eight years, was his true disciple. Franz Liszt (1811–1886) was present at the first successful performance of the *Symphonie fantastique,* and seldom has a seed fallen in more fertile ground. Liszt brought into the open what Berlioz had only implied: music could profit by cooperation with other arts, especially poetry and drama. Liszt discarded the term "symphony" for all but two of his large orchestral works; instead he called them symphonic poems and gave them suggestive or dramatic titles.

There are thirteen symphonic poems in all, twelve written between 1848 and 1857 and the last one, *Von der Wiege bis zum Grabe (From the Cradle to the Grave),* written in 1881–82, only a short time before the composer's death. Several titles suggest that the music is connected with a literary work, although the exact nature of the connection is never clear. Thus two Liszt symphonic poems, *Ce*

The young Franz Liszt

qu'on entend sur la montagne (*What One Hears on the Mountain*) and *Mazeppa*, are "after Victor Hugo," *Tasso* is "after Byron," *Die Ideale* "after Schiller," and so on. Stimulation of a mood for composer and listener seems to be the purpose of Liszt's literary references. His compositions often rely heavily on organizational procedures native to the traditional symphony: distinctive themes, plausible schemes of key relationship, enlargement by thematic manipulation, and, most vital of all, a systematic plan for recall of important thematic elements. The term "parasymphonic" is here used to describe the symphonic poem because it did indeed derive many qualities from the traditional symphony and flourished alongside it for more than a century.

The symphonic poem was a form whose time, obviously, had come. Liszt's pioneer examples assume importance as early specimens of what proved to be an uncommonly durable and prolific musical type. Most of the composers whose symphonies have already been discussed turned from time to time to the freer form of the symphonic poem. Other important nineteenth-century composers bypassed the symphony altogether, choosing to cast all their large-scale orchestral works in the newer, more flexible mold. After Liszt, the degree of cooperation between the nonmusical subject of inspiration and the resultant music varies from composer to composer. But every composer who made even a labored or nebulous literary reference was bowing to the nineteenth century's definite predilection for "the word." They were also tending toward the popular ideal of the *Gesamtkunstwerk* (total, or composite, art work), which found more explicit expression in compositions of Wagner and Scriabin.

With different composers the symphonic poem assumed different guises. Sometimes extensive "sound-painting" was employed, so the composition became a descriptive episode, although music can, of course, be descriptive in only a subjective and tentative way. The French have always preferred music with verbal allusions, so the symphonic poem was an especially felicitous form for them. Saint-Saëns' *Le Rouet d'Omphale* (*Omphale's Spinning Wheel*) and *Danse Macabre* and César Franck's *Le Chasseur maudit* (*The Reprobate Huntsman*) are three descriptive examples that are still played from time to time.

A number of nationalist composers—or those with strong patriotic leanings— chose the symphonic poem as a framework for fond meditations on the fatherland. Bedřich Smetana, one of the founders (along with Dvořák) of the Bohemian nationalist school, wrote a series of six symphonic poems, *Ma Vlást*, or *Mein Vaterland* (*My Country*), of which only "The Moldau" is often heard today. And Sibelius, whose symphonies have already been discussed, wrote a number of symphonic poems, all more or less nationalistic: *The Swan of Tuonela*, *Finlandia*, *Pohjola's Daughter*, and *Tapiola*.

The group of Russian composers known collectively as the "Great Five" was mostly responsible for the spectacular rise of Russian music during the second half of the nineteenth century. All of them were ardently nationalistic, and because all but one (Balakirev) were amateurs with little formal training in music, they found the uninhibiting framework of the symphonic poem ideal for their large-scale orchestral works. At least three of the Great Five had intuitive gifts for brilliant orchestration; many of their compositions are especially vivid and colorful. Mily Balakirev (1837–1910) wrote *Russia*, into which he incorporated authentic folk melodies. Modest Mussorgsky (1839–1881) wrote *A Night on Bald Mountain* to evoke the celebration of a Russian version of Walpurgis Night. He also wrote a series of piano pieces, *Pictures at an Exhibition*, which, in an orchestral version by Ravel, has now achieved the status of a symphonic poem. Most important of all the Five because of his influence on subsequent generations of Russian composers was Nicolas Rimsky-Korsakov (1844–1908), who, as head of the St. Petersburg Conservatory, was Stravinsky's mentor. Two of Rimsky's most important orchestral works may be classed loosely as symphonic poems: his *Capriccio Espagnol* is a marvelous tour de force of orchestral usage in which most of the instruments have an opportunity to emerge as virtuosos; *Scheherazade* is a four-movement suite based on episodes from *The Arabian Nights*.

Aside from Liszt, two composers of symphonic poems emerge as the most important, primarily because of their intrinsic musical excellence: Richard Strauss (1864–1949) and Claude Debussy (1862–1918). Debussy, a genuinely radical composer who epitomizes all the best in the resurgence of French music, adapted the form as shaped by Berlioz and Liszt to the exigencies of changing French taste and the special language of French impressionism. Representative works of Liszt, Strauss, and Debussy have been chosen for discussion here to demonstrate the versatility of the symphonic poem.

Liszt: Les Préludes

Liszt wrote the original version of *Les Préludes*, which was to prove the most durable of his thirteen symphonic poems, in 1848. At that time he wrote it as an actual prelude to his choral work *Les Quatre Eléments*. Six years later he revised it into an independent piece with a program whose origin has been the subject of considerable controversy. The score indicates "After Lamartine," and a line from that contemporary French poet ("What is our life but a series of preludes to that unknown song the first solemn note of which is sounded by Death?") has generally been seen as the inspiration of the tone poem. But a Hungarian scholar, Emile Haraszti, writing in the French journal *Revue de Musicologie* (December 1953) has argued persuasively that the program of *Les Préludes* stems from the texts of the cantatas comprising *Les Quatre Eléments*. The title of Haraszti's essay tells its own story: "Genèse des Préludes de Liszt qui n'ont aucun rapport avec Lamartine." ("Origin of Les Préludes of Liszt which has no relationship with Lamartine.") Haraszti's view has the virtue of suggesting that the program of *Les Préludes* was not as foreign to the music as had been supposed.

Les Préludes needs to be examined on three levels of organization if Liszt's total plan is to be apprehended. The first, and probably the least important, is the relationship of the program to Liszt's music. This program is quasi-autobiographical and appears to suggest four periods or influences in the life of man. The probable correspondence of these to sections of the music is as follows:

Meas.	1–108	"Youth and Love" (*Andante, Andante maestoso*)
	109–99	"Early Problems and Struggles" (*Allegro ma non troppo, Allegro tempestoso*)
	200–343	"Pastoral Joys" (*Allegretto pastorale*)
	344–419	"Final Struggle and Triumph" (*Allegro marziale animoto, Tempo di marcia*)

The sequence of tempos and moods parallels that of the four movements of many symphonies, although each section is much curtailed in length.

Another aspect of the organization, an extremely important one, concerns a technique of composition that was very useful for Liszt: motivic transformation. In this piece, a three-note motive given out in strings at measure 3 is the germ of all the principal thematic members in the piece. Shown below (Ex. 9-1) is the germ motive (X) and the six transformations that evolve from it during the course of the symphonic poem. The designations Theme 1a, 2, etc., are used because the large plan of *Les Préludes* is a modified sonata-allegro, and these designations will be needed presently when the outline of that design is discussed. As will be observed in Ex. 9-1, the thematic members designated "1" conform most closely to the germ motive, showing all its essential melodic characteristics.

EXAMPLE 9-1   Liszt, *Les Préludes*, germ motive (X)
                                   and its transformation into thematic elements

a) X, meas. 3–4

Vn I & II

b) Theme 1a, meas. 35–36

c) Theme 1b, meas. 47–50

d) Theme 2a, meas. 70–73

e) Theme 1c (midtheme), meas. 109–14

f) Theme 1d (martial transformation), meas. 346–49

g) Theme 2b (martial transformation), meas. 370–73

Theme 2a (Ex. 9-1d) shows its principal affinity with the germ motive in the initial notes of successive figures, which are marked with asterisks in the example: G♯–F♯–B outlines a descending second and rising fourth, as did *X*, the model. In its innate quality, Theme 2a offers the customary contrast to the more militant Theme 1; but it too becomes militant when recast as 2b.

The third aspect of organization is the modified sonata design that emerges as the form of the main portion of the work, beginning with *Andante maestoso* (meas. 35). The 34-measure section before the *Andante maestoso* is an introduction, following the model of numerous symphonies in their first movements. This primary Andante is devoted entirely to exploration and expansion of the motive in its original guise (Ex. 9-1a, *X*).

The principal themes as shown in Ex. 9-1 are dispersed in a free sonata-allegro plan with a "mirror" Recapitulation in which the reprise of Theme 2 precedes that of Theme 1. The closing section recalls Theme 1a almost intact as it had occurred at the outset of the design. This modified sonata-allegro plan, in which the tonal dualism of C-E for the two themes in Exposition is mirrored by A-C in Recapitulation, is shown below.

	Exposition				*Midsection*	*Recapitulation*				
Measure of occurrence	35	47	55	70	109 ⟶	260	296	346	370	405
Theme	1a	1b	1b	2a	1c plus development	2a	2a	1d	2b	1a
Key	C	C	E	E	Area of transient tonality	A	C	C	C	C

Supplementary and supportive materials, which serve to enlarge and unite the design, are not indicated in the skeletal plan shown above. Many of these derive from the arpeggio that concludes the initial presentation of the germ motive (meas. 3–5).

Much of the interest and laudable tension of this design stems from the fact that several sections as suggested by changes of tempo or expressive marking do not coincide with fresh key areas or with the beginning of a principal thematic element. For example, the new key of E major during the Exposition arrives first in connection with a restatement of Theme 1b; and the key of A that signals the Recapitulation is prepared by 59 measures of fresh material (*Allegretto pastorale*, meas. 200–59) before Theme 2a is restated in A (meas. 260) to confirm the validity of this section of reprise. It must be pointed out, too, that Liszt may have borrowed his key scheme from Beethoven's "Waldstein" Sonata, Op. 53—although Beethoven's piece does not have a mirror Recapitulation.

Strauss: Till Eulenspiegels lustige Streiche (Till Eulenspiegel's Merry Pranks)

Not only was Richard Strauss among the most gifted and versatile composers of the waning nineteenth century; he was also an intensely practical artist, one who recognized with rare candor what he could do successfully and what the taste of his day would support. Born when Wagner and Liszt were flourishing, Strauss lived to see the overt rejection of most nineteenth-century musical mores. In a sense, Strauss outlived his time, for his living presence among the serialists and atonalists of the 1930s and 1940s postponed a properly retrospective evaluation of his music, particularly those compositions written toward the close of the previous century. And several of these deserve to be ranked among the strongest examples of the type pioneered by Berlioz and Liszt.

As a young man, Strauss probably sensed the potential dangers of the highly chromatic harmony and casual form favored by his older contemporaries, for he had a brief go with Neoclassicism in some of his early songs and chamber works. Realizing, however, that a successful artist does well to adopt the posture of his time, Strauss turned, in his middle twenties, to writing symphonic poems. There are seven, beginning with *Aus Italien* (1887) and culminating with *Don Quixote* (1898). No composer has used this form with greater aplomb and distinction. In some instances, Strauss's title and program are as extrinsic as Liszt's, serving merely to establish a state of mind. *Tod und Verklärung (Death and Transfiguration)* of 1889 and *Also sprach Zarathustra (Thus Spake Zarathustra)* of 1896, which was inspired by Nietzsche, are typical examples. Like other Romantic composers, Strauss was prone to be autobiographical: *Ein Heldenleben (A Hero's Life)* is the most consummately arrogant but at the same time disarmingly attractive of all self-portraits in music. And something of the composer, too, must emerge in several of Strauss's protagonists: in Don Juan and Don Quixote, but especially in Till Eulenspiegel.

In several of his symphonic poems, Strauss accomplishes what Berlioz and Liszt merely attempted: he plausibly sketches a series of episodes in sound. When this is the case, knowledge of the background program and a willingness to relate it specifically to the music are essentials for the perceptive listener. *Till Eulenspiegel* (1895) is probably the most graphic of these musical narratives, and it could well be the most durable of all orchestral pieces of the late nineteenth century. It has been chosen for discussion here to represent the symphonic poem as realized most characteristically by Strauss.

The narrative background of *Till Eulenspiegel* is derived from medieval German folklore, which probably has an origin in fact. Strauss's Till is an engaging rogue who indulges in outrageous pranks, but emerges between forays as a lovable, fallible, sometimes pathetic character. He epitomizes the conflict of the simple fellow with his intellectual superiors, of the nonconformist with the establishment. Although Till lived in the fourteenth century, he was still timely in Strauss's day and he is even more so now—which may help explain the extraordinary timelessness of the music he inspired.

Instead of the more pretentious sonata design, Strauss chose a rondo form for *Till*. The alternation of principal with deviant materials that is implicit in the rondo is especially useful for depicting the kaleidoscopic changes in Till's mood. In its total format, however, *Till Eulenspiegel* shows an unbalanced ternary design: the material of the preliminary 5 measures is recalled near the close of the composition and is extended there into a 26-measure *Epilog*. Placed in between is Strauss's massive free rondo design, the principal corpus of the work.

Till, the protagonist of this symphonic yarn, is characterized by two themes. The first, representing the "straight" side of our hero, belongs natively to the horn, although this theme is transferred on occasion to other instrumental contexts. As shown in Ex. 9-2, this "Till 1" theme is based on the F major triad enlivened with a discreet number of embellishing nonharmonic notes.

EXAMPLE 9-2   Strauss, *Till Eulenspiegel*, "Till 1" theme, meas. 6–12

The other principal theme, "Till 2," emerges at measure 46, after a general pause (Ex. 9-3). This is marked *lustig* (merry) and is related to "Till 1" through its third, fourth, and fifth notes: in both themes these constitute a cluster of three chromatic tones interposed between more widely spaced intervals.

In retrospect, we see the opening motive of the piece, which many writers have likened to the storyteller's "Once upon a time," as a prefiguring of "Till 2."

The first 74 measures state Till 1 and Till 2 and extend each in turn by elementary developmental processes. At measure 75, eliding with a weak F ca-

EXAMPLE 9-3   Strauss, *Till Eulenspiegel,* "Till 2" theme, meas. 46–47

dence, the first deviant section commences. After 6 measures, however, Till 2, somewhat altered, intervenes to suggest the hero's first masquerade; his flight is implied when the opening rhythmic figure of Till 2, ♫, is made the subject of a continuing sequence series (meas. 96–102) that sounds frenetic because it completely displaces the prevalent 6/8 measure. A full F cadence (meas. 110–11) terminates this episode. There follows a 66-measure episode in the style of an interpolated development, ahead of the first change of meter: from 6/8 to 2/4, at measure 179. This "square" rhythm is established to carry one of the most outrageous of Till's masquerades—as a priest. After 10 bars, this "priestly" theme is interrupted by Till 2, adapted to the continuing 2/4 meter (meas. 189–95). This affront to the supreme established authority, the Church, is countered with prefiguring of still another new motive—that of impending retribution (meas. 196–200). The new motive uses the three chromatic notes found in both Till 1 and Till 2 as the basis for successive figures ♫♩ , scored in very close harmony in muted horns, trumpets, and five solo violins; this passage is typical of Strauss's imaginative but eminently practical orchestration. The brief foreboding of punishment to come is displaced by Till 2 and what surely must be a nose-thumbing gesture in a long glissando chromatic scale for a solo violin, which leads to reestablishment of the 6/8 meter (meas. 208).

After a brief, leisurely interlude, a "love" theme is introduced (meas. 229ff). This new subject, which is concocted from the opening figure of Till 1 and marked *liebeglühend* (ardently), suggests the swooning condition of our hero by use of a long portamento for flute, clarinet, and violin. The new "love" motive alternates with Till 1 in a subsequent long development. A new deviant section is introduced by the "Philistine" motive (meas. 272ff). A major point of reprise occurs with the firm cadence of F major (meas. 428–29) and the immediate introduction of Till 1, completely intact in horn, as at the outset.

The next large portion, which intermingles most of the previous materials in a skillful mélange, represents, jointly, the climax of Till's escapades and the grand coda of the rondo form. This romp is halted at measure 576 with a subject representing Till at the bar of justice. The scoring of this "justice" motive is especially colorful: a snare-drum roll in the background supports a massively realized F minor triad scored so that the open fifth (F-C) is consistently sounded in pairs of similar instruments, serving to emphasize the primitive quality of the interval. The third of the chord, A♭, lies in strings (except double basses) and horns. The effect is wonderfully ominous, or *drohend* as the score indicates. The hero responds with Till 2, but the sentence of justice is reiterated, and the portion climaxes in a recall of the "retribution" motive, again in muted brass and strings.

The most literal tone-painting of the piece comes at measures 613–18: a sheer drop in the interval of a major seventh (F to G♭) is variously understood to represent Till's sentencing, or his execution; and a small (D) clarinet sounding Till 2 in an ascending arpeggio perhaps suggests that Till's soul escaped after all.

In the light of the intensely dramatic character of Strauss's tone poems, it comes as no surprise that he turned from them to opera, which is, after all, the consummate dramatic form.

Debussy:
Prélude à l'Après-midi d'un faune
(Prelude to the Afternoon of a Faun)

A few compositions of the nineteenth century have acquired the status of landmarks or catalysts, which makes them significant beyond whatever their intrinsic worth may be. Beethoven's "Eroica" Symphony and Wagner's *Tristan und Isolde* are two such pieces, and Debussy's *Prelude to the Afternoon of a Faun* (1892–94) is another. This small orchestral *scène*, which belongs to the genre of the symphonic poem, was a sensation in its own day, and it was Debussy's most influential work. Debussy's revolutionary attitude toward sound and his highly personal musical language, as first demonstrated in the *Faun*, have affected most subsequent composers, even those of the present time.

Two initial comparisons between Strauss's *Till* and the *Faun* will serve to stress differences between Debussy and his contemporaries: Strauss's piece occupies 657 measures, but the *Faun* requires only 110; the former uses the rondo, the most partite of musical forms, whereas the latter is not so much formless as indivisible. Perhaps the *Faun* can be truly perceived only in memory, which is the one means of achieving immediate totality for an art work that takes place in time. In several aspects of his *Faun*, Debussy shows himself to be an eclectic, for traces of numerous contemporaries—Grieg, Wagner, Mussorgsky, Saint-Saëns, among others—as well as of exoticism are detected. Debussy's very individual style (and that of his followers) is called impressionism. This term links Debussy with French painters and poets of his day, who sought to evoke mood and atmosphere in the graphic arts and literature. In music at any rate, impressionism militates against the excessive size, concrete imagery, and elaborate, cerebral plans cultivated by German composers of the late nineteenth century.

The immediate inspiration of Debussy's composition was an *Églogue* (idyll) of the French poet Stéphane Mallarmé. There is firm evidence that Debussy contemplated a group of pieces of which the present *Prelude* was to be the first.[1]

---

[1] See William W. Austin's essay "The History of the Poem and the Music" in his critical score of the piece (New York: Norton, 1970), p. 11.

The *Faun* as we now know it was complete at least by the fall of 1894; it was first performed at a concert of the Société Nationale on December 23 of the same year.

The effect on Debussy of Mallarmé's long, suggestive, erotic poem was quite different from that of literary works on the composers of German tone poems: the verbal stimulation served to arouse sensual images in Debussy's mind, and his music is the means of perpetuating these impressions (Mallarmé's poem commences "Ces nymphes, je les veux perpetuer") in episodes that unfold continuingly, in colorful, evocative, but often diaphanous textures. The listener, in preparing to hear Debussy's *Faun*, would do well to read Mallarmé's poem, but to retain only veiled recollection of it as he listens to its musical reflection.

Because Debussy's *Faun* is conceived as a totality, an understanding of any specific portion is dependent on realizing it in total context. The matter of tonality, still an active means in Debussy's music, will serve to illustrate this. Tonality exists in the *Faun* on two planes, the linear and the vertical (harmonic); and the two do not necessarily coincide. In light of its conclusion (meas. 106–10), the *Faun* appears to have E major as its harmonic focal point; it is significant that this terminal key of E is confirmed by the conventional dominant-to-tonic bass movement of B to E (meas. 105–06). If, however, we examine the opening arabesque of the flute (Ex. 9-4), we find that a C-sharp tonal center is generated by establishing C♯ as a focal point in the line.

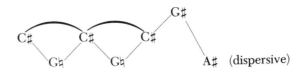

This arabesque concludes on A♯, which is supported by the first harmonic structure of the piece, C♯-E-G♯-A♯, which may be termed a "chord of the added sixth" (A♯ is an added sixth above the triadal root, C♯). Immediately after this chord is sounded in oboes and clarinets, the horn sounds the note E, thus giving early prominence to the pitch that will prove to be the ultimate cadence point of the music. In a broad sense, the vacillation between C♯ and E and the varying contexts given each of these pitches reveal the dual tonal orientation of the music.

The flute arabesque is the recurrent factor in the *Faun;* it gives the impression that instrumental timbre here replaces more traditional means (theme or key) of recall. The varying contexts given this arabesque do much to determine the relative tension at any given point. At the first recall (meas. 11), the initial C♯ is posed over a D major triad, which is a tensive, dissonant relationship that serves to isolate the melodic element from the harmonic texture. At the second recall 10 measures later (meas. 21), the tension decreases when the harmonic context for the initial C♯ is the seventh chord C♯-E-G♯-B, which may be interpreted as another chord of the added sixth: E-G♯-B-C♯. At measure 26, C♯ is

EXAMPLE 9-4   Debussy, *Afternoon of a Faun,* meas. 1–4

posed over the ninth chord E-G♯-B-D♮-F♯, again giving it the sound of an added sixth over the chord root. An episode of contrasting material that begins evolving about measure 34 reaches a climax at measure 55, with the key of D-flat major (enharmonic of C-sharp) and a strong new theme. At measure 79, the point of minimum tension is achieved when the flute arabesque returns, transposed to begin on E, over clear E major harmony. At measure 94, the arabesque returns to its original C♯ starting point; here the note C♯ again acquires the sound of an added sixth (paralleling the context of the note A♯ at measure 4 since the underlying harmony is essentially E major. This context of an added sixth for the note C♯ is confirmed in the last 2 measures where the melodic interval C♯–G♯ in the flute overlies the cadential E major harmony in harp and low strings.

Instrumental timbre is of extraordinary importance in the *Faun,* first through the role of the flute as a ritornello element for the persistent returns of the opening arabesque. The harp acquires stature through the effective use of its glissando to underline principal harmonic points. Several of the harmonies may well have been plotted to permit use of the harp glissando through tuning pairs of adjacent strings as homophones. At measure 4, for example, the harp can be tuned as follows to carry the chord of the added sixth cited above (C♯-E-G♯-A♯) in glissando: A♯ B♭-C♯ D♭-E F♭-G♯. The effect of the long (four-octave) glissando here and elsewhere is diffusive and nebulous. The horn generally has an opposite effect and tends to anchor important pitches. The bright color of Debussy's orchestra emanates from the woodwinds; the strings are likely to be relegated to a background role. The scoring after measure 55 typifies the French orchestral tutti: each choir has a unique part and doubling between choirs is almost never permitted. The effect is a stratified texture in which each choir maintains its separate integrity; rarely is the integrated orchestral sound favored by German composers found here, or in other French scores.

The suppleness of Debussy's rhythm has been the subject of much comment, but it is important to note that Debussy wrote in most of the flexibility; for a conductor to add to this with personal whims of tempo variation can court disaster in performance. The tutti beginning at measure 63 (*pp subito*) furnishes an excellent example of simultaneous disparate rhythms that emphasize the stratification by choirs. The strings have the basic 3/4 rhythm but, after the first measure, disperse it in syncopated rhythms (hemiola = $\frac{3}{4}$ ♩. ♪♫ | ♩ ♪♩ ♪ etc.); the woodwinds play triplets, giving nine notes to the measure, while the harps play sextuplets, giving eighteen notes to the measure.

After his *Faun,* Debussy wrote two other compositions that belong to the genre of the symphonic poem: *Nocturnes* (1899) and *La Mer* (*The Sea,* 1905). In his later years, Debussy followed the example of several of his earlier peers (Beethoven and Brahms, for example) in turning to chamber works. He died at 55, during the bombing of Paris at the end of World War I. As for the symphonic poem, it has continued to be useful for each generation of twentieth-century composers. The rivalry between it and the symphony is but another aspect of the very old controversy concerning the relative merits of absolute versus representative music.

PART THREE

Symphonic Types
during the Twentieth Century

10

The Symphony in the
Twentieth Century

When the twentieth century was little more than a decade old, the "guns of August" marked the beginning of the first of the world wars of our time. In remarkably clairvoyant fashion, trends in music for half a century before 1914 had foreshadowed events in the social and political spheres, although few people were prescient enough to so read them. The rise of a fervently nationalistic group in Russia and the entrance of Russian composers into the mainstream of Western music can be seen as presaging the emergence of Russia as a great power. The opposition of French composers led by Debussy to a two-century German hegemony in music is reflected in the central conflict of the War of 1914, which was between France and Germany. And the gradual erosion of most time-honored organizational factors such as tonality, regular metric grouping, and hierarchical designs—all observed in music we have examined—can be seen as paralleling the rejection of monarchical systems of government and of the capitalist system in favor of communes. Carrying this analogy to its logical musical conclusion, the twelve-tone system and serialism, which eventually supplanted the notion of key for many composers, constitute a "communism among pitches," as Eaglefield Hull, the English theorist, sagely remarked.

Two compositions first performed in 1912–13 epitomized the direction that musical winds were blowing. Although neither is in the direct line of the symphony, they brought two composers who were to be largely responsible for trends in twentieth-century music into early prominence; and they show clearly some of the problems the symphony was to encounter during the next half century. One of the works is *Pierrot Lunaire* (*Moonstruck Pierrot*), the first piece by Arnold Schoenberg (1874–1951) to attract widespread attention. *Pierrot* summarizes

Schoenberg's style up to the time of World War I, and it reveals the dead end to which unorganized chromaticism was leading. *Pierrot* is based on a cycle of 21 grotesque but symbolic poems by the Belgian Albert Giraud, used in a German translation by Otto Erich Hartleben. The medium employed combines a solo voice with a small instrumental group that varies from piece to piece. The voice part is in *Sprechstimme* (speaking voice), which was a somewhat novel sound in 1912 but had derived from melodrama (speech over music), a device used in a number of earlier operatic scenes, including one in Beethoven's *Fidelio*. The aspects of *Pierrot* that relate, although none felicitously, to the future of the symphony are these:

1. The piece is written for small ensemble groups. This shows a reaction to the excessive size of the orchestra required for almost any of the late nineteenth-century symphonic pieces. And it surely relates to the fact that the complicated textures employed in much new music were more audible if performed by fewer instruments.
2. The music relies heavily on Giraud's imagery. This continues the trend away from absolute music, of which the symphony is the consummate type.
3. The musical elements in *Pierrot* tend to be miniscule and detached. Line (that is, melody) is generally replaced by a succession of fragile figures, or even single pitches, often sounded staccato in the piano or one of the orchestral instruments.
4. The musical syntax of *Pierrot* is undeniably atonal. Since the basic structure of the sonata (and the symphony is a sonata for orchestra) is grounded in contrast of key, the new incursion of atonal music was ominous for the symphonic form.

Presently we shall examine one of Schoenberg's symphonies, which were all of the chamber variety. For the moment, it will suffice to observe that this twentieth-century master's composition on the eve of World War I was truly prophetic.

The second of the landmark works, first performed in 1913, was Igor Stravinsky's *Le Sacre du printemps* (*The Rite of Spring*). Its subject is the celebration of spring (fertility) in a series of primitive, pagan rituals. Stravinsky (1882–1971) was a pupil of Rimsky-Korsakov, as has been observed. His earliest compositions of importance were ballets: *Firebird* (1910) and *Petrushka* (1911), both written in collaboration with Diaghilev and his Ballets Russes, which had been taking Paris by storm. *Le Sacre* also was written for the Ballets Russes, and its first performance in Paris has become one of music's legendary occasions. Those who were affronted or filled with consternation by Stravinsky's bold music literally attacked the performers, the composer, and their partisans, so that a musical donnybrook ensued. The result was to catapult *Le Sacre* into the public eye in a fashion that could not have been more effective if the event had been planned by a Madison Avenue impresario. Within a short time, Stravinsky's polychords, brutal, pounding rhythms, and ruthless melodic fragmentation had provoked avid interest and heated controversy in sophisticated musical circles. More than any other single composition, *Le Sacre* brought many details of what was to be a new musical language to the attention of concerned people.

Two aspects of *Le Sacre* pertain specifically to the history of the symphony. First, this work quickly escaped its original ballet frame, and combined portions were most often performed as an autonomous orchestral piece; as such, it belongs to the genre of representative music and the symphonic poem. Second, Stravinsky demonstrated in it that radically new versions of such old components as harmony, rhythm, and linear material could be made plausible and, more important for the symphony, could be accommodated within the framework of a piece for large orchestra. Stravinsky himself later graphically demonstrated this accommodation in three pieces he specifically titled "symphony."

No earlier disruption had affected music so immediately and profoundly as World War I, probably because no previous conflict had involved all the countries active in the music scene. With the onset of the war in 1914, public concern for music went into eclipse for five or six years. This hiatus was followed by a regrouping of the forces that were to govern musical trends through the 1920s and 1930s. Most important of the changes brought about by the war was the interruption of the powerful German hegemony, not so much through animosities aroused during the war as through the emigration of most gifted German composers of the new generation, several of them to the United States. Both Schoenberg and Paul Hindemith (1895–1963) were among this group of émigrés. Although these two men were active and influential as teachers in the United States, their influence was of quite a different quality dispensed in the midst of a polyglot culture than it might have been in an indigenously German situation.

In France, Debussy's role as musical leader was taken over in the 1920s by a group of composers born mostly in the 1890s. Jean Cocteau was their early spokesman and, at the outset, six of them were grouped, almost inadvertently, by the French critic Henri Collet. "Les Six" came into being as a journalist's effort to establish a French counterpart for the Great Five in Russia, but only three of them attained stature as major composers: Darius Milhaud (1892-1974), Arthur Honegger (1892–1955), and Francis Poulenc (1899–1963).

England had been enjoying the start of a renaissance late in the nineteenth century. Edward Elgar (1857–1934), Gustav Holst (1864–1934), and Fredrick Delius (1862–1934) were leaders, all of them composers of merit, although not major symphonists. Their slightly younger countryman, Ralph Vaughan Williams (1872–1958), belongs essentially to the post–World War I generation, however; his symphonies, which are some of the first of note in the period now under consideration, will be discussed presently.

The two countries of special vitality between the world wars were to emerge as superpowers and adversaries after World War II: Russia (the U.S.S.R.) and the United States. The activity begun by the Great Five in Russia was maintained, even augmented, during the early years of the twentieth century. After the Revolution of 1917, Stravinsky, who must be included on anyone's roster as one of the three or four most significant composers of the twentieth century, became an émigré; with his detachment from his native country, he took on international

status. A large group of gifted composers did remain in the U.S.S.R., however. Two of them, Miaskovsky and Prokofiev, were among the few symphonists to carry on in the old tradition.

Sustained interest in developing an indigenous art music in the United States began just after World War I. During the earlier years, the impetus flowed from two groups: the francophiles, those who had made the pilgrimage to Paris after Melville Smith and Virgil Thomson discovered the efficacy of Nadia Boulanger's tutelage; and the Prix de Rome winners, starting with Howard Hanson and Leo Sowerby who took the first awards in 1921. A little later, several young Americans studied with various of the émigré Germans who came to take up residence in the United States. In consequence, American music of the 1920s and 1930s had quite a cosmopolitan flavor; but self-conscious Americanism, too, was professed in the works of several composers. American music of those between-the-wars decades was in somewhat the same stage of maturation as Russian music fifty years earlier.

The remainder of this chapter is devoted to a discussion of representative twentieth-century symphonic works, grouped according to the nationality of their composers.

England

Sir Edward Elgar

As has been remarked, England has been experiencing a splendid musical renaissance during the twentieth century and Sir Edward Elgar (1857-1954) is looked upon as its real progenitor: the first native British composer in 200 years (since Purcell) to achieve international acclaim and recognition. While the majority of his important works are choral—cantatas, oratorios, and the like written in deference to England's long-standing preference for vocal music—the composition on which his reputation now rests is for orchestra, the so-called *Enigma Variations*,

Twentieth-century composers:
Igor Stravinsky, Aaron Copland,
and Ralph Vaughan Williams.

originally titled simply "Variations on an Original Theme." Elgar, who had a typically English, dry sense of humor, asserted for years that the theme on which the variations were based was the counterpoint to a well-known air; he never divulged, however, whether the counter-point had actually existed or had been expeditiously improvised by him. Since this aroused avid interest among musical aficionados, hunting or guessing the "Enigma" theme became a sophisticated pastime in Edwardian days. Even as late as 1953, the American periodical *Saturday Review* staged a contest offering a prize for the most plausible solution to the "Enigma" riddle. Very likely the whole furor was a product of Elgar's whimsy; but if he had wished to assure long life to his *Enigma Variations*, Madison Avenue could have done no better.

EXAMPLE 10-1   Elgar, *Enigma Variations*, theme

The *Variations* had their première under Hans Richter in London, June 19, 1899. They open with an intriguing "questing" theme, which is followed by fourteen variations. Each bears the initials or the nickname of some friend of Elgar's — at first these were secret but were eventually divulged. Here is the list with a word about each variation.

1. *C.A.E.*: Alice, Elgar's wife, characterized by a tender, expressive passage.
2. *H.D.S.P.*: H. D. Stuart Powell, a pianist. Vigorous and athletic, parodying Powell's indiosyncracy of exercising his fingers before a concert.
3. *R.B.T.*: Richard Baxter Townshend, an actor. The woodwinds mimic his ability to change his voice to a squeaky falsetto.
4. *W.M.B.*: William M. Baker. Vigorous and headstrong with stress on trumpets and timpani.

193

5. *R.P.A.*: Richard P. Arnold. Moody with a lovely counter-melody, representing Arnold's dual personality.
6. *Ysobel*: Isabel Fitton, an amateur violist. Mostly viola solo.
7. *Troyte*: Arthur Troyte Griffith, a friend with an explosive personality.
8. *W.N.*: Winifred Norbury—a stately lady.
9. *Nimrod*: August Jaeger, who was wont to wax eloquent on the grandeur of Beethoven's slow movements.
10. *Dorabelle*: Miss Penny. Mimics her hesitating manner of speech.
11. *G.R.S.*: George Roberts Sinclair. Probably a portrait of Sinclair's bulldog.
12. *B.G.N.*: Basil G. Nevinson, a cellist.
13. * * *: Lady Mary Lugon, subtitled "Romanza."
14. *E.D.U.*: A self-portrait, since his wife called Elgar "Edoo."

At the close, the opening theme returns, exultantly, followed by a brilliant, presto finale.

Gustav Holst

Gustav Holst who, along with Ralph Vaughan Williams, carried the English renaissance in musical composition begun by Sir Edward Elgar into the twentieth century, commenced life as Gustav von Holst (1864-1934). He was the son of a Swedish father and an English mother, both of them talented amateur musicians. Holst removed the "von" from his name after the onset of World War I made things German anathema in England. He spent a busy musical life, teaching at a number of institutions including the Royal College of Music, composing assiduously, though mostly weekends, even traveling once to the United States where he lectured and conducted at Harvard and the University of Michigan (he conducted his *Planets* at the May Festival of the latter institution in 1923).

Holst's interest in matters astrological and oriental probably began during his friendship with Sir Arnold Bax, a fellow English composer and an amateur astrologist. This interest, along with Holst's devotion to English folksong, brought color to many of his works. Holst composed his suite *The Planets* during the period 1914 to 1916. A holiday in Algeria just before the onset of World War I had quickened his interest in the exotic, and his rejection for military service for physical reasons perhaps gave him more free time for compositions. Even so, *The Planets* did not receive its first performance until September 29, 1918, just before the close of the war. This informal performance was a gift from his friend Balfour Gardiner and was conducted by the distinguished Sir Adrian Boult. *The Planets* is surely Holst's most enduring work, although the composer did not consider it his best composition and continued to be astonished at its popularity. A composer should pray not to be a success, averred Holst, "then you are in no danger of repeating yourself."

A glance at the score of *The Planets* marks it as typical of much of the serious music from the period of the two Great Wars. This period was launched by the revolutionary Stravinsky ballet *The Rite of Spring*, first performed in Paris on May 29, 1913, and it lasted until well after the close of World War II in 1945.

Music of this period, if it were to receive serious attention, had to be pretentious and complicated, often showing change of time or key signature every few measures. If written for orchestra, the music usually required an enormous complement of instruments, with emphasis on such quasi-exotic members of the percussion section as gong, glockenspiel, celeste, tambourine, and so on. Also plentiful were special effects for the strings. Holst's score shows all these characteristics, and his choice of a programmatic subject — seven astral bodies surrounding the sun — is one to suggest use of exotic colors. The seven movements are discussed below.

1. *Mars, the Bringer of War* is in 5/4 time and starts with a clatter produced when all strings are played "col legno" (struck with the bowstick), supplemented by two harps, gong, and six timpani played with wooden sticks. The uneven rhythm established in these opening bars persists during much of the piece, but the other instruments of the maximum-sized orchestra enter gradually, each new part involving syncopation or some other device to complicate the total sound. Toward the end of the movement, the organ enters in chords to fill any aperture in the sound mass. Surely the ancient god of war must delight in this uproar invoked in his name!

2. *Venus, the Bringer of Peace* offers welcome relief after the bellicose opening. Various colorful instruments are used thinly, often in amiable dialogue. Percussion is limited to the gentler harp, glockenspiel, and celeste.

3. *Mercury, the Winged Messenger* is fleet and playful, having the conflicting rhythms of 6/8 and 3/4 used in close proximity. This conflict (hemiola) is intensified in a later portion written in 2/4 time for all instruments except a solo violin which maintains the primary 6/8 measure.

4. *Jupiter, the Bringer of Jollity* brings back the fuller orchestration of the opening episode, but individual parts are less harsh. A lively syncopated tune heard first in horns suggests English folksong. Other syncopated snippets in various instruments add to the jollity. Only toward the close do all instruments converge for a few passages of full orchestral tutti.

5. *Saturn, the Bringer of Old Age* is said to have been Holst's favorite movement, although the composer was barely entering middle age when he wrote it. Marked *Adagio*, the movement's sense of uncertainty and diminished vigor is generated at first by halting, syncopated chords lightly scored with harp harmonics, low flutes and bassoon. Slow-moving figments of melody in strings underlie these chords. The vigor of the piece increases but only sporadically. The harp dominates the closing section at first with animated passage work, but lapses at the close to harmonics as at the start.

6. *Uranus, the Magician*, in Holst's realization, becomes more like Merlin, a conjurer and seer, than the ruler of the world which he was in classical mythology. As opening color trumpets and trombones play a four-note motive in unison; this motive comprises the eerie intervals of the augmented fourth (the wicked medieval "tritone") and the minor seventh, each note marked by a fermata which indicates a hold beyond specified duration.

This motive is repeated, more rapidly, by two tubas. After a pause, the piece starts in earnest with bassoon chords in 6/8 time. These are reminiscent of the well-known piece *The Sorcerer's Apprentice* and the borrowing, if it is such, is surely suitable. Other woodwinds and strings enter gradually, the xylophone being added occasionally for piquancy. Toward the center of the piece are several spectacular changes of register when notes in the highest octave plunge to the lowest depths, with bass tuba and timpani stressing the drop. Eventually an orchestra tutti is achieved: the climax has a full organ glissando through four octaves, helping produce a smashing *fff* (triple forte, extremely loud). Then the movement tapers off in eerie colors.

7. *Neptune, the Mystic* returns to the rhythm of a 5/4 measure, as in the first movement, this time with the direction that the time units are to group 3 + 2. A chorus of female voices, which is reserved for the later portions of the movement, is added to the huge orchestra. Woodwinds and harp are colorful at the opening. Tension increases with very rapid passage work in harps and strings. Toward the end of the movement, the chorus enters, at first on a wordless, sustained note G. Soon the voices undertake a short imitative episode, accompanied by very light harp harmonics and woodwinds. The celeste has a few rapid runs just before the close, which is quiet, in chorus, harps, high violins, and bass flute. At the end, the composer specifies, "this bar is to be repeated until the sound is lost in the distance."

Ralph Vaughan Williams

Ralph Vaughan Williams (1872-1958), the youngest of the English symphonists to be considered here, finished his First (*Sea*) Symphony in 1910 at the age of 38. *A Sea Symphony*, by comparison with many contemporary compositions (Mahler's last symphonies and Debussy's *La Mer*, for example), seems conservative, even retrospective. But Vaughan Williams was to write eight more symphonies, the last in 1957-58, and attention must be given to a composer who evinced such confidence in a form that might have seemed anachronous. Vaughan Williams' Second (*London*) Symphony (1914; revised 1920) is an appealing, individual work; it shows that drawing back from pretentiousness and radicalism was not impossible in the years just before the Great War. *A London Symphony*, which endures as the best liked of Vaughan Williams' nine, is presented for detailed discussion here.

Before he turned to writing art music, Vaughan Williams was engaged in a number of enterprises that gave him identity with the common folk in Great Britain and with peculiarly English musical concerns. He was active in editing the new English Hymnal, and he came to admire the work of Cecil Sharp, who was the first to be seriously concerned with retrieving and preserving England's heritage in folk song and dance. Quite early, too, Vaughan Williams developed esteem for the music of the last great generation of English composers—those of the seventeenth century, including Henry Purcell and John Blow. With such a diversity of interests, Vaughan Williams became a natural eclectic. If any nationalist aura emanates from his *London Symphony,* it is no self-conscious veneer but a reflection of deeply rooted preferences, and it is never propagandistic.

Although *A London Symphony* is in the general line of program symphonies, only occasionally is it directly representative; no continuous plan invests the entire work. The symphony was first performed in 1914, but was revised after the war in 1920. In its new edition, some of Vaughan Williams' concern for the amateur performer shows in a notation he added concerning certain reductions and substitutions in instrumentation that "are possible; but they should not be used except in case of absolute necessity." He wished his music to be adaptable for performing groups of modest endowments, which links him with his forebears (Purcell wrote *Dido and Aeneas* for a girls' school) and sets him apart from some of his more arrogant contemporaries.

The *London Symphony* has four movements dispersed in the traditional order. The key scheme for the entire work revolves around G, although there are striking departures, and a number of passages are organized by nontonal means. A principal theme is likely to constitute a "thematic group" in which a succession of short, disparate ideas coalesce through the simple fact of following closely upon one another. The prevalent texture is homophonic (that is, melody with supportive harmony), although a few sections are multilinear. Even in this early work, Vaughan Williams uses some strikingly dissonant harmonies; but since the harmony is often detached from the more conspicuous melodic part, it does not necessarily disturb a pervasive sense of key.

FIRST MOVEMENT: *Lento/Allegro risoluto*

The Lento preface to the first movement (which is recalled during the Epilogue at the close of the symphony) is the only directly representative portion: most listeners will find a suggestion of London's fogs and mists in its nebulous, contemplative sound; and Big Ben's chime, sounded in harp and clarinets (meas. 31–34), seems to confirm the allusion. But the Lento also shows some definite musical traits that were to become Vaughan Williams hallmarks in later symphonies. One is emphasis on the sixth scale degree of the prevalent key (in this case, E for the key of G) and the plotting of various contexts to permit its frequent use. At times the sixth degree is used as a neighboring tone to D, the dominant; at other times it is used as a means of direct linear approach to the tonic note through the scale succession 5–6–8 (for example, meas. 13, the first violin line, D–E–G). The result of this emphasis on the sixth is a vaguely modal (nontonal) and sometimes pentatonic flavor. A second important trait in the Lento is the use of pandiatonic linear counterpoint, in which the individual lines use the tones of a diatonic scale, but with random dispersion. A third prophetic trait is the frequent injection of hemiola into the 3/2 rhythm. For example, measure 1 conforms to the indicated 3/2 grouping, but measures 2 and 3 group as for 6/4 time: $\frac{3}{2}$ ♩ ♩ ♩ | ♩ ♩ ♩ | ♩ ♩ ♩ |. Such plasticity in the metric structure is equally responsible with nontriadic pitch combinations for the general "misty" atmosphere. The juncture of the Lento with the sonata-allegro part of the movement (*Allegro risoluto*) is in a texture (meas. 35–37) made up of an E pedal point in trombone and tuba, a bare, "white-key" motive (D–G–A–D–E–G) in horns, and, over all, a multiple trill in woodwinds derived from notes of the horn motive.

The meter changes to 2/2 and the first principal theme of the *Allegro risoluto* begins emphatically (marked *fff*) after a general pause. This theme (Ex. 10-2) has as its chief melodic component a chromatic motive that is slightly reminiscent of the "retribution" motive of Strauss's *Till:* it begins on G and ends on E♮–E♭, again stressing the important relationship between the first and sixth scale degrees. Also, the E♮–E♭ suggests a mixed mode (major-minor) in the key of G. The harmonic support for this motive is a strikingly dissonant chord that can be termed an "augmented major seventh chord": E♭-G-B♮-D.

The intensity of this opening idea is gradually dissipated until, at measure 63, a quiet transitional theme is introduced in clarinets, horns, and violas, with a livelier variant to follow 12 measures later in oboes and violins (*Pochettino animato*).

A thematic group beginning at measure 112 (*Poco animato*) replaces the more

EXAMPLE 10-2   Vaughan Williams, *London Symphony*/I, meas. 38–40, Theme 1

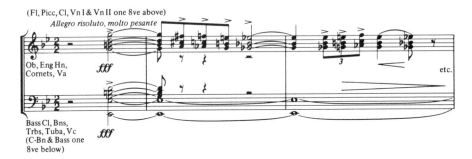

conventional second principal theme. The successive components of this group are as follows: (1) Theme 2a, an incisive rhythmic motive in brass and woodwinds emphasizing the key of B-flat major (the relative major key to G minor) and the "Scotch-snap" rhythm so common in folk song: ; (2) Theme 2b, a lively linear theme extended through constantly repeated rhythmic figures, also in the manner of folk song; (3) Theme 2c, a broader idea (*Largamente*, meas. 133ff.), scored mostly tutti. The cadence of the Exposition section (meas. 147) confirms B-flat major as the second principal tonal level; but immediately afterward the taking of G♮-G♭ in bass instruments introduces the same emphasis on the sixth degree and suggestion of mixed mode in the key of B-flat as was found in the first area in the key of G.

The Midsection of this design (meas. 166–287) reaches an important point when an area centered on C♯ emerges (meas. 202–46). The pitch C♯ is an augmented fourth (tritone) distant from G, the central key level of the movement. Vaughan Williams seems here to be reflecting the practice of many contemporary atonalists who liked to use the tritone relationship as symbolic of key negation. Since measure 202 is almost exactly the middle of the movement, the composer may well have sought to mark this point with the most radical departure in pitch from the initial keynote, G.

The Recapitulation, from measure 288 (*Tempo alla* I), recalls most of the prominent materials, with traditional transpositions. The final cadence, unequivocally in G major, is approached through the notes E♭–D–G in bass instruments, a final reference to the sixth degree and the minor mode.

SECOND MOVEMENT: *Lento*

This movement, in an unbalanced ternary (ABA′) form, has two principal thematic components. Each has certain folk traits—notably, ingenuousness and repetitiousness. Vaughan Williams' freely atonal setting for the first of these themes tends, however, to belie the folk impression. As seen below (Ex. 10-3), Theme 1 emanates from the harmonic background provided by the strings. This background comprises two sets of three minor triads moving in totally parallel motion: E-G-B/F♯-A-C♯/G♯-B-D♯: A♭-C♭-E♭ (G♯-B-D♯)/B♭-D♭-F/C-E♭-G. The folk-like melody in English horn derives its notes from the second set of three triads and thus shifts the focus, with seeming ease, from A flat minor to C minor. Such feigned simplicity is found often in Vaughan Williams' later works.

EXAMPLE 10-3 Vaughan Williams, *London Symphony*/II, meas. 1–8, Theme 1

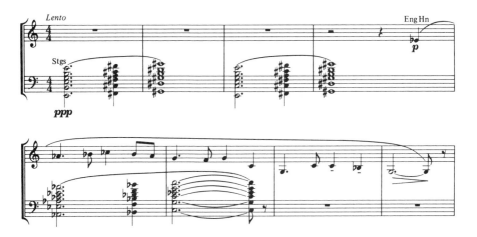

The progression of chord roots, as seen above, derives from a whole-tone scale: E-F♯-G♯(A♭)-B♭-C.

The second principal theme, given out by muted violas (meas. 59–64), is unaccompanied; thus its more genuine simplicity is not diluted by ambiguous accompanying harmony. Its rhythm again features the Scotch-snap (designated by asterisks):

THIRD MOVEMENT: *Scherzo (Nocturne)*

Those people who choose to find the *London* primarily a program symphony have suggested that the Scherzo alludes to night life in the great city—perhaps the jostling crowds of the theater district and the colorful haunts of Soho. The style of the Scherzo is traditional, with a 6/8 measure used until 9/8 takes over for the contrasting Trio section (*Poco animato*). The predominant key is D minor, used generally with the modal-sounding natural seventh degree C♮.

FOURTH MOVEMENT: *Andante con moto/Maestoso alla marcia/Epilogue*

Many suggestions of recall of elements from previous movements are found during this Finale. But, until the Epilogue, these recollections have to do with details rather than with literal repetition. For example, the prefatory *Andante con moto*, which begins on a B-flat major triad, moves through a chromatic bass line to pause, just before the Maestoso, on E♮-E♭, in reflection of many points in the first movement. And the cadence of the Maestoso section (meas. 51–53) is taken in a succession of parallel triads whose roots form a whole-tone tetrachord, reminiscent of the chords at the beginning of the slow movement. Two of the numerous motives in the Allegro section after measure 54 seem to be derived from materials in the first movement, although the reference is indirect. This Allegro section also sees the temporary restoration of G as the implied key.

The Finale has only one conspicuous and fully formed new theme, which begins with the *Maestoso alla marcia* (Ex. 10-4). This is given out by clarinets, bassoons, violas, and cellos and derives its pitches from a combination of the Dorian and Mixolydian modal scales, both of which use the flat seventh degree: C–D–E♭–E♮–F–G–A–B♭. The E♭-E♮ juncture, occasioned by the combined modes, recalls numerous earlier instances of these notes used consecutively.

EXAMPLE 10-4   Vaughan Williams, *London Symphony*/IV, meas. 15–22 principal theme

Once this theme has been stated and developed, the Finale becomes a potpourri of new and recalled materials, until the principal theme is recalled briefly after measure 119. The section just ahead of the cadential Lento (meas. 163–71) recalls the chromatic motive of Theme 1 of the first movement. The cadential Lento itself recalls two more elements of the first movement: the harmony Eb-G-B♮-D on which the *Allegro risoluto* began and, posed over it, Big Ben's chime in G, played by the harp. The Epilogue restores the contemplative mood of the opening Lento but not its actual material until measure 200, where the movement begins to relax toward the final *niente*.

Among Vaughan Williams' seven symphonies written after the *London*, the Fourth, in F minor (1935), is the best known and perhaps the strongest. Although twenty years had intervened between the two works, several of the traits in the *London* are found again in the Fourth Symphony. But a number of new idioms should also be cited, for example: (1) themes based on successive melodic fourths—at the beginning of the second movement and in the principal theme of the Scherzo; (2) use of imitation to vary the texture, most notably in the *Epilogo fugato* that closes the piece; (3) expansion in the use of devised scales, produced most often by combining tetrachords from two modes. In the second movement, for instance, the first theme (meas. 10ff., first violin) is derived from a scale that combines the lower tetrachord of the Lydian mode with the upper one of the natural minor: F–G–A♮–B♮ C–Db–Eb–F.

Lydian   Natural minor

The total mood of the Fourth Symphony is one of confidence and vitality. Unfortunately, it was written at a time when the serialists and atonalists had the public ear, and it seems to have faded from the common repertory.

Benjamin Britten

Benjamin Britten (1913-76) has been a major influence in sustaining the musical renaissance in England. Unfortunately for the present prosperity of the symphony, Britten seems not to have found it a very useful form, for his only full-scale symphonic composition is a youthful work: the *Sinfonia da Requiem*, first played by the New York Philharmonic in March, 1941. The bizarre and unfortunate circumstances surrounding the early history of this work may well have disenchanted the composer with the type. The *Sinfonia* was commissioned in 1939 by the Japanese government to mark the 2,600th year of the reigning dynasty in Japan. Britten, a lifelong pacifist, chose to base his work on portions of the Latin Mass for the Dead, although no musical material is quoted and only a general mood is suggested by the titles of the three movements: "Lacrymosa," "Dies Irae," and "Requiem Aeternam." The Japanese government rejected the work as unsuitable. Because of the time of its premiere, it has come to be associated with the darkest days of World War II and the composer's horror of all conflicts.

Britten's musical language for this symphony is unmannered, even simple as compared with that of many slightly older composers of the day. Each of the three movements, which are played without pause, is basically tonal. Each concludes with a sonority based on D, although the consonance of the D major triad is withheld until the very close. The texture is predominantly linear; when chords do intervene, they are likely to be structured with interlocking fourths, fifths, and seconds. Lines are often conspicuously noncontiguous, such as the craggy part for alto saxophone after rehearsal numbers 3 and 9; since the surrounding parts here move stepwise and in parallel motion, the contrast is striking. An instance of genuine pointillism (notes widely spaced to encompass different octaves) occurs in harps and bass strings at the opening of the "Requiem Aeternam," as support for a tranquil melody in flutes. The "Dies Irae," Britten's grim testament to the tragedy of all war, commences with the interval of a fourth (B♭-E♭) sustained in muted trumpets, overlaid by the note A taken as a piercing

figure (𝄞♩ , etc.) in flutes and piccolo. A *saltando* (with springing bow) figure in strings soon enters, and the strings, covering the full gamut of special effects, are the backdrop for the entire movement. At *Alla marcia* (No. 26) the sound is notable. A heavy march beat of four quarters to the measure is maintained in strings, the staggered entries taken down-bow with appoggiatura; this is reinforced by harps with piano, and each fourth beat is stressed by bass drum. Over this background rides an anguished line in alto saxophone. The bitter, acrimonious temper of this "Dies Irae" contrasts notably with the well-known settings by Verdi and Berlioz, who appear, in retrospect, to revel in the dramatic aspects of Judgment Day.

Britten's two remaining compositions called "symphony" belie the traditional concept of the form, but this is true of many other so-called symphonies of the 1940s through the 1960s. These works are the *Spring Symphony* (1949), a setting of twelve poetic texts for soloists, chorus, and orchestra; and *Cello Symphony* (1964) written for Mstislav Rostropovich, which is virtually a cello concerto.

France

Darius Milhaud

Two members of the group still called, rather casually, *Les Six* have proved to be prolific symphonists. Darius Milhaud (1892-1974) postponed the writing of his first symphonic work until he was a middle-aged, mature composer, with much of his youthful experimentation either discarded or assimilated into a strong, characteristic musical language. Milhaud's First Symphony, which was performed in 1940 by the Chicago Symphony, is a work in four movements featuring materials gleaned from his native Aix-en-Provence. In his Second Symphony (1946), Milhaud used five movements, as follows: "Peaceful," "Mysterious," "Sorrowful," "With Serenity," "Alleluia." Milhaud's Fourth Symphony (1948), is clearly programmatic, with four movements designated "Insurrection," "To the Dead of the Republic," "The Peaceful Joys of Liberty Regained," and "Commemoration 1948"; but the patriotic subject was made inevitable by the fact that the French government commissioned the work to commemorate the centenary of the revolution of 1848.

Milhaud continued to find the symphony a useful form. In 1962, his Twelfth ("Rural") Symphony was performed by the San Francisco Symphony. An important asset of his music is that he continued to communicate successfully with even conservative audiences, probably through the elegant, direct address of his very French style. His music often appears to be as chromatic as Schoenberg's; but he generally organizes pitch into clearly opposing "systems," as, for example, two key levels, or a modal versus a pentatonic texture. Of most consistent interest is the vitality of his rhythms, which explore every intricacy without losing contact with a basic, audible metric grouping.

Arthur Honegger

Arthur Honegger (1892–1955) was born in France of Swiss parents in the same year as Milhaud and was also a member of Les Six. His first orchestral piece to receive wide recognition was in reality a symphonic poem, *Pacific 231* (1924), which portrays in gloriously robust fashion Honegger's fascination with the giant American locomotive. The motor-rhythms, the wide, jerking intervals, and the bold instrumentation fascinated Americans in particular, as did also Honegger's candid assertion: "I have always loved locomotives passionately. For me they are living beings whom I love as others love women and horses."

Honegger's First Symphony came in 1930 and his last (Fifth) in 1951, only four years before his death. His Symphony No. 3 (the "Liturgique") is a product of the last year of World War II. As did Benjamin Britten in his wartime symphony, Honegger took the mood for each of the three movements from a liturgical text. The opening, "Dies Irae," from the Mass for the Dead, is a heavy, marching movement, which uses a modified sonata-allegro design. Three palpable themes, all military in character, appear during the Exposition section—at rehearsal numbers 1, 4, and nine bars after 4. As the climax of the Recapitulation, in lieu of Coda, Honegger introduces a new, sustained theme in trombones and tuba (11 bars after rehearsal number 19), overlaid by pervasive eighth-note rhythm in other parts. "De Profundis Clamavi" ("Out of the depths I cried to thee," Psalm 129) illustrates the symphony's cyclic qualities, since several motives from the first movement are recalled in transformed guise. The general contours of the sustained theme from the first movement might be detected in the lavishly embellished flute line at the close. "Dona Nobis Pacem" again uses a marching theme at the start, in bass clarinet and string basses, to a constant quarter-note beat in piano (bass register) and drums. A contrasting part featuring the chromatic glissando in winds and piano intervenes three times. A quiet Adagio concludes with the embellished cyclic theme sounded now in the fourth octave register by piccolo.

Honegger's Symphony No. 4 (1946) is called *Deliciae Basilienses* (*Delights of Basel*) because it quotes tunes traditional to that Swiss region. His Symphony No. 5 is subtitled *Di tre re* because each of the three movements concludes on *re* (D) in the bass register—as was true in Britten's *Sinfonia da Requiem.*

Olivier Messiaen

One of the most radical of modern French composers and a broadly influential teacher is Olivier Messiaen (1908-92). His mystic concepts, which derive as much from Eastern mysticism as from orthodox Catholicism, have made his music seem abstruse, difficult for the layman to comprehend. His single symphony, *Turangalîla* (roughly translated, *Love Song*) of 1946–48 is so vast a work as to intimidate any but the most intrepid listener. The performance time for the ten movements is close to an hour and a half. Required in addition to the largest conventional orchestra are piano (with a truly formidable part) along with glockenspiel, celesta, and vibraphone; all manner of exotic percussion instruments; and the *Ondes Martenôt,* an electronic instrument providing timbres that dominate the passages in which it is used. Discussion of a work of this length and complexity is outside the scope of this book; but the composer has furnished a lucid and revealing analysis for the recording by the Toronto Symphony Orchestra, which may be consulted by those interested in the early employment of electronic means.

Germany and Austria

Paul Hindemith

Of all the major composers of the first half of the twentieth century, Paul Hindemith (1895–1963) alone evolved a personal style that adjusted without constraint to the exigencies of traditional forms. A significant number of his compositions are sonatas and string quartets, but three of them are symphonies. Hindemith was a first-rate performer, and he appeared often in this country as soloist on the viola or viola d'amore. His lifelong experience in playing string instruments (as opposed to piano for most composers) probably induced the linear orientation of his musical texture.

Hindemith's opera, *Mathis der Maler* (*Matthias the Painter*), completed in 1934, immediately aroused both interest and controversy. A suite of three episodes from this opera, bearing the designation *Symphonie,* has turned out to be the most durable of all Hindemith's compositions. While this fine orchestral piece is thoroughly autonomous and has no real need for a program, familiarity with the circumstances of the opera plot can make the music especially communicative. Hindemith's Mathis was Matthias Grünewald, a sixteenth-century German painter, whose altarpiece for the Church of St. Anthony at Isenheim may still be viewed in the museum at Colmar, south of Strasbourg, France. Three panels of the altarpiece inspired the three movements of the Symphony *Mathis der Maler.*

FIRST MOVEMENT: *"Engelkonzert"* (*"Angel Concert"*)

This music forms the prelude to the opera, and it returns midway in that work, during Mathis's inspiration for the "Angel concert" panel. As the opening piece of the symphony, the format of the music is close to that of the traditional symphonic first movement with slow introduction.

The clue to Hindemith's plan probably lies in the text of the opening folk tune given out by trombones early in the introduction: "Es sungen drei Engel" ("Three angels were singing"). During the main portion of the movement, three characteristic themes are presented. The implication is, no doubt, one theme for each angel; but the ideas occupy the places in the design assigned traditionally to the first and second principal themes and a closing theme. The simple, powerful folk song of the introduction remains the dominant force in this first movement, however, and it serves to fuse disparate elements during sections of contrapuntal development.

The introductory portion of "Engelkonzert" is a model of Hindemith's rational structure. During the preliminary 8-measure phrase, a strong suggestion of G minor/major is generated, and the pause is taken on a chord of interlocked fifths with D and F♯ in the outside parts, suggesting dominant harmony. Immediately following this, the "Es sungen" theme (Ex. 10-5a) enters in trombones but in the key of D-flat with supportive linear counterpoint for that key in strings. At measure 16, the key implication slips away from D-flat when the cadence note

EXAMPLE 10–5   Hindemith, Symphony *Mathis der Maler*/I, principal themes

a) "Es sungen drei Engel," meas. 9–16

b) Theme 1, meas. 39–47

c) Theme 2, meas. 98–106

d) Closing theme, meas. 135–39

is D♮ rather than the anticipated D♭. Throughout the movement, the mainly "white-key" passages tend to imply G, while those with profuse accidentals center around F-sharp, or C-sharp–D-flat.

Beginning at measure 230, the "Es sungen" theme enters in a 3/2 measure, thus conflicting metrically with the continuing 2/2 grouping in the rest of the orchestra; the result is that this powerful theme sounds even more prominently than usual.

SECOND MOVEMENT: *"Grablegung"* (*"Entombment"*)

This mournful episode parallels the Pietà panel of Grünewald's altarpiece. Several musical devices produce, symbolically, the sense of weight and tension. (1) The high range of the orchestra is curtailed, so that even violins and flutes play mostly in the first and second octaves. (2) Various combinations of the long-short metric foot (♩ ⅞♪⠄♩ ⅞ ♫⠄♩. ♪ etc.) permeate the texture. Such rhythms have long been associated with dramatic or tragic episodes, especially in opera. (3) Intervals of the fourth, fifth, and second predominate in both linear and harmonic structure; the brighter consonances of the third and sixth are sparsely used.

The movement is essentially binary (ABA'B), with the opening idea (meas. 1–9) recalled (meas. 26–33) in expanded form and a changed pitch context. The concluding cadence is exceptionally broad and shows Hindemith's predilection for plagal endings. At the conclusion of the part designated A' (meas. 33), an

F-sharp major triad in full orchestra occurs. During the remainder of the movement, the note C♯ is constantly present, and final repose is taken on the C-sharp major triad, so that a massive IV–I cadence occurs, beginning in measure 33.

THIRD MOVEMENT:
"Versuchung des heiligen Antonius" ("Temptation of St. Anthony")

St. Anthony, patron of the Isenheim church for which Grünewald painted his altarpiece, was a fourth-century hermit who lived in the Egyptian desert. The devil, in order to frighten him and drive him from his solitude, "would appear to him in the most hideous shapes; but the Lord made him formidable to his foes; one word from his mouth reduced these prodigies to nothingness."[1] Grünewald painted a vivid scene in which swarms of horrid creatures surround and torment the venerable hermit.

Hindemith has captured the spirit of the painting in gruesomely evocative sound, and listening to this movement for its descriptive qualities alone is rewarding. The climax of the movement is attained after a fugal passage scored mostly for strings (meas. 407–66). The traditional Latin sequence for the feast of Corpus Christi, "Lauda Sion Salvatorem," enters in upper woodwinds, above the fugal subject in first violins (meas. 467–518). This is followed by a closing phrase captioned "Alleluia." The implication is that St. Anthony dispelled his devils with the ringing old words of faith: "Zion praise the Savior, praise thy shepherd and king, in hymns and canticles."

Since this is one of Hindemith's finest movements, a few comments about musical structure are needed. An 18-measure introduction is in the style of a cadenza-recitative, basically for strings and marked *Sehr langsam, frei im Zeitmass* (Very slow, free in tempo). This introduction suggests two sections but without break: measure 10 starts a recall of the material of the first 6 measures, but a fifth higher and augmented by addition of woodwinds. The lines, derived freely from twelve-tone pitch material, have contours of the "cheironomic" kind found so often in music of this period: that is, they move as if by hand (*cheir*) signals—up, down, up, up, and so on—with complete casualness about the pitches used. Since the movement closes in a clear D-flat cadence, it is significant that the starting pitch of the first cadenza is A♭ and the first point of arrival, marked by longer notes, is D♭ (meas. 3–5). Each segment has a highest and lowest pitch.

At *Sehr lebhaft* (Very fast), a brilliant rondo in 9/8 time begins. Massed strings carry a simple, legato theme, while woodwinds and brass provide a continuous and agitated rhythmic background: ♩♪ ♩♪ ♩♪ | etc. After measure 87, a slightly contrasting section develops, although the basic rhythmic pulse continues. At *Langsam* (meas. 193) begins a section of total contrast with a strong theme in violas. The fast tempo is restored at measure 235 and the pace is more and more frenzied until it is "regimented" by the first fugal entry (meas. 407). The climax and conclusion achieved with the traditional "Lauda Sion" chant, cited above, acquires a semblance of cyclic form when the notes of the opening cadenza-recitative are underlaid to the passage as an ostinato in horn.

[1] From the entry for the Feast of St. Anthony in the *Saint Andrew Daily Missal.*

Arnold Schoenberg

No other composer of the twentieth century has had so pervasive an effect on his peers as Arnold Schoenberg (1874–1951). Born only ten years later than Richard Strauss, he inherited the heavy burden of the German Romantic tradition, and his earlier works, such as *Verklärte Nacht* (*Transfigured Night*, 1899), amply reveal that heritage. Schoenberg's important solution of the dilemma of unorganized chromaticism was the "twelve-tone system," alternatively called "serialism," which has had its effect on every composer of consequence in the past seventy years.

After the mid-1920s, much of Schoenberg's music was ordered within the twelve-tone system. A detailed résumé of the premises of that concept is not possible here. But a general remark about it will help to explain the scarcity of works for large orchestra in Schoenberg's later repertory. Serialism is, in its very essence, a linear system, and it tends to be effective to the degree that the composer is able to concentrate on particularities. The symphonies and symphonic poems current during Schoenberg's youth (those of Brahms and Mahler, for example) are structured to stress exactly opposite qualities: vertical structure and simultaneities, as well as the broad gesture at the expense, often, of detail. Having such symphonies in his immediate background may have caused Schoenberg to reject the full-scale symphony as a vehicle for a big serial work, although his *Variations for Orchestra*, Op. 31, is at once a serial piece and one of the composer's most admired compositions.

At any rate, Schoenberg wrote only two compositions that have place in this account. Because his Chamber Symphony No. 1, Op. 9 (1906), emphasizes the singularity of each instrumental part, it becomes more chamber music than orchestral piece: the woodwind choir is comprised of fifteen soloists, and the strings, detached from their traditional role as the foundation of the orchestra, play mostly in special effects—pizzicato, harmonics, *col legno*, and so on.

Schoenberg's Chamber Symphony No. 2, Op. 38, straddles the earlier and the closing portions of the composer's career: the first movement was composed in 1906 and reorchestrated in 1935; the second movement was completed in 1940; and the entire work was first performed on December 15 of that same year, by the New Friends of Music in New York. The second movement is not a serial work and many portions are candidly Neoclassical in derivation.

The orchestra, which has the conventional Classical instrumentation with addition of piccolo (alternating with second flute), marks this piece immediately as not chamber music like the First Chamber Symphony. Scrutiny of almost any of the tutti passages (in the first movement, meas. 32ff. and 81ff., for example) confirms this, for it reveals consistent doubling among instruments, which is rarely found in a genuine chamber piece. In this case, the title "Chamber Symphony" refers to the use of fewer players in the string choirs, and perhaps to the modest length and general unpretentiousness of the work.

The first movement, Adagio, sounds through-composed, despite the recall of initial material (flute, meas. 95); a few seminal components permeate the texture of the entire piece. Two of these concern pitch: (1) the semitone—in pairs of notes (meas. 1, all parts, and throughout) or occurring in chains up to eight (meas. 14–17, first cellos); (2) "affective" falling intervals, generally sixths, fifths, and fourths. Three other pervasive ideas concern rhythmic texture: (1) the anacrusis (upbeat) and consistent off-beat entries; (2) syncopation; (3) traditional contrapuntal artifice, as at measures 74 and 75 where the bassoon part is in diminution of the English horn and clarinet parts.

For people who find Schoenberg's sound abstruse, the lack of audible punctuation, generated by the very devices cited above, is a deterrent to clarity. The linear texture of most Schoenberg music is closer to that of a contrapuntal composition of Bach or Josquin than it is to the clearly phrased fabric of Classical and most Romantic music.

Each of the movements of the Chamber Symphony No. 2 is tonal: the first movement shows six signature flats; this implication of E-flat minor is confirmed by the opening interval (B♭–E♭) and by the concluding cadence. Often during the course of the piece, the Phrygian second (F♭) is present, as part of the network of semitones. In contrast, the clear G major for the opening of the second movement (*con fuoco*) sounds extraordinarily bright, its one-sharp key signature far removed from the six flats of the first movement. The instrumental color serves to heighten the brightness: a thin background of pizzicato in strings, a staccato part in bassoon, and an accented figure in cellos is overlaid with fragmentary linear parts, mostly in woodwinds. The linear parts throughout this piece reveal far fewer semitones than in the first movement; falling intervals, however, are still plentiful. The melodic figures for both horn and trumpet provide bright splotches in the texture (especially, meas. 205ff. and meas. 219ff.). Rhythmic complexities, generally involving hemiola (meas. 334ff., 352ff., 428ff., for example), infuse sinuousness in the metric structure. At measure 445, the key signature changes to that of the first movement (six flats), and the final 45 measures have more frequent semitones and affective intervals than the earlier portions of the movement. These two somewhat indirect allusions impart a slight sense of *da capo* and subtly link the two disparate movements.

The United States

Howard Hanson

The first American composer to achieve international stature as a symphonist was Howard Hanson (1898-1981). Hanson's First ("Nordic") Symphony was completed while he held his Prix de Rome: it was performed at Rome on May 17, 1923, with the composer conducting. The success of this symphony seemed to presage a golden age for music from American composers of the new generation, and the next two decades were to see a heartening interest in the works of a sizable group of talented younger men. As for Hanson, he was able, from 1924 onward, to exert powerful influence on the direction of American music through his post as director of the Eastman School of Music and through his establishment there of the American Composer Concert Series. For forty years, this institution gave serious readings to new works of young American composers.

The "Nordic" Symphony is a fervent, skillfully constructed work, one that compares favorably with many symphonies already discussed, such as those of Sibelius and Dvořák. Its conspicuous devices were to be those of many American composers of the next two decades:

1. Both linear material and harmony are likely to show modal derivation. The reference to one or another of the Church modes is generally quite candid (as compared with the more indirect suggestion observed in works of Vaughan Williams, for example); and stress is given to the member of the modal scale that marks it as different from the traditional major or minor. The opening theme in cellos at the start of the "Nordic" Symphony is typical. Here the mode is transposed Dorian, taken from E as *finalis:* E–F♯–G–A–B–C♯–D♮–E. The two characteristic Dorian notes are the raised sixth (C♯) and the natural seventh (D♮). As this 4-measure theme takes shape, the apex is reached at the juncture D–C♯, and the fourth-measure cadence stresses the low seventh degree with the melodic progression F♯–D–E.

2. Frequent changes of time signature are used. At the opening of the first movement, there are three changes in the first 8 measures: 5/4, 9/4, 5/4, 6/4; similar fluctuation persists throughout the movement. This mannerism produces a kind of "eye music" that gives an outward semblance of complexity. In most cases, metric change is unnecessary and Hanson himself discarded such mannered writing within a few years.

Howard Hanson conducting his Sixth Symphony at Philharmonic Hall. New York, in 1968.

3. Change of tonal focus is generally accomplished by direct juxtaposition, typically involving movement of a semitone. At measures 14 and 15 a change of focus from E to B-flat is so effected; at measures 57 to 58, a change from A-flat to C-sharp involves partly enharmonic, partly stepwise progression.

4. The orchestration is in the German style. Several writers have found the influence of Sibelius, but it should be pointed out that Hanson, too, is a Nordic, and, in any case, Sibelius's orchestration is German-oriented. The most conspicuous characteristic of German (as opposed to French or Russian) scoring may be seen in almost any passage for full orchestra, where the various choirs fuse through sharing similar material. The result is a composite timbre that could suitably be designated "the orchestra." The following passages in the first movement of the "Nordic" Symphony illustrate such a tutti: measures 24ff., 50ff., 89ff.

5. At the opening of the third (and final) movement of the "Nordic" Symphony, the tritone interval F♯–C♮ is given prominence, and Hanson is thus in tune, for a few bars at least, with contemporary atonalists who used the tritone as a symbol of key negation.

Hanson's activities as teacher and conductor continued to exert a strong influence on American composers in the decade before World War II. That his symphonies continued to be respected is attested by the five that followed the "Nordic": they were written over a span of four decades, and each was composed as the result of a specific commission by a major American symphony orchestra. The Boston Symphony commissioned the Second ("Romantic") of 1930 and the Fourth ("The Requiem") of 1944. The Third of 1938 was written for the NBC Symphony, and the Fifth ("Sinfonia Sacra") of 1955 for the Philadelphia Orchestra. During its 125th anniversary year, 1967–68, the New York Philharmonic commissioned and first performed Hanson's Sixth Symphony.

The decade of the 1930s was a heady time for young American musicians. Many talented composers were finding what seemed then to be an indigenous, expressive style as they sought consciously to escape the bonds of their European training. An important aspect of musical activities in the United States during the 1930s was that American composers found several persuasive, articulate spokesmen in such fellow composer-critics as Henry Cowell (1897–1965) and Virgil Thomson (1896-1989). An examination of concert programs of leading American orchestras reveals a heartening number of premiere performances of new works in the years just before and during World War II. A large number of the works were candidly entitled "Symphony"—an affirmation that this form, despite its vicissitudes, was still viable. The Americans seem, in fact, to have found it preferable to the symphonic poem, perhaps because they had come to it but lately.

Many of the European composers who had produced the most important earlier twentieth-century compositions had emigrated to the United States by the 1930s. Their more sophisticated, but often more jaded music acted as a foil and perhaps as an incentive for the younger Americans.

Some American composers who were especially active during the 1930s are cited below, and a representative early symphony from each is discussed.

Walter Piston

Although Walter Piston (1894-1976) was trained mostly in Paris, his compositions are not widely known outside the United States. But he has long been a respected and influential voice in American music. From his teaching post at Harvard, as well as through his textbooks and articles, Piston has made clear his admiration for orderly, lucid, rational music. This point of view is the most tangible reminder of his French training.

His Symphony No. 1, completed in 1937 and performed the next year by the Boston Symphony Orchestra, is one of his best. In the discussions of this and other symphonies that follow, attention is concentrated on the distinctive features of each.

For the first time in any work examined thus far, rhythm, rather than pitch or key, emerges as the vital factor in the comprehensive plan of the Piston Symphony No. 1. In this three-movement work, the outer movements are marked by a relentless, driving "beat" maintained in continuing notes of equal duration; not only does the middle movement lack such a beat, but even the normal measure groupings tend to be obscured by syncopation or other types of rhythmic displacement. The first movement in particular is organized by the temporal element.

FIRST MOVEMENT: *Andantino quasi adagio/Allegro*

During the introductory Andantino (meas. 1–28), the beat is maintained in eighth notes, so grouped within the 4/4 meter as to cloud it, and to give the illusion of shifting stress. The grouping for the first few measures is characteristic:

At the Allegro, where the meter changes to 3/4, the beat is again in eighth notes, but the tempo is twice as fast as in the Andantino ($\downarrow = \downarrow$). The grouping of eighths varies in different instruments, but the violins carry the predominant part with eighth notes typically dispersed as follows (meas. 29–34):

As can be observed in the above, the group increases from two, to four, to seven. Ultimately (meas. 39–41), the group increases to nine eighth notes; after measure 47, a continuous grouping of six eighth notes to the measure, maintained for

11 measures, generates the first sense of climax. The beat becomes thinner and more discursive between measures 60 and 79, when linear material gradually takes over. As the movement continues, the presence or absence of the eighth-note beat and its dispersion are the most conspicuous audible means of textural distinction. Melodic materials, which are simple and freely twelve-tone, play a secondary role in organizing this energetic movement.

SECOND MOVEMENT: *Adagio*

The total absence of the pervasive, relentless beat is the prime characteristic of this movement. The entire Adagio (only 157 measures) tends to sound continuously composed, through rhythmic displacement and elision of sections.

A 5-measure melody given out by English horn, unaccompanied, at the beginning is typical of many themes in contemporary works. The notes that comprise it give contour, but do not suggest affinity with any particular key or even harmony, as is the case with traditional themes in Classical and Romantic music. Such melodies are often called cheironomic (see p. 207), and in such themes, a highest and lowest pitch can give a sense of delimiting the span. Temporal values are more than commonly important in suggesting emphasis, cadence, and other necessary elements of melodic syntax. Similar contour melodies in this movement are found in violins (meas. 12–17 and 27–32), horn (meas. 45–53), and flute (meas. 64–73, 84–93, and 96–102).

The harmonic structure is thin and often nontriadic, with intervals of fourths, fifths, and octaves given prominence through dispersion of the notes. The final cadence is taken on an F-sharp minor triad approached by a succession of C♯s in the double basses (meas. 143ff.), but this is the only point of strong tonal orientation.

THIRD MOVEMENT: *Allegro con fuoco*

The relentless beat is restored at the very start of this movement and is maintained through many sections to the end. Eighth notes again are the pervasive value, but now they are twice as fast as in the Allegro of the first movement, since the time signature is 2/2. This beat has twice undergone "duple diminution": the proportion between the Andantino and the Allegro of the first movement was ♩=♪ ; between that Allegro and the Finale, ♩=♩ . Piston has sought recourse in time-honored (fifteenth- and sixteenth-century) metric devices to give this symphony an unusually clear sense of direction and climax.

At the beginning of the final movement, however, the most audible beat lies in the continuing quarter notes in bassoons and double basses. These quarter notes tend briefly to cover the eighth-note movement in upper strings. As the movement progresses, the eighth-note movement comes to dominate, and after about measure 14 it is seldom suppressed.

The final cadence is a model of simplicity but is taken through nontonal means. C, the note of termination, is first proposed openly at measure 319 in bassoons, double basses, and timpani. Gradually a digressive passage takes over, but a clear C is restored at measure 333 and maintained to the close.

Roy Harris

During the decade before World War II, Roy Harris (1898-1979) was often described as the most "American" of our native composers. Perhaps Harris's birth in Oklahoma, then the newest of our states, along with his scanty early training in music, helped foster that image. Whatever its origin, this early judgment has not been sustained by eventual, more considered opinion. For Harris is not conspicuously different from other American composers of his generation—in his musical language, his intention, or, in the end, in his accomplishment. Indeed, one might question whether there is, or ever was, an "American" style in music. But regardless of that, Harris's mature music shows a striking affinity for such old-line contrapuntists as Josquin and Bach; he himself has pointed out this honorable lineage.

The first important performances of Harris's works occurred just at the start of the 1930s, and he became interested in many of the devices that engaged his American contemporaries: studied use of the Church modes for color, flexible metric organization, and, above all, dependence on the temporal factor to systematize and vitalize his music. Several compositions of the 1930s exploited Harris's interest in time. The best known is his *Time Suite* (1936), in which the various units are "One Minute," "Two Minutes," and so on.

Harris's *Third Symphony*, known alternatively as the "Symphony in One Movement," had its premiere performance at Boston in February, 1939. A young student at Harvard wrote a review of the work for *Modern Music* in which he expressed a "strong desire to hear the Harris again, because it greatly excited me." The young man, whose name was Leonard Bernstein, was to have ample opportunity to do this, for he has conducted many performances of this and other Harris compositions.

The designation "in one movement" may be seen to indicate that no portion is autonomous, as is the case with the various movements of most traditional symphonies. But the subsections of the composition are discernible even though junctures are well disguised. The fact that portions follow one another without obvious interruption imposes a relentlessness on this comparatively brief (about seventeen minutes) piece.

The composer's announced plan for the symphony is helpful chiefly because it indicates the mood he imputes to each portion, and the "Section" designations used below follow the composer's outline.

SECTION I: ("Tragic") *Con moto*

This totally linear episode, which serves as an introduction, is scored for instruments of dark color: violas, cellos, basses, bass clarinet, and bassoon. The focal pitch is G, although all twelve semitones are introduced, gradually and in relaxed rather than pointed fashion.

SECTION II: ("Lyric") *Measures 57 to 208*

The score has no new verbal direction here, but the section takes on a more active character through the quickened tempo, which is almost twice as fast: ♩ = 72–80 mm., virtually ♩ = ♩ as compared with the introduction. The whole episode sounds continuously evolutionary; the few changes from duple to triple meter are scarcely perceptible and the indicated adjustments in tempo are subtle rather than overt. Harris's affinity with sixteenth-century Flemish composers is evident in the overlapped sections and the sense of unbroken flow. Two points of increased intensity (meas. 89–91 and 186–93) keep the portion from somnolence.

SECTION III: ("Pastoral") *Measures 209 to 415*

Most of this core section of·the symphony is constructed on an undulating background of arpeggios in the strings; above these occur successive melodic segments in various wind instruments. After measure 271, the vibraphone adds an occasional chord for color. The texture changes at measure 387 when the string arpeggios are replaced by simple eighth-note figures in woodwinds, underlaid with pizzicato strings.

SECTION IV: (Fugue-"dramatic") *Measures 416 to end*

The use of a fugal finale is in the tradition of many of Harris's illustrious (and obviously admired) forebears: Beethoven, Mozart, and Bach, as well as Renaissance contrapuntists. Even the double time signature 3/2 6/4, with its suggestion of hemiola, shows potential recourse to typical sixteenth-century metric complexities. The fugal subject, given out by strings with occasional reinforcement from brass, makes immediate use of the metric dualism shown in the time signatures:

The first section gives prominence to brass and, especially, timpani. At measure 432, the rhythmic figure ♩♩♪ 7 (marked with an asterisk in the rhythmic design of the fugal subject shown above) begins to intrude in the string ·background; this figure and its retrograde (7♪♩♩) become more and more pervasive up to measure 503 where a lyric episode ensues. The climax of the fugue accumulates gradually, but measures 567 to 634 constitute the real apex through the prominence given the brass.

The matter of tonality in this fugue is adroitly handled: at the outset, the fugal subject gives prominence to members of the D major triad; although the lengthy working-out of the fugue ranges from nontonal to polytonal, the final cadence of the movement is taken on the G minor triad. Hence a widely separated V–I gesture for G minor encloses the entire fugal finale. The immediate approach to the cadential G minor triad is, however, through the single pitch C♯, which recalls the level stressed during Section III, the core of the work, and also the tritone interval.

Samuel Barber

Samuel Barber (1910-81) wrote a number of symphonic poems and symphonies. His Symphony No. 2 offers an opportunity to contrast an American wartime symphony with those of Britten and Honegger. It was commissioned by the United States Army Air Force, first performed by the Boston Symphony Orchestra in 1944, and broadcast to the Armed Forces throughout the world by shortwave radio. Each of the three movements is a candidly independent piece, uncommonly cogent because it is developed from such simple materials.

FIRST MOVEMENT: *Allegro non troppo*

The four seminal ideas of this movement are distinctive primarily through their rhythmic qualities. Two of them occur during the first 8 measures and can be viewed as constituting Theme 1. Theme 1a (meas. 1–5) has a syncopated motive stated in upper woodwinds and piano; at measure 4, upper strings enter with a related motive but in faster values:

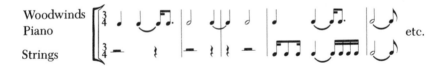

Throughout this motive, the only intervals used, in both linear and vertical structures, are seconds and sevenths; the resultant sound is arresting and incisive. Theme 1b (meas. 6–8) combines the piano with bassoons and uses a slightly less energetic rhythm and less intense melodic intervals, so that a sense of relaxation after Theme 1a ensues.

A new section (meas. 29, *A tempo, agitato*) adds a new rhythmic idea— sixteenths in low strings that group varyingly for shifting metric stress:

At measure 57, a slight variant of this develops: $\frac{3}{8}$ ♩ ♪♪♪♪♪♪ , and these two patterns in alternation dominate the remainder of Area I (to meas. 100). Area II has other, but derived, background rhythms; throughout the movement, melodic material tends to be subverted by these obsessive rhythmic figures. Recapitulation and coda, respectively, are suggested when Theme 1a enters at measure 360 and again 23 measures short of the close.

SECOND MOVEMENT: Andante, un poco mosso

As was the case in the first movement, the piano has an important role in this Andante. Whereas it was employed for percussive effect in the Allegro, here it is used mostly in sustained style. Theme 1, at the outset, is given to piano in its low register along with muted cellos and basses. This theme is chorale-like and entirely white-key derived until violas enter at measure 5 with a complicating line that shows G♯, F♯, and C♯; the slight tension recedes when this complicating line drops out after 5 measures, replaced by an English horn melody that is again white-key derived, but spaced in wide intervals. Such gradual change in the character and focus of long melodic lines, which is accomplished without disturbing the effect of continuous flow, is a characteristic trait in Barber's best music. Even the change of key signature to six flats (meas. 50) is prepared during 6 measures when the white-key lines gradually acquire flat inflections, and the legato temper of the music is undisturbed by the conversion.

THIRD MOVEMENT: Presto, senza battuta/a tempo

The brilliant opening flourish for violins and violas, in equal but unmeasured (senza battuta) eighth notes, is reminiscent of Vivaldi. At A tempo, the principal theme of the Finale is lined out by horns, underlaid with a counterpoint derived from the opening flourish. The entire Finale is in the general style of a rondo because of the frequent alternation of materials. A first climax comes in a brilliant fugal episode for strings at about the middle of the movement; but a new section of unsystematized recall and alternation (Allegro risoluto, come prima) brings back nonimitative texture and makes the fugal episode the core rather than the climax of the Finale.

Aaron Copland

No American composer has matched the ability of Aaron Copland (1900-90) to communicate with audiences of every degree of sophistication at every stage of his career. His success may stem from his willingness to write unpretentious works as well as major compositions: listeners accustomed to the Copland "sound" in, for example, Appalachian Spring or one of the Hollywood scores are able to go along with it easily in the symphonies. Sometimes the very unpretentiousness of his style has tended to obscure the solid compositional craft that supports it.

Copland's Symphony for Organ and Orchestra was performed in 1925 with Nadia Boulanger at the organ. Its somewhat noisy, mannered sound, typical of much American music in those days, is attested by Lawrence Gilman, who wrote in the New York Herald Tribune, "Mr. Copland is a child of his time. Naturally enough, his speech is the atonal, polytonal speech of today." Although he wrote a number of tone poems and a Short Symphony, which was heard only arranged as a sextet (1939), Copland did not write a full-scale symphony again until 1946. His Symphony No. 3 was performed that year by the Boston Symphony Orchestra.

The Symphony No. 3 has four movements: *Molto moderato, Allegro molto, Andantino quasi allegretto,* and *Molto deliberato,* thus conforming to Classical models more closely than many works of the day. A few comments about the first movement, which is surprisingly tonal, may suggest why Copland's music is so immediate. Although three easily identifiable thematic components emerge during the early portions of the *Molto moderato,* they are less conspicuous than the pitch plan in organizing the movement. Up to rehearsal number 4, the texture is clearly rooted in E realized as a mixed mode. During the three bars preceding 4, an easy change of focus to A minor (via F) is effected. At number 5, the focus changes to E-flat, which is the maximum distance in terms of tonality from E, the key of the opening, and also a tritone away from A. E-flat and A alternate as tonal centers until number 15, where E is restored, eventually with allusion to opening material.

The *Allegro molto* is a Scherzo with Trio, full of what have been called Copland's "nervous" rhythms. The Andantino exploits metric flexibility, both through changing time signatures (5/4, 3/4, 2/4, C) and, more subtly, through free organization within the measure. The *Molto deliberato* is the most conventionally organized of the four movements: it uses a sonata-type design, and like the first movement, is clearly laid out in tonal areas. The central portion has quotations from Copland's *Fanfare for the Common Man* (1943).

Russia

There is something paradoxical in the enthusiasm Soviet composers of the interwar generation evinced for the symphony. Living in a society that was bent on rejecting many traditional institutions, these composers chose the most convention-laden and restrictive of musical forms for a sizable proportion of their large works. Their activity was responsible in no small measure for keeping the idea of the symphony viable.

Nikolai Miaskovsky

Nikolai Miaskovsky (1881–1950) is a name not even included in many Western music history books, yet he was a vital link between the nineteenth-century nationalists and the Russian composers of the past two generations. Soon after World War I he took a prestigious post at the Moscow conservatory, where he influenced directly a number of talented younger composers, including Khatchaturian and Kabelevsky. Miaskovsky wrote 27 full-scale symphonies, the largest repertory since Haydn. The symphonies are skillfully crafted and easy to listen to. They are scarcely works in the mainstream of symphonic literature, but they had considerable influence on Russian taste during the 1920s and 1930s, when Soviet audiences were seldom in touch with the compositions of such radical composers as Schoenberg and Stravinsky. Miaskovsky's continuing confidence in the symphony must have influenced his younger contemporary, Sergei Prokofiev (1891–1953), who wrote seven symphonies.

Sergei Prokofiev

Sergei Prokofiev (1891-1953) was fortunate in completing the superb training offered at the St. Petersburg Conservatory in 1914, just before the Russia he had known disintegrated. On graduating, he received the Anton Rubinstein Prize (a grand piano), although his interest was already turning toward a career as a composer. He remained in Russia until 1918, when the terrors of the 1917 Revolution made a longer stay there unwise. During the early years (1915-16) of World War I Prokofiev had composed his *Classical Symphony* which has become one of the best known orchestral works of the twentieth century. He wrote his little masterpiece at a crucial juncture in his development as an artist—a time when his early determination to become a virtuoso pianist (he was a formidable prodigy at an early age) was in conflict with his ever increasing interest in composition. Whether the *Classical Symphony* was written as a fond parody of symphonies of Mozart and Haydn has never been clear, despite the apologia Prokofiev himself provided in his autobiography. The symphony has the Classical complement of four movements: *Molto vivace, Gavotte, Larghetto, Allegro.* Each one is succinct, dry, and amusing in its apparent burlesque of Classical traits. Although the total mood is closer to that of an eighteenth-century serenade such as Mozart's *Eine kleine Nachtmusik* than a full-scale symphony, two consequences may have surprised the composer more than anyone else. This youthful work caught on in a way that tended to divert attention away from Prokofiev's subsequent serious symphonies, and later it seemed as much a caricature of a certain labored type of "modernism" current during the war as it was a parody of Haydn and Mozart.

Prokofiev spent the first eight years after World War I traveling widely to London, Paris, Japan, and America. He was warmly received, primarily as a concert pianist. But he returned permanently to Russia in 1933, where his international experiences probably made more difficult his conformity with the Soviet proscriptions concerning art.

Prokofiev's Fifth Symphony, completed in 1944 but premièred a year later, was a landmark work for the composer. Most importantly, it was his first fully successful symphony. Each of the previous four was marred by qualities most apparent to the composer himself. The year 1944 was a relatively happy one in Russia, for, with the German invasion repelled, the country was free to live a more normal life. When it became known that Prokofiev planned a new symphony, the official Soviet critics urged that it carry a political message relating to Russia's victory; but the composer resisted. "It has none," he said, "unless a hymn to the human spirit could be called such." The opening movement is presented with exultation, its opulent, darkly colored first theme apparently so cherished by the composer that he used it again in his masterpiece *Cinderella.* A delightful *Allegro marcato* follows, its lyric mid-section again prefiguring parts of *Cinderella.* An agreeable *Adagio* has a curious recollection of the opening figure of Beethoven's "Moonlight Sonata." A bridge passage leads to the finale (*Allegro*) filled with trochaic (long-short) rhythmic figures, until a grand coda in the manner of nineteenth-century Romantic symphonists brings the work to a close.

Prokofiev's Fifth Symphony was an impressive success at its première in Moscow on January 13, 1945, with the composer conducting. Today, fifty years later, it retains much of the quality that brought it such kudos at its first hearing.

Twice in his later career as a symphonist Prokofiev sought refreshment in writing orchestral pieces for young audiences. His *Peter and the Wolf* (1936), a "fairy tale" written for narrator and orchestra, has delighted listeners of all ages and has helped familiarize them with the instruments of the orchestra. In the early plans for his Seventh Symphony, written during the last year of his life, Prokofiev reverted to the simpler frame of his earlier, most successful works. Although this symphony exceeded its intended address to the young, it shows, even in its eventual form, unpretentiousness and preference for the then unfashionable principles of tuneful themes, clearly delineated, energetic rhythms, and unabashed reliance on key for organization.

Dmitri Shostakovich

The most successful Russian symphonist of the twentieth century was surely Dmitri Shostakovich (1906-73). His Symphony No. 1, composed when he was nineteen, is among the best works of its type written during the post–World War I period. It brought Shostakovich immediate attention from audiences in the West, and, even today, it remains a refreshing, vital piece.

Shostakovich apportioned his Symphony No. 1 in the traditional four movements, three of them predominantly lively, but the third one a contrasting Lento. The key of F minor/major is affirmed in the final cadences of the two outside movements; the second movement confirms A and the third, D-flat. These constitute the kind of tonal "mirror" around F found often in works of nineteenth-century composers: D♭ F A. Having provided this entirely conventional large framework for his symphony, Shostakovich proceeded to draw consistently on freely chromatic materials to enrich the texture, even during statement of themes. Generally, its rhythmic character is the distinctive trait of any thematic component.

FIRST MOVEMENT: *Allegretto/Allegro non troppo*

This relatively short movement (311 measures) is refreshing because, while it shows the routine plan of a modified sonata-allegro, the themes are unpretentiously breezy and the orchestration uncluttered. It would be tempting to conclude that Shostakovich, too, was reacting to the pretentiousness of many turn-of-the-century works; yet Shostakovich himself was to lapse into ostentation a few symphonies later.

The Exposition section presents three themes and develops them minimally. The first (Ex. 10-6a) is given out by trumpet, but with the counterpoint of bassoon as an integral part of the idea. Theme 2 (Ex. 10-6b) enters in clarinet at *Allegro non troppo* and bears a strong enough resemblance to Theme 1 to be considered a derivative. Theme 3, in flute, enters at measure 97 and has the lyric character

EXAMPLE 10-6   Shostakovich, Symphony 1/I, Themes 1, 2, 3

a) Theme 1, meas. 1–5

b) Theme 2, meas. 58–61

c) Theme 3, meas. 97–105

of the Classical second theme (Ex. 10-6c). While none of the themes is clearly tonal of itself, Theme 2 suggests F minor through the supportive harmony in strings, and the bass line in Theme 3 suggests A-flat.

As the Midsection begins (meas. 145), three quartets of soloists formed from the first violins, second violins, and violas reduce the string sound. The particularity of texture that results is a distinctive effect. At measure 209, a mirror Recapitulation commences, and the three themes as shown above recur in the order of 3 (meas. 209), 2 (meas. 259), and 1 (meas. 289).

SECOND MOVEMENT: *Allegro*

This lively episode, in mood a Scherzo with Trio (*Meno mosso*, meas. 37), uses the piano to augment the percussion choir. The writing for all instruments is brilliantly idiomatic, but the piano in particular gives a brittle articulateness to the frequent transitional scale passages (meas. 13, 95–96). The piano also takes its turn at stating the Scherzo subject (meas. 22, 97ff.), and its two-octave white-key glissando provides a trenchant new timbre (meas. 106–07). In the glittering final statement of the Scherzo subject (meas. 113ff.), the piano joins the upper strings and woodwinds for a massive unison, while horns provide counterpoint in the theme of the Trio converted from the original 3/4 time to the 4/4 of the Scherzo. Such compositional acrobatics by the nineteen-year-old Shostakovich foreshadow the formidable musical architecture he was to develop in later symphonies.

THIRD MOVEMENT: *Lento/Largo*

In design, this Lento has a conventional ternary (ABA') form. Its first theme (oboe, meas. 1–16) is organized through several standard twelve-tone principles for ordering pitch. Largely by means of the phrasing in the oboe part, this theme (Ex. 10-7) sounds continuously composed throughout its 25-measure span, and the pitch content could seem, to the casual scrutiny, miscellaneous.

EXAMPLE 10-7   Shostakovich, Symphony 1/III, meas. 1–16, Theme 1

But this theme is made plausible and saved from randomness by at least three maneuvers: (1) The opening bars are recalled, virtually intact, at measures 9–10; and measure 5 foreshadows measure 13. Such unsystematized recall of small elements unifies without being restrictive. (2) Eleven of the twelve semitones of the octave have been employed by measure 5; far from being haphazard, these pitches generate a strong affinity for F. (3) The entire line has a contour suggested by its highest and lowest points and by adroit placement of notes of conspicuously longer duration.

In the middle portion of the design (Largo, meas. 47) the oboe presents a brief new theme having the march-like character often associated with Soviet music, but the background in strings is freely chromatic.

FOURTH MOVEMENT: *Allegro molto/Lento/Allegro molto*

This movement, less imaginative than the preceding three, has an introductory portion of 30 measures; then, at restoration of the *Allegro molto* there is a sprightly but stereotyped rondo-like theme. This is recalled in a later portion of the design, after introduction of a contrasting idea (*Meno mosso*, meas. 109) that was actually prefigured at measure 91, before the change of tempo.

This Finale is marked by persistent changes of key signature and tempo. The shifts of key signature are frequently superfluous; but by giving this movement the outward look of complexity, the young Shostakovich probably sought to show he was not out of tune with his age. For, as Howard Hanson remarked with some disillusionment, "the Nineteen Twenties marked the heyday of the atonalists and any composer under seventy-five who wrote an undisguised triad was considered a traitor to the cause."[2]

Shostakovich wrote fifteen symphonies in all, but never, it seems fair to state, has he managed to fulfill the bright promise of his First. The Second (1927) and Third (1930) are clearly patriotic works, since they bear the subtitles "October" and "May First." In the Fourth (1936), Shostakovich attempted a return to absolute music, but he withdrew the work after Soviet critics branded it academic and reactionary. (It was, however, played in 1962.) The Fifth through the Ninth returned to patriotic subjects and a parallel naïveté of structure. His Symphony No. 10 has an interesting but traditional origin, since many motives derive from the German letters at the start of Shostakovich's name: D, S (Es = E♭), C, H (B♯).[3] The immediate product is the figure D-E♭-C-B, which strongly implies the key of C minor. Symphony No. 13 (1961), scored for bass soloist, male chorus, and orchestra, uses words by the young Soviet poet Yevtushenko and is a passionate appeal against anti-Semitism.

Shostakovich was, first of all, a symphonist, as his fifteen works of this genre attest, although he also wrote vital music in most of the important large forms—

---

[2] Quoted in New York Philharmonic-Symphony Program Notes for January 17–18, 1946.
[3] The letters of Bach's name (B♭ A C B♮) served several composers as a motive. Also, a number of Russian composers saluted their patron, Belaiev, with a quartet based on an acrostic sounding his name: B♭ A F (Be-la-ef).

operas, concertos, and chamber music. His Tenth Symphony, completed in 1953, was a landmark, not only for the composer but also for the Russian people since 1953 was the year of Stalin's death. For Shostakovich, the Tenth Symphony marked his emergence from the ignominy of his second (1948) castigation by the Communist Party's Central Committee. At last he felt released to write as his own muse dictated and, as usual, he wrote with great speed. Of the Tenth Symphony's four movements the first three seem to reflect the tragedy of the composer's five-year ostracism. One critic has commented that they reflect, successively, three moods of tragedy: pensive, fierce, and wistful. The finale is an anomaly, seeming to emerge in a spirit of forced gaiety, with little affinity for the three movements that have preceded it. The close does, however, confirm the concentricity around the pitch E posed at the opening of the first movement and powerfully authenticated by a glittering E closure.

In the opening Moderato a simple quarter-note figure, emerging dourly in bass strings, permeates the early part of the movement, which gradually increases in intensity. Although the opening clearly suggests the key of E minor, the movement soon becomes freely chromatic. Return to the initial level of E is postponed until the final cadence which is recessive, approached through a duet in two piccolos.

The second movement, Allegro, bursts forth in an abrupt change of mood, projecting a march-like theme. Throughout the movement, the kind of "two" rhythm characteristic of so much Russian music provides continuity. Woodwind instruments and segments of the string choir often move in paired thirds or sixths with dissonant brass harmony in between. Many long passages are propelled by repeated motives, or by figuration over a pedal point. The final cadence to B-flat is taken at maximum dynamic strength, anticipating in its means the brilliant E cadence of the finale.

The third movement, Allegretto, returns to a gentler mood, beginning with a dour little air in the first violins. English horn and clarinet provide sporadic doleful moments. A pouding midsection leads to a recall of the opening theme. The cadence is quiet and recessive.

The finale has an Andante as preface to the Allegro, the main portion of the movement. This finale is virtually autonomous, giving the impression of an afterthought. Shostakovich remarked that, though it was finely wrought and in good taste, he feared it was somewhat distracting in mood. Be that as it may, the movement is a marvelous concoction for the orchestra. Toward the close it is marked by Shostakovich's "motto" blared forth in horn and trombone: the notes D-Eb-C-B. This is a kind of acronym of Shostakovich's name, using the German letter indications of the pitches of the motto: D-Es-C-H. The composer used this signature in many other works.

Igor Stravinsky

Almost everyone looks upon Igor Stravinsky (1892–1971) as one of the three or four giants of twentieth-century music, and many regard him as peerless. Stravinsky comprehended and used, during his 65-year creative life, several radically different styles. These ranged all the way from the flamboyant, bold manner of his first ballets, through the Neoclassicism of his middle years, to the modified serialism he used toward the end of his life. But transcending the manner of any particular work or period is an essential vitality that is unique and unmistakable: it is the sound of Stravinsky.

Stravinsky's First Symphony, Op. 1, written in 1907, is a youthful exercise, interesting mostly for its promise. His Symphony of Winds (1921) is a strong, individual work that, like his Symphony of Psalms (1930), uses the term "Symphony" in a special, somewhat loose context. Stravinsky's two works that indubitably belong to this account are his Symphony in C (1940), which is a masterly piece in the Classical tradition, and his Symphony in Three Movements (1945). Both these symphonies were written after Stravinsky had emigrated from Russia.

The Symphony in Three Movements is eclectic in the sense that it recalls many of the sounds and techniques that its composer had found useful or expressive during the past. It was written for the New York Philharmonic-Symphony Society "as an homage and appreciation of my twenty years' association with that eminent musical institution." The symphony was performed at an All-Stravinsky Program on January 26, 1946, with the composer conducting. In his brief note of dedication, Stravinsky pointed out that the symphony has "no program nor is it a specific expression of any given occasion." (However, Ingolf Dahl, himself a composer of distinction, provided a set of illuminating notes for the Philharmonic program. Reading them will prove useful for anyone with special interest in this symphony.)

The orchestra required for this piece is large. It includes peripheral woodwinds to extend the pitch compass (piccolo, bass clarinet, contrabassoon) and, in the percussion choir, both piano and harp, along with bass drum. A few general comments about the score will point out several sources of Stravinsky's characteristic "sound." Especially important is the scarcity of devices for clouding the pulse at the start of a measure; syncopation tends to be within rather than across the measures, and the consistent use of the anacrusis and other types of off-beat entry tends to strengthen the measure accent when it does arrive. A major source of Stravinsky's bright, articulate sound is the French type of scoring, which delineates the individual orchestral timbres rather than merging them. A third feature, in the first movement in particular, is the casualness in occasional recall of elements; Stravinsky appears to be subverting any suggestion of sonata design.

FIRST MOVEMENT: *No verbal indication, but* $\quad \downarrow = 160$ ($\downarrow = 80$)

The first movement unfolds with the kaleidoscopic diversity of a series of ballet episodes. But a few elements that do recur (in an unsystematized framework) take on the quality of seminal ideas. The first of these is the rising scale passage of measure 1; this is always given to strings reinforced by woodwinds and, generally, by piano glissando. This scale passage is the principal instigation of the first 14 measures, but it is not heard again until measure 388 and also 399; in each of these cases there is but a single entry, which prevents any sustained sense of recapitulation.

In his notes, Dahl cites the interval of a third with its inversion, the sixth, as another seminal element. This is prominent first in the horn motive (meas. 22) and is transferred to the bass strings 10 bars later. A surprising number of chords in the piano are structured from thirds—seventh chords or triads with an added dissonant note. At measure 81, thirds are plentiful in the eighth-note figures of upper strings, as well as in the bass part, which consistently alternates the notes G and B. At measure 132, a brief figure in cello recalls the horn motive, but with the intervals reversed so that the sixth precedes the third. The piano part beginning at measure 150 (also measures 209 and 216) is derived from the horn motive, as are sporadic melodic figures throughout the piece. The relentless, pounding rhythms, which are Stravinsky hallmarks from his ballet period onward, are plentiful in this movement. Sections beginning at the following measures are typical examples: measures 20, 31, 81, 148 (horns and piano), 327 (recall of 31), 378 (a climax, recalling 148), and 391 (pizzicato in low strings).

SECOND MOVEMENT: *Andante*

The opening accompaniment figure in strings derives from the first-movement rhythm heard initially at measure 148 (horns); the association of F♯ with F♮ (cello-bass pizzicato) gives the figure pungency. Over it, flute and harp cooperate in a succession of motives with G major orientation. At measure 54 (*Piu mosso*), a theme in the very low register of the flute turns out to be an embellished version of the harp's repetitious figure, measures 25 to 33. But at measure 54 the harp accompanies the flute with a part essentially in G-flat (F-sharp), which recalls the F♯-F♮ conflict of the opening measures. In this movement, a discernible Recapitulation (meas. 92) suggests ternary design.

THIRD MOVEMENT: *Con moto*

The Finale is even more of a collage than the first movement: sections are uncommonly brief and succeed each other with studied unreasonableness. (Beethoven invoked a similar heterogeneity in several of the movements of his last quartets—the first movement of Opus 130, for example.) In such structure, elements are interdependent primarily because they are so clearly not autonomous. Identifying sections of parallel, or special, character may prove useful in apprehending this bold piece.

I. Sections of march-like character
   1. Meas. 1–27: This opening episode constitutes a small three-part design (ABA′) with measures 13 to 17 as the contrasting phrase. The outside sections feature a heavy four-pulse, with the piano the predominant timbre. The iambic ("Scotch-snap") rhythm occurs in a number of contexts:

   2. Meas. 60–67 and 77–84: Both of these are episodic.

3. Meas. 88–98: Here a theme in bassoons seems related to the motive of thirds and sixths in the first movement as well as to the opening portion of this movement.

4. Meas. 172–76 and 183–end.

II. Material based on repetitious figures and surrounding tones

1. Meas. 13–17 (*B* in first March section): Both second violins and violas have continuing figures surrounding a single pitch: second violin = E–F–G–F–E–F, etc.; viola = C–D–E–D–C–D, etc. This sinuous type of line might have been suggested by the letter-writing episode in Mussorgsky's *Boris Godunov*.

2. Meas. 28ff.—first bassoon: Here G is the surrounded note, but the line is less obvious because the interval of a fourth occasionally intervenes.

3. Meas. 50 ff.—first violin: Here B is the surrounded note.

4. Meas. 88ff.—all accompanying parts: Here E is the center of movement.

III. Figures based on disjunct lines or pointillism (octave displacement for one note of an interval)

This type of line is most conspicuous in the section beginning at measure 105 (*L'istesso tempo, tranquillo*). Here the first 8 measures are transitional, the chief components being the interval of a tenth in bassoon and complementary parts that are very widely dispersed (oboe, trombone, tuba, bass strings). The principal material, which arrives at measure 113 (*Alla breve*), sounds like a fugue subject, but is aborted before anything like a consistent exposition is achieved. This subject is shared by piano and trombone (Ex. 10-7) and features both disjunct lines and pointillism.

EXAMPLE 10-7   Stravinsky, Symphony in **Three Movements/III**, meas. 113–23, fugal subject

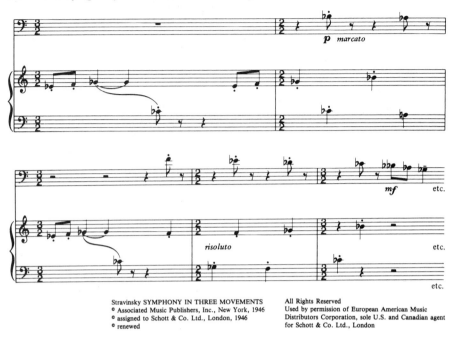

The final cadence of the movement, which occurs after a general pause (meas. 196), is the essence of simplicity. The notes that are to comprise the terminal chord (Db-F-Ab-Bb-Eb) are present during the active figuration that precedes it; the implied chordal dualism is most apparent in trumpets, which have Db, plus Eb-Ab, and violins, which have the same pitches stressed by measured tremolo. The sense of cadence comes from a simple cessation of motion and intense prolongation of the final chord, which retains both dissonant members (Bb and Eb), but is solidly rooted on Db.

Some Perspectives

The role of seer is always a dangerous one, and anyone who ventures to predict the ultimate judgment concerning art works of his own time is probably brash or foolish. Even so, it is impossible to close this account of the symphony without a few observations concerning the last few decades.

During that time, music in general has been subject to a bewildering infusion of new ideas. Because large bodies move slowly, the orchestra has experienced more difficulty than most mediums in assimilating the radically new. As a result, the symphony has not been a favored form for avant-garde composers; most of the symphonies of the 1950s and 1960s have been written by composers who were also writing them a decade or so earlier, and Americans have favored the symphony more consistently than any other group. However, Shostakovich had his Fourteenth performed during 1971; and when this turned out to be, in essence, a song cycle, it emphasized the long road the symphony has traveled since its "sonata for orchestra" days of the eighteenth century.

The New York Philharmonic Orchestra, conducted by Loren Maazel.

Three lines of development have seemed to be major influences in shaping important music of the 1950s and 1960s. The first is the adoption by so many composers of the serial technique to order pitch. After more than a half century of development, use of the twelve-tone row is not necessarily mannered, and composers have learned to construct their fundamental row so as to produce the kinds of sounds they need for any particular piece. The principle of serialism has been extended, too, to such other elements as rhythm and dynamics. While orchestral pieces like the symphony are less easily organized by serial means than pieces for smaller groups, excellent symphonies by Roger Sessions, Ross Lee Finney, and Roberto Gerhard (to name but a few) demonstrate that an accommodation is possible.

A second important development is the use of the electronic tape, a totally prepared and mechanical means, to supplement (or supplant) the timbres available from conventional instruments. The tape may be seen as the climax of a tendency that began late in the nineteenth century: the usurpation by the composer of the performer's prerogative to interpret freely. In works by Bruckner, Mahler, even Debussy, for example, virtually every passage is provided with a profusion of interpretive markings, to the annoyance of the performer. The logical end of this explicitness is the tape prepared by the composer, which totally eliminates both human performer and variance in realization. The orchestra and the symphonic forms have scarcely welcomed the electronic tape into their fold, but a kind of uneasy cohabitation has been achieved in a number of works.

Any arresting idea is likely to breed a reaction. "Aleatory" (random or unprepared) sound, a development of the late 1950s, may be seen as the antithesis of the prepared tape. In restoring important rights to the performer, aleatory passages recall a condition of most music before about 1750: the page seldom indicated the total sound and performers routinely supplemented the written part with such extemporized factors as realization of the basso continuo, embellishment of the melodic line, and cadenzas. When a composer includes an aleatory passage in a contemporary piece, he indicates an interval during which some or all performers are directed to play at will; if the composition is for orchestra, the conductor suspends his beat during the aleatory passage. The aleatory technique brings exciting prospects for expanding the temporal scope of a composition without necessarily increasing its complexity. Performers trained to respect "the page" have had difficulty in adjusting to the idea of improvisation, but time can remedy this.

With such enlivening new notions afloat, we can but await the advent of a Beethoven or Bartók who can assimilate the new means and prove them to be communicative. Meanwhile, we may well direct attention toward a group of composers active in Poland during the 1950s and 1960s. In 1960, Krystof Penderecki (b. 1933) wrote his *Threnody for the Victims of Hiroshima*, which quickly became well known. Written for strings alone, the *Threnody* evokes radically new sounds from this most traditional of orchestral choirs. Extremes of pitch are pushed to the borders of noise when the performer places his finger as high as possible on the string, close to the point of crossing with the bow; exact pitch is largely abandoned. The result is an anguished tone color totally suited to the lamentable inspiration of the piece. Every possible variation in bow attack and pizzicato is included, resulting in an appreciable augmentation of the dynamic palette achieved by Mahler and Bartók. Elsewhere, tone-clusters (groups of contiguous pitches between given pairs of notes) give an illusion of stratified texture as they progress in broad bands of sound. Penderecki's temporally derived formal plan imposes order on the infinitely varied timbres.

The *Threnody* brought avant-garde Polish composers immediate and worldwide recognition. Penderecki's older peer, Witold Lutoslawski (1913-94), provided during the 1960s a number of compositions for orchestra that might herald a renaissance of the symphony in Poland. His *Venetian Games* of 1961 was Lutoslawski's first venture into aleatory writing. Despite its title, this composition has closer affinity with the Classical symphony than most new works: it has four movements and employs conventional instrumental forces, although often in unconventional ways. The composer says he used "Games" in his title because of the aleatory passages and "Venetian" in deference to the site of its premiere. The first movement alternates composed and aleatory passages, whereas the second uses the piano in an improvisatory manner. The flute is the leader in the even more extemporaneous third movement, with the other instruments providing discreet (but free) support. In the Finale, an aleatory core is prefaced by a "straight" introduction; the apex of the movement is formally composed.

Proof that Lutoslawski's *Games* might herald a trend lies in the same composer's Symphony No. 2 (1966–67). It is significant first that the conventional term "Symphony" is used; and examination of the score shows the instrumentation to be that of the large, Bruckner-Mahler orchestra, with the addition of piano and celesta. A further scrutiny of the score might cause a certain disquietude for any conductor or performer nourished exclusively on Haydn through Debussy. There are, first of all, the frequent aleatory sections, which need remain troublesome only until the idea of improvised playing is accepted. Lutoslawski's sign for an aleatory passage, $\bigtriangledown$, corresponds to the last downbeat of the conductor before the *ad libitum* portion begins. Notation is simplified by at least two means: (1) an accidental applies only to the note it precedes, so that ♭♩♩ designates B♭ and B♮; (2) note heads are eliminated during repetition of the same pitch. Some of the indications in the score are revealing; for example, "The duration of the fermata is decided by each player, thus movement of parts will not begin at the same time," or "This tempo concerns only the wind instruments. The strings continue independently." The symphony is cast in two large units entitled "Hesitant" and "Direct." The effect of this piece is electric, especially when performed by a group of uninhibited young

Aleatory passages from *Venetian Games,* by Witold Lutoslawski.

players of the present generation. Aleatory music is "now" music, and the young are conditioned for it by the improvisatory nature of jazz and other popular types of music.

In closing this account of the symphony during the twentieth century, it seems appropriate to speak of three composers who have, during the two decades prior to the time of this writing (1994), composed symphonies that, for quite different reasons, have captured the interest of both critics and "lay" listeners. The earliest composed of the works is the Symphony No. 3, subtitled "Symphony of Sorrowful Songs," by Henryk Górecki (born in Poland, 1933). It was written in 1976 and has established an extraordinary vogue and familiarity, chiefly through its recordings.

Górecki's Symphony No. 3 has three movements, all marked *Lento*, and is a striking example of minimalism, a style favored by a number of contemporary composers. Minimalism may be seen as reaction to the hyperactivity of most music of the last century or so, music the vitality of which depends on a continuous series of musical "events." Górecki's symphony uses a minimum of pitches, repeated interminably over a constant pedal figure, which is seldom relieved. The "events" of the first movement comprise only the rising dynamic, and the apex of the movement is the entry of a soprano voice, prepared by several lengthened tones and a bell tone from the percussion. The voice has its own rising dynamic that peaks in a high-pitched portion of consummate anguish. The movement falls away from this climax, moving slowly and deliberately to the monotone texture of the beginning.

The second and third movements continue the *Lento* tempo of the first, but are propelled mostly by the expressive voice part, which is dispersed *seriatim*. In both movements, the orchestral bass is the audible support for the more active upper parts, but minimal pitch content is a continuous factor.

*   *   *   *   *   *   *   *

The First Symphony by John Corigliano (born 1938) is the next work to be cited in this closing statement concerning the symphony form as it is emerging in this last decade of the twentieth century. Corigliano wrote this First Symphony in response to a commission for a piece to honor the centennial of the Chicago Symphony Orchestra. It was first performed by that group March 15, 1990, with Daniel Barenboim conducting. The composer wrote an informative essay to accompany a recording of the work made at that first performance. Many of the comments that follow are based on that essay.

This symphony, in three movements and an *Epilogue*, was inspired by the death from AIDS of many of Corigliano's close friends. He compares his composition to the famous quilt, each panel of which memorializes a person who has died of AIDS. The first movement of the symphony is titled "Apologue: of Rage and Remembrance" (an *Apologue* is an allegorical narrative usually conveying a moral). The movement ("Ferocious") begins with the note A sounded on the open strings of violins and violas (this note will conclude the symphony). Soon the full orchestra enters with a slow beat from the timpani, suggesting a kind of "musical heartbeat." The dynamic and tempo increase, to climax with violins in their highest register.

A middle section of the ternary (ABA) form features an offstage piano playing Isaac Albéniz's *Tango*, which was a favorite piece of the dead friend who is being memorialized. Subtly the first section returns, climaxes with a "near hysterical" repetition of a dissonant chord, and stops suddenly without preparation. The movement resumes and maintains a *forte* dynamic until a final dying away. The close recalls the *Tango*, then ends on a forlorn high A.

The second movement — *Tarantella*—suggests the "South Italian dance played at continuously increasing speed." It was said that by dancing it a kind of insanity caused by the tarantula bite could be cured. However, Corigliano informs that the friend being memorialized died as a result of AIDS-induced dementia.

The third movement — *Chaconne: Giulio's Song*—memorializes a college friend, a cellist, with whom Corigliano often improvised. He says that discovering an old tape they had made in 1962 yielded the idea for the extended cello solo that follows an opening played by cellos and basses and the chords of the *Chaconne*. A series of short motives recalling other dead friends and a return of Giulio's theme are interrupted and overpowered by a solo trumpet playing the motto note A. Other brasses join in, then all the strings, finally two sets of chimes tolling the 12 tones, all with the persistent rhythm of a funeral march. This dissolves slowly into a solo cello playing an A, which introduces the final *Epilogue*, a fantasy of recollection resembling those used often by nineteenth-century composers.

*   *   *   *   *   *   *   *

Alfred Schnittke (born 1934), who is the third and last composer to be cited in this "coda" to the history of the symphony, is perhaps the most frequently played of any living composer — but in Europe. In the United States, acquaintance with his music is just now (1994) gaining momentum. Schnittke once described his ancestry thus: "I feel I am a German, a Russian, and a Jew." He was born in Engels in central Russia, but now lives in Hamburg, Germany. His family had no interest in music. His own musical orientation commenced late: when he was twelve years old, he acquired an accordion and serious interest in music followed through lessons in piano and composition. Despite this late beginning, Schnittke has come to embrace in his own music virtually every style in the history of Western music, with music of the Baroque period perhaps the most influential (the harpsichord is virtually his *signum*). Schnittke is now spoken of often as "heir to Shostakovich," and we recall that Shostakovich was first of all a symphonist who left a legacy of fifteen symphonies at his death in 1975. Schnittke spent his earlier years as a composer in Russia, surviving the strictures of the Soviet League of Composers, which group proscribed any but "optimistic" music. He was a young, impressionable composer during Shostakovich's prime and had just arrived at the peak of his own creative life at the time of the older composer's death.

During the month of February 1994, Schnittke's Sixth Symphony had its New York première with the National Symphony, Mstislav Rostropovich conducting. A few days later, the New York Philharmonic with Kurt Masur conducting gave Schnittke's Seventh Symphony its world première. Like all his recent works, the

Seventh is a leak and desolate episode, full of empty pauses followed by angular "melodies," especially for winds and brass. The first movement is chiefly for strings, the second for winds and percussion. The third movement is the most amply scored but is full of strange sounds and unpredictable points of arrival. No doubt Schnittke's music reflects the aura of this last decade of the twentieth century.

*   *   *   *   *   *   *   *

As we confront the last decade of the twentieth century, the most urgent problem is a practical one. The symphony orchestra as we know it and as it has developed through two centuries is a permanent ensemble with relatively fixed instrumentation. Composers from Haydn through Stravinsky have simply accepted this and written their orchestral music accordingly. Composers of the last twenty years or so have been less willing to be governed by such invariableness and have shown a marked preference for a flexible or mixed medium. A means must be found to make the symphony orchestra less rigid, perhaps by organizing smaller ensembles within the permanent large body, and playing other works than the massive productions that use the total complement of players. Complicating factors such as job security for orchestral musicians and public taste make a solution difficult. But compromise is the stance of our day, and all interested persons—composers, conductors, performers, and listeners—must give a little if music is to thrive and progress.

A Postscript

The progress of the symphony over some two and a half centuries, from modest beginnings about the mid-eighteenth century to the grandiose productions of such composers as Mahler and Messiaen — all of this has been discussed in the foregoing parts of this book. Quite a different development, touching all kinds of Western music, *including* the symphony, remains to be mentioned in this Postscript. Perhaps this could be called *retrograde* development — that is, re-acquaintance with music written before the eighteenth century and its effect on some compositions of our own time. It all started with Bach, probably instigated by Mendelssohn's prophetic performance of J. S. Bach's *St. Matthew Passion* at Leipzig in 1829. The fascination with music's past grew from that occasion, until, by the mid-twentieth century, modern editions and transcriptions of works of most major composers of a time as remote as the Renaissance and the Middle Ages back to the twelfth century were available for study and performance.

In this country, especially in the half century since the end of the Second World War, groups have been formed specifically for the performance of early music, groups called variously Collegium Musicum, Pro Musica Antiqua, and so on. Such ensembles are now part of the curriculum of every major school of music, and a number of professional groups are conspicuous on the concert circuit. Not surprisingly, the less familiar sounds heard in this music have engaged the interest of a number of contemporary composers, who welcome these unfamiliar sounds as a means of revitalizing their own scores. One of the most enthusiastic and successful of these "borrowers" is Charles Wuorinen, an American born in New York in 1938. And one of his recent compositions inspired by one of these early works has been chosen to close this account of the symphony and its near-relatives.

Wuorinen's early source for his composition is a musical landmark work by Guillaume de Machaut (ca. 1300-77) — his *Messe de Notre Dame* (Mass of Our Lady), which is the first (known) polyphonic setting by a single composer of texts comprising the Ordinary of the Catholic Latin Mass. These texts are *Kyrie*, *Gloria*, *Credo*, *Sanctus*, and *Agnus Dei*—to which Machaut added the words of dismissal of the Mass: *Ite missa est* (go, the Mass is ended). Machaut's Mass is the progenitor of hundreds of Mass Ordinary compositions, right down to those of Haydn, Mozart, Beethoven, and even Stravinsky. Now it has spawned quite a different progeny, by a composer of our own time, in Wuorinen's pseudo-symphony, which he calls *Machaut mon chou*. Machaut's Mass is the sole source and inspiration for Wuorinen's composition, which was commissioned and premièred by the San Francisco Symphony Orchestra and dedicated to its conductor, Herbert Blomstedt. As for Wuorinen's title, we may recall that the French often use the word "chou" (literally "cabbage") as an informal term of affection or endearment, much as we might say "my pet," or "my sugar plum." Since Wuorinen is clearly an admirer of Machaut, his "mon chou" is doubtless an appelation of affection, one which would have delighted the worldly Frenchman if we are to judge by the amatory, sensuous nature of many of Machaut's own poetic texts.

As remarked, Wuorinen has derived his composition entirely from Machaut's Mass of 600 years ago, the most obvious change being the compression of the earlier six-movement choral work into an impressive three-movement instrumental piece that could easily be designated a symphony. All the conventions and clichés of fourteenth-century music are retained, even accentuated in the reworking. Like all medieval music, Machaut's Mass movements were conceived linearly, each of the several parts having its own linear shape and maintaining its independence until the cadence point. As in most medieval music, the tenor voice is the most important. In Machaut's Mass, the tenor is generally derived from some well-known Gregorian chant that can still be traced in modern liturgical books of the Catholic Church. In his scoring, Wuorinen often stresses the tenor by assigning it to the trombone. To hear this music sensitively, the hearer should concentrate on its horizontal, not its vertical (chordal) aspects. As the ear grows more accustomed to the medieval sound, the tenor voice will frequently extrude and assume the leadership role its fourteenth-century composer allotted it. The rhythmic structure is much more complicated than that found in much of today's music. Because of the independence of the several lines, syncopation and two/three conflicts are often encountered, especially in fast-moving parts.

Wuorinen's redistribution of the material of the several movements of Machaut's Mass is as follows. The first movement of his three-movement "symphony" is the longest and most impressive. It suggests a tripartite (ABA) structure. Part 1 is a straight tutti instrumentation of the opening *Kyrie* of Machaut's Mass. Part 2 derives first from the "Ite missa est," then from the "Christe" portion of the *Kyrie* movement. Part 3, the close of the first movement, uses the last *Kyrie* of the Mass, again in full instrumentation. The middle movement is a quiet setting of the *Sanctus*. The finale shows the most modification of Machaut's material and is brilliantly scored, using first a portion of Machaut's *Credo*, then most of his *Gloria*. A restatement of the opening *Kyrie* acts as a coda for Wuorinen's "symphony."

Machaut mon chou, composed in 1988, is not Wuorinen's first recourse to early music. Previously he had reworked a famous fifteenth-century German song collection into a composition he called *Bearbeitungen über das Glogauer Liederbuch* (Elaboration of the Glogauer songbook). And he used one of Machaut's lovely chansons *Vergine bella* in his *Percussion Symphony*. A number of other twentieth-century symphonists have used such medieval and Renaissance sounds as chords moving in parallel motion, modal harmony, and rhythmic complexity, especially that involving two-three interrelationships (hemiola) to add interest to their compositions. Thus, as the twenty-first century approaches, we may expect that the fruits of continuing exploration of our remote musical ancestors will be assimilated in new symphonic forms.

With the population of our country growing ever more multi-ethnic, a certain tension between the symphony, which is essentially a European creation, and a considerable segment of our newer citizens may be expected. Thus a very important problem for symphonists as we approach the twenty-first century is one of assimilation of elements from a diversity of cultures, flexibility to experiment, and openness to change.

Suggested Reading

The books cited in the 1st edition are updated with citations to new editions, supplemented by more recent publications chosen as useful for the general reader. There is no attempt to be comprehensive — consult your local library and these books for reference to other readings. (Note that some of the *New Grove* spinoff books, assigned to one of the chapters below, may also pertain to another.)

General

Berry, Wallace. *Form in Music.* 2nd ed. Englewood Cliffs, N.J.: Prentice-Hall, 1986.

Boyden, David D. *An Introduction to Music.* 2nd ed. New York: A. A. Knopf, 1970.

Geiringer, Karl. *Instruments in the History of Western Music.* 3rd ed. New York: Oxford University Press, 1978.

Lang, Paul Henry, ed. *The Symphony, 1800-1900: A Norton Music Anthology.* New York: Norton, 1969. Includes scores of symphonies by Beethoven, Schubert, Berlioz, Mendelssohn, Schumann, Tchaikovsky, Brahms, Bruckner, Dvořák.

LaRue, Jan. *Guidelines for Style Analysis.* 2nd ed. This publisher, 1992.

The New Grove Dictionary of American Music. Ed. H. Wiley Hitchcock and Stanley Sadie. 4 vols. London: Macmillan, 1986.

The New Grove Dictionary of Music and Musicians. Ed. Stanley Sadie. 20 vols. London: Macmillan, 1980. S.v. "Symphonic poem," by Hugh Macdonald; "Symphonie concertante," by Barry S. Brook; "Symphony," by Jan LaRue, Nicholas Temperley, and Stephen Walsh; plus articles on individual composers, some updated in the *New Grove* spinoffs cited below.

Norton Critical Scores, with analysis and commentary (New York: Norton):
Haydn, *Symphony No. 103 in E-flat Major*, ed. Karl Geiringer (1974).
Mozart, *Symphony in G minor, K. 550*, ed. Nathan Broder (1967).
Beethoven, *Symphony No. 5 in C minor*, ed. Elliot Forbes (1971).
Schubert, *Symphony in B minor ("Unfinished")*, ed. Martin Chusid (1968).
Berlioz, *Fantastic Symphony*, ed. Edward T. Cone (1971).
Debussy, *Prelude to "The Afternoon of a Faun,"* ed. William W. Austin (1970).

The Norton/Grove Concise Encyclopedia of Music. Ed. Stanley Sadie. New York: Norton, 1988.

Randel, Don Michael. *The New Harvard Dictionary of Music.* Cambridge: Harvard University Press, 1986.

Stedman, Preston. *The Symphony.* 2nd ed. Englewood Cliffs, N.J.: Prentice-Hall, 1992.

_____. *The Symphony: A Research and Information Guide.* Vol. 1: *The Eighteenth Century.* New York: Garland, 1990.

Ulrich, Homer. *Symphonic Music: Its Evolution Since the Renaissance.* New York: Columbia University Press, 1952.

Chapter 1

Burney, Charles. *A General History of Music*. London, 1776-89; ed. with critical and historical notes by Frank Mercer, New York: Dover, 1957.

Chapter 2

Anderson, Emily, transl. and ed. *The Letters of Mozart and His Family*. 3rd ed. London: Macmillan, 1985.

Carse, Adam. *The Orchestra in the XVIIIth Century*. Cambridge, England, 1940; reprint, New York: Broude Bros., 1969.

Einstein, Alfred. *Mozart: His Character, His Work*. Transl. Arthur Mendel and Nathan Broder. New York: Oxford University Press, 1945.

Geiringer, Karl, in collaboration with Irene Geiringer. *Haydn: A Creative Life in Music*. 3rd ed. Berkeley: University of California Press, 1982.

Landon, H. C. Robbins. *Haydn Symphonies*. London: BBC, 1966.

————. *The Symphonies of Joseph Haydn*. London: Universal Edition, 1955.

The New Grove Haydn, by Jens Peter Larsen. New York: Norton, 1983.

The New Grove Mozart, by Stanley Sadie. New York: Norton, 1983.

Chapter 3

Brown, Maurice J. E. *Schubert Symphonies*. London: BBC, 1970.

Deutsch, Otto Erich, ed. *The Schubert Reader*. Transl. Eric Blom. New York: Norton, 1947.

Einstein, Alfred. *Schubert: A Musical Portrait*. Transl. David Ascoli. New York: Oxford University Press, 1951.

Grove, Sir George. *Beethoven and His Nine Symphonies*. London, 1898. 3rd ed. New York: Dover, 1962.

The New Grove Beethoven, by Joseph Kerman and Alan Tyson. New York: Norton, 1983.

The New Grove Schubert, by Maurice J. E. Brown. New York: Norton, 1983.

Thayer, Alexander Wheelock. *The Life of Ludwig van Beethoven*. 3 vols. New York, 1921; reprint, London: Centaur Press, 1960. Rev. and ed. Elliot Forbes, Princeton: Princeton University Press, 1964.

Tovey, Donald F. *Beethoven*. London: Oxford University Press, 1945.

Chapter 4

Abraham, Gerald, ed. *Schumann: A Symposium*. London, 1952; reprint, Westport, Conn.: Greenwood Press, 1977.

Schauffler, Robert Haven. *Florestan: The Life and Work of Robert Schumann*. New York: H. Holt and Co., 1945.

Chapter 5

Geiringer, Karl, in collaboration with Irene Geiringer. *Brahms: His Life and Work*. Transl. H. B. Weiner and Bernard Miall. New York, 1947. 3rd enlarged ed., New York: Da Capo, 1982.

Schoenberg, Arnold. "Brahms the Progressive." In *Style and Idea*. New York: St. Martin's Press, 1975.

Chapter 6

The New Grove Late Romantic Masters: Bruckner, Brahms, Dvořák, Wolf, by Deryck Cooke, et al. New York: Norton, 1985.

Newlin, Dika. *Bruckner, Mahler, Schoenberg*. Rev. ed. New York: Norton, 1978.

Redlich, Hans F. *Bruckner and Mahler*. London: J. M. Dent, 1955.

Schoenberg, Arnold. "Gustav Mahler." In *Style and Idea* (see chapter 5).

Walter, Bruno. *Gustav Mahler*. Transl. James Galston, with a bibliographical essay by Ernst Krenek. New York: Greystone Press, 1941.

Chapter 7

Barzun, Jacques. *Berlioz and the Romantic Century*. 2 vols. 3rd ed., rev. New York: Columbia University Press, 1969.

Berlioz, Hector. *Memoirs*. Ed. Ernest Newman. New York, 1935.

Cooper, Martin. *French Music from the Death of Berlioz to the Death of Fauré*. New York: Oxford University Press, 1951.

Chapter 8

Abraham, Gerald. *Studies in Russian Music*. New York: Charles Scribner's Sons, 1936.

————. *The Music of Sibelius*. New York: Norton, 1947.

Beckerman, Michael. "Dvořák's 'New World' Largo and *The Song of Hiawatha*." In *19th-Century Music* 16, no. 1 (summer 1992): 35-48.

Cowell, Henry and Sidney. *Charles Ives and His Music*. New York: Oxford University Press, 1955.

Gray, Cecil. *Sibelius: The Symphonies*. London: Oxford University Press, 1935.

The New Grove Russian Masters 1: Glinka, Borodin, Balakirev, Musorgsky, Tchaikovsky, by David Brown, et al. New York: Norton, 1986.

Newmarch, Rosa. *The Music of Czechoslovakia*. New York, 1942; reprint, New York: J. & J. Harper, 1969.

Tibbetts, John C., ed. *Dvořák in America, 1892-1895*. Portland, Ore.: Amadeus Press, 1993.

Weinstock, Herbert. *Tchaikovsky*. New York: A. A. Knopf, 1959.

Chapter 9

The New Grove Early Romantic Masters 1: Chopin, Schumann, Liszt, by Nicholas Temperley, Gerald Abraham, Humphrey Searle. New York: Norton, 1985.

The New Grove Early Romantic Masters 2: Weber, Berlioz, Mendelssohn, by John Warrack, Hugh Macdonald, Karl-Heinz Köhler. New York: Norton, 1985.

The New Grove Turn of the Century Masters: Janáček, Mahler, Strauss, Sibelius, by John Tyrrell, et al. New York: Norton, 1985.

The New Grove Twentieth-Century French Masters: Fauré, Debussy, Satie, Ravel, Poulenc, Messaien, Boulez, by Jean-Michel Nectoux, et al. New York: Norton, 1986.

Newman, Ernest. *The Man Liszt*. London, 1954.

Searle, Humphrey. *The Music of Liszt*. London, 1954; rev. reprint, New York: Da Capo, 1966.

Vallas, Léon. *Claude Debussy: His Life, His Works*. London, 1933.

Chapter 10

Abraham, Gerald. *Eight Soviet Composers*. New York: Oxford University Press, 1943.

Austin, William W. *Music in the 20th Century, from Debussy through Stravinsky*. New York: Norton, 1966.

Hindemith, Paul. *A Composer's World*. Cambridge: Harvard University Press, 1952.

The New Grove Modern Masters: Bartók, Stravinsky, Hindemith, by Vera Lampert, et al. New York: Norton, 1984.

The New Grove Russian Masters 2: Rimsky-Korsakov, Skryabin, Rakmaninov, Prokofiev, Shostakovich, by Gerald Abraham, et al. New York: Norton, 1986.

The New Grove Second Viennese School: Schoenberg, Webern, Berg, by Oliver Neighbour, Paul Griffiths, George Perle. New York: Norton, 1983.

The New Grove Twentieth-Century American Masters: Ives, Thomson, Sessions, Cowell, Gershwin, Copland, Carter, Barber, Cage, Bernstein, by John Kirkpatrick, et al. New York: Norton, 1988.

The New Grove Twentieth-Century English Masters: Elgar, Delius, Vaughan Williams, Holst, Walton, Tippett, Britten, by Dian McVeagh, et al. New York: Norton, 1986.

Sessions, Roger. *The Musical Experience of Composer, Performer, Listener*. Princeton: Princeton University Press, 1950.

Slonimsky, Nicolas. *Music Since 1900*. 5th ed. New York: Schirmer Books, 1994.

Stravinsky, Igor. *Poetics of Music*. Transl. Arthur Knodel and Ingolf Dahl. Cambridge: Harvard University Press, 1947. Bilingual ed., 1970.

Symms, Bryan R. *Music of the Twentieth Century: Style and Structure*. New York: Schirmer, 1986.

Watkins, Glenn. *Pyramids at the Louvre: Music, Culture, and Collage from Stravinsky to the Postmodernists*. Cambridge: Harvard University Press, 1994.

_____. *Soundings: Music in the Twentieth Century*. New York: Schirmer, 1988.

Glossary*

Boldface terms within a definition are also glossary entries.

Added sixth (*chord of the*). A chord consisting of a triad with a major sixth added above the root, as C-E-G-A, F♯-A-C♯-D♯.

Agogic stress. Stress by duration, as with notes of conspicuously longer value.

Antiphonal (*performance*). Two groups scored to oppose each other, as strings versus woodwinds, brass versus strings, and so on. Antiphonal performance is most effective in alternation.

Appoggiatura. In melody, a dissonant ornamental note (often written as a note of smaller size) that falls on the beat.

Arco. Played with the bow (the opposite of **pizzicato**).

Arpeggio. In the manner of a harp; generally, sounding of chord tones in rapid succession rather than simultaneously.

Atonal. Without tonality (key).

Augmented sixth (*chord of the*). Most commonly, a variant of the chord of the **added sixth.** In this case, the sixth above the root is augmented—that is, increased by one semitone. Examples are A♭-C-E♭-F♯, E♭-G-B♭-C♯. By extension, the chord of the augmented sixth includes the so-called French sixth: in C major, D-F♯-A♭-C, which is used in "position of the sixth" with A♭ and F♯ the lowest and highest members, respectively.

Augmentation. The restatement of material with increased rhythmic values, most often doubled. ♩♫ = ♩♩♩ in simple augmentation.

Bar. Measure bar, or the content of a measure.

Basso continuo. The continuous bass part of Baroque music, generally played by a low-pitched string instrument with harpsichord to realize the implied harmony.

Bitonal. In two keys.

Cembalo. Harpsichord; in French scores, *clavecin;* in German, *Clavier.*

Chromatic. The opposite of **diatonic;** describes tones foreign to a given key, used to embellish diatonic tones.

Cheironomic. Describes melodies organized by shape and direction (as if by hand signals) instead of according to a certain key or harmony. From *cheir,* "hand."

Concertato (*style*). In the style of a concerto, especially the **concerto grosso.**

Concerto grosso. Literally, a large (orchestral) concerto. In the Baroque period, the performers were divided into a large body (the *concerto grosso* or, alternatively, *ripieno*) and a small body of soloists (the *concertino*).

Cross-relations. The use of a certain pitch in variant inflections (e.g. C-C♯, E-E♭) in different parts, either simultaneously or in close juxtaposition.

Cyclic theme. A theme that occurs in several, or all, movements of a symphony or other large work.

Da capo (D.C.). A direction to return to the beginning. The ternary form (ABA) is often called a "da capo form."

---

* Standard musical terms, such as tempo indications, are not included; only terms especially pertinent to orchestral music, or special terms used in the analyses, are included.

Diatonic. Within a major or minor key. Diatonic is the opposite of **chromatic,** and diatonic music is likely to have few added accidentals (chromatics).

Diminution. The opposite of **augmentation;** restated with diminished rhythmic values, most often halved. ♩♫ = ♫♫ in simple diminution.

Divisi. Divided; a direction given most often to a string choir, indicating that the players are to divide for playing notes of a chord or a multipart musical section.

Duodecuple (or **dodecuple**). Pertaining to twelve. Duodecuple music treats the twelve notes of the octave as all equal, in a kind of "musical communism," as opposed to **chromatic** music, which regards seven notes (of a **diatonic** scale) as prime, and the remaining five as secondary or decorative.

Enharmonic. With the same sound but a different spelling. This may involve single pitches, such as A♭-G♯; entire keys, such as D-flat and C-sharp; or, especially, chords, such as the dominant-seventh chord C-E-G-B♭, which equals the **augmented-sixth** chord C-E-G-A♯.

Fermata. A sign for a pause: ⌒.

Figuration. Passage-work such as **arpeggios,** scales, and so on. Certain figurations are idiomatic to each instrument.

Figured bass. A system of figures often added to the **basso continuo** part in Baroque music, to guide the keyboard player in realizing the harmony.

Fugal. In the style of a fugue. The term is generally used to describe a texture during which voices enter successively but with the same motive (sometimes at various pitch levels). "Fugal" and "imitative" are more or less synonymous terms. Prolonged strict imitation is called canon.

Glissando. A sliding effect produced by playing a series of adjacent tones in very rapid succession. This is most effective on the harp or the piano, but it is possible on a string instrument.

Harmonic rhythm. The speed (or rhythm) of harmonic change.

Head-motive. A highly distinctive musical idea, occurring at the outset of a part and generally useful in various contexts. The **appoggiatura** motive at the beginning of Mozart's G minor Symphony is a fine example.

Hemiola (or **hemiolia**). Rhythmic complexity based on the ratio 2:3. In modern times, the commonest expression of hemiola is in the simultaneous use of a duple compound (6/8) and a simple triple (3/4) measure.

Homophones. Tuning of adjacent strings, especially on the harp, as **enharmonics** to produce identical pitches, as A♭-G♯.

Imitative (*entries* or *style*). See **Fugal.**

Legno, col. Played with the stick of the bow.

Linear counterpoint. Musical texture organized by the shape of lines and their relation to each other, rather than by specific pitch relationships, as in ordinary counterpoint.

Louvered texture. An orchestral texture that (figuratively) opens and closes to give a sense of ventilation and light. In such texture, instruments or choirs move in and out frequently, to avoid opaqueness.

Motto. An epigrammatic musical idea, usually stated at the outset of a piece. A motto is generally longer than a **head-motive.**

Nonharmonic tone. A note outside the basic harmony, generally dissonant, and always for embellishment.

Passacaglia (and **chaconne**). A recurring 8-measure pattern, used mostly as the bass in sets of variations.

Pitch (*octave designations of*). Exact pitch within the octaves covered by the ordinary orchestral score is designated as follows, each pitch taking the designation of the C below it.

Contra	Great	Small	"Middle" One-line	———————	Two-line	Three-line	Four-line
CC	C	c	c′		c″	c‴	c⁗

Pizzicato. Plucked (as opposed to bowed) playing of a string instrument. **Arco** indicates that the ordinary method of playing is to be resumed.

Polyphonic. Several-voiced, a term used to describe contrapuntal or multilinear music.

Polyrhythmic. In several rhythms or meters.

Polytonal. In several keys.

Ponticello, sul. Played near the bridge on a string instrument.

Portamento. Passage from one tone to another in a continuous glide through the intervening tones, but without articulating them as with **glissando.**

Ritornello. A musical segment that returns at intervals during a design, helping to organize it.

Rubato. Modification of the strict time pulse, to achieve litheness and expressiveness in performance.

Serialism. A plan for organizing pitch into "tone rows" for ordering **duodecuple** music. Initiated by Schoenberg, serialism has now been extended to other elements, such as rhythm and dynamics.

Seventh chord (*means of designating*). A seventh chord (a four-note chord constructed in thirds, such as G-B-D-F) is commonly designated by naming the basic triad plus the size of the seventh between the root and seventh. Thus G-B-D-F is a "major-minor seventh chord," D-F-A-C♯ a "minor-major," B-D-F-A a "diminished-minor," C-E-G♯-B an "augmented-major," and so on.

Sordino, con. With mute, a device for softening or muffling the tone, especially of a string or brass instrument.

Timbre. Tone quality; the distinctive sound of any instrument.

Tonality. The condition of having key. Compounds are **bitonal** (in two keys), **polytonal** (in several keys), etc.

Transpose. To restate material at another pitch level.

Tritone. The augmented fourth (by inversion, the diminished fifth), an interval containing three whole-steps. The *diabolus in musica* of early times.

Tutti. Literally "all," an indication in orchestral music that the entire ensemble is used.

Twelve-tone. A synonym for **duodecuple.**

Index

Boldface type indicates that a composition has a major analytical discussion in the text.

About the Author

LOUISE E. CUYLER *was born in Omaha, Nebraska, and graduated from high school there, having studied violin for seven years with Emily Cleve Gregerson. She entered the Eastman School of Music in 1926, earning the B.Mus. in violin in 1929, and that year was appointed to the faculty of the University of Michigan to establish a new Department of Theory. She taught at Michigan until becoming professor emeritus in 1975.*

During World War II she joined the American Red Cross Overseas Service, with duty in New Caledonia (a French island in the South Pacific) as club director and liaison with the Army Special Service. After the war she obtained the Ph.D. in musicology at Eastman in 1948, with a dissertation on Heinrich Isaac's Choralis Constantinus *(posthumously published in 1550), book III, her edition of which was published by the University of Michigan Press in 1950. At Michigan, she was promoted to full professor in 1953, chair of the Musicology Department in 1956, and received the Distinguished Faculty Award in 1973. Other major publications are an edition of Isaac's* Five Polyphonic Masses *(University of Michigan Press, 1956), and* Maximilian I and Music *(Oxford University Press, 1972). Colleagues and former students contributed to* Notations and Editions: A Book in Honor of Louise Cuyler, *edited by Edith Borroff (Wm. C. Brown, 1974; reprint, Da Capo, 1977).*

Louise Cuyler was a Fulbright Senior Research Scholar and Lecturer in Belgium, 1953-54, and also held guest professorships at the University of Washington, Stanford University, Smith College (William Allen Neilson Chair), Indiana University, and the University of California-Santa Barbara. She served the American Musicological Society for over twenty years on its Council, including eight terms (1955-71) as its national secretary.

Since retiring to Carmel-by-the-Sea, California, she has remained active with the Monterey County Symphony, for which she served twelve years as member of the Symphony Association Board, and continues as annotator of the program books. She was named Benefactor of the Arts by the Monterey Cultural Council in 1991 and 1994.